BHARAT RATNAS

BHARAT RATNAS

Edited and Compiled by
Dr. R.K. Pruthi
Executive Editor
LSRF

Life Span Publishers and Distributors
New Delhi 110 002

First Published 2015

ISBN 978-93-81709-46-7

Price: **Rs. 600**

Published by:

LIFE SPAN PUBLISHERS AND DISTRIBUTORS
4782/23, Ansari Road, Daryaganj,
New Delhi-110 002
Phones: 9811597982, 9013763525, 9868347115
E-mail: lifespandelhi@gmail.com
http://sites.google.com/site/lifespanpublishers/
http://lifespanpublisher.webs.com/

PRINTED IN INDIA

Published by Rakesh Pruthi for Life Span Publishers and Distributors, New Delhi - 110 019, Printed at Rajdhani Printers, Delhi.

Contents

Preface

This book on Bharat Ratna gives an account of life, career and achievements of the recipients of the award. It is the highest civilian award, instituted by the Republic of India. Details of the life stories of recipients along with nature, characteristics and the history of the award, will be an asset in every home and library

R.K. Pruthi

Preface

Introduction

Bharat Ratna (Jewel of India) is the highest civilian award of the Republic of India. Instituted on 2 January 1954, the award is conferred "in recognition of exceptional service/ performance of the highest order", without distinction of race, occupation, position, or sex.

As per original statutes for the award, only the fields of art, literature, science along with public services were made eligible. However, in December 2011, the Government of India broadened the criteria to include "any field of human endeavour".

Recommendations to award the Bharat Ratna are made by the Prime Minister to the President, and a maximum of three people may be awarded in a year. The recipient receives a *Sanad* (certificate) signed by the President and a peepal-leaf–shaped medallion; there is no monetary grant associated with the award. The recipients of the Bharat Ratna rank seventh in the Indian order of precedence, but are constitutionally prohibited from using the award name as a title.

The first recipients of the Bharat Ratna were politician C. Rajagopalachari, scientist C.V. Raman and philosopher Sarvepalli Radhakrishnan, who were honoured in 1954. Since then, 45 individuals have been bestowed the award including 11 posthumous declarations.

The original statutes did not provide for posthumous awards, but they were amended to allow so in January 1955. In 1966, former Prime Minister Lal Bahadur Shastri became the first individual to be honoured posthumously.

Though usually conferred on Indian citizens, the Bharat Ratna has been awarded to one naturalized citizen—Mother Teresa in 1980—and to two non-Indians—Pakistan national Khan Abdul Ghaffar Khan in 1987 and South African Nelson

Mandela in 1990. The most recent recipients are C. N. R. Rao and Tendulkar who were honoured in 2013.

History

On 2 January 1954, a press communique was released from the office of the secretary to the President of India to institute two civilian awards—Bharat Ratna and the three-tier Padma Vibhushan, classified into "Pahela Warg" (Class I), "Dusra Warg" (Class II), and "Tisra Warg" (Class III). The Bharat Ratna is termed as the highest civilian award of India, followed by Padma Vibhushan classifications. A year later on 15 January 1955, the Padma Vibhushan classifications were altered into three different awards; the Padma Vibhushan, the highest of three awards followed by the Padma Bhushan and the Padma Shri.

The award was briefly suspended twice; first time in 1977 and again in 1993. When Morarji Desai sworn in as the fourth Prime Minister of India in 1977, his government withdrew all personal civil honours on 13 July 1977 and the past recipients of the awards were asked not to use the awards as a title. The awards were reintroduced on 25 January 1980 when Indira Gandhi again became the Prime Minister in 1980. The civilian awards were suspended again in 1993 when two Public-Interest Litigations were filed, one in Kerala High Court and another in Madhya Pradesh High Court, to challenge "the constitutional validity" of the awards. This time it took three years till the awards were reintroduced by the Supreme Court of India in December 1995.

Regulations

In terms of Article 18 (1) of the Constitution of India, the recipients cannot use the award as a prefix or suffix to their name. Although, recipients may use either "Awarded Bharat Ratna by the President" or "Recipient of Bharat Ratna Award" as an expression to indicate that they have been honoured with the award. The holders of the Bharat Ratna rank 7th in the Indian order of precedence.

The award can be considered to be conferred only if the recipient's name is published in *The Gazette of India*—a public journal and an authorized legal document of the Government of India, and a recipients' register maintained under the direction of the President. Only the President is given an authority to cancel and annul the award. If the award is cancelled and annulled, the recipient is required to surrender the medal with his/her name removed from the register. The President can restore the award if the cancellation and annulment has been withdrawn. It is required to have a notice of cancellation or restoration of the award to be published in *The Gazette of India*.

1

Chakravarti Rajagopalachari (1878 – 1972)

Known as C.R. or 'Rajaji' to millions, Chakravarti Rajagopalachari was close to Gandhiji. In fact Gandhiji referred to him as, "the keeper of my conscience". A stalwart who imbibed Gandhiji's ideology and practised it privately, and publicly, he worked for the Congress Party for more than half a century. Rajaji, fell out of Congress, formed his own 'Swatantra' Party, because he was more than convinced that the ruling Congress had totally deserted Gandhi's principles and was turning 'despotic'. He symbolizes the disillusionment, the close associates of Gandhi witnessed two decades after gaining independence.

Life

Rajaji was born in Thorapalli village of Salem District, Tamilnadu on 10th of December 1878. His father Chakravarti Venkataraya Iyengar hailed from Tamilnadu. His mother Singaramma came from Kuppam in Chittoor, in Andhra Pradesh. Rajaji himself had his schooling in Hosur and higher education in Central College of Bangalore of Karnataka.

As a student he developed great love for literature and later bloomed into a distinguished writer in Tamil and English. As was the custom, Rajaji had to marry early. His wife passed away after giving birth to three sons and two daughters. He started the legal practice at Salem after obtaining Law degree from Madras. His entry into politics, coincided with zeal for social reforms. He became Chairman of Municipal Council of Salem and started a crusade against caste system, and drinking of alcohol. He faced opposition from both ends, conservatives and the oppressed. But he was successful in introducing civic reforms.

Political Career

His entry into national politics followed. In 1906 he attended Indian national Congress held at Surat. He actively supported Lokamanya Tilak. By 1918, the rift between *moderates* (Gokhale group) and *extremists* (Tilak group) was conspicuous. Rajaji had leaning for the latter. He worked for Tilak and Dr. Annie Besant.

With Tilak's death in 1920, leadership of freedom movement, passed on to Gandhiji. Rajaji by then had moved to Madras to practice at High Court and had built up a lucrative practice in no time. In the city, he could organize a whole team of radicals for social and political reforms.

Rajaji had met Gandhiji on earlier occasions, and soon became a member of his inner circle. He gave up legal practice and plunged into freedom movement. He organized provincial congress on sound footing. He was one of the first to court arrest as 'Satyagrahi'. Next quarter of a century he suffered jail-term, five times. He wrote several books during his internment, and edited 'Young India' during Gandhiji's imprisonment. He toured the entire country for the propagation of Gandhiji's constructive programs. Very soon his name reckoned among forefront leaders.

According to Gandhi's wish, he established an ashram in the famine-stricken village of Pudupalayam in Salem district and started *swadeshi* i.e., production of *khadi* cloth, campaign of eradication of untouchability and drinking. The *Dandi* March had a replica in the south led by Rajaji. The March from Tiruchi to Vedaranyam was an eye-opener to British Government. The freedom movement had caught the masses. The government order not to supply food and water to marchers went unheeded. Village after village welcomed the *satyagrahis*. Such was the organizing skill of Rajaji. He was acknowledged provincial leader of Madras after his jail-term.

Gandhi-Irwin pact and Government of India Act 1935, followed. Partial provincial autonomy and self rule was declared. Rajaji became premier of Madras Presidency.

Now, he had powers to implement the social reforms, he was striving for. The famous Meenakshi Temple of Madurai was opened to Harijans. Prohibition followed. He rescued farmers from the clutches of the land-lords by bringing in Agriculturists' Debt Relief Act. Sales tax, an innovation in revenue collection in India was introduced by Rajaji.

Quit India movement was declared and Rajaji resigned only to be arrested. He was released after the Second World War was over.

India became free. He became the first Indian Governor General after Lord Mount Batten in 1948. Nehru wanted Rajaji to become the first President of free India as well. But Rajaji wanted 'retirement' from active politics and returned to Madras.

But, there could be no retirement to a leader of his stature, transparent personality and unquestionable caliber. Under pressure from admirers and followers he again had to served as Chief Minister for two years (1952-54).

Rajaji's Vision of India

Rajaji was a visionary. He knew what were India's prime ailments. He was against the formation of linguistic states.

He thought, that would weaken India. He recommended manageable administrative zones. He was for retaining of English language as Official medium of Indian Union. He thought that for a country of multilingual existence, English was the remedy. He was also against the 'permit-license-quota-raj' which was taking roots.

We all know very well how the three factors Rajaji spoke against, worked havoc. The third one had the ugliest picture during Indira Gandhi's emergency period (1975-77).

As a great humanist, Rajaji could not bear the bombing of Hiroshima and Nagasaki. In his later years he became a vehement opponent of Nuclear Weapon Tests. He wrote a book, 'Mankind Protests' which became quite popular. Mr. Khruschev as Head of Soviet Russia got it translated into Russian for wide circulation in his country. At the age of eighty-four, Rajaji undertook his only trip abroad, to plead with world statesmen to give up nuclear testing. He also met President Kennedy in this connection.

Rajaji was a prolific writer. He has written stories for children, He wrote about religion, philosophy, history, world events etc. He has translated Ramayana and Mahabharata. His analysis of Hinduism, Bhagavad-Gita and Indian Culture make an absorbing reading.

Rajaji knew Kannada well. One of his closest friends was Navaratna Rama Rao, also a well known writer and civil servant. Ram Rao has written some intimate memories of Rajaji in his memoirs, 'Kelavu Nenapugalu' a modern Kannada classic.

Death

Rajaji breathed his last on 25th December 1972 at the age of 94.

2

Dr. C.V. Raman

Dr. C.V. Raman was one of the greatest scientists of India, who was awarded the 1930 **Nobel Prize in physics** for his work on the scattering of light and for the discovery of the 'Raman Effect', which is named after him. Chandrasekhar Venkata Raman, commonly known as C.V. Raman was born on November 7, 1888 at Tiruchirapalli in Tamillandu. His mother tongue was Tamil. He was the second child of Chandrasekhar Iyer and Pravathi Ammal. His father was a lecturer in mathematics and physics. Raman was a very brilliant student right from his childhood.

Education

At an early age, Raman moved to the city of Vishakhapatnam, which is situated in state of Andhra Pradesh, where his father accepted a position at A V N College. Raman's academic brilliance was established at a very young age. At the age of twelve, he finished his matriculation education and entered A V N College and two year later moved to the prestigious presidency college in Madras (Chennai). When he was fifteen he finished at the head of the class too received B. A. with honours in physics and English. In those days, it was a system of government that students who did well academically were typically sent to abroad (England) for additional studies. Because of Raman's poor health, he was not allowed to go abroad and he continued his studies at the same college. In 1907, barely seventeen, Raman received his Master degree with honors. He got first position in the University in M.A. In the same year, he married Lokasundari Ammal with whom he had one son, Radhakrishnan.

He completed his education in Visakhapatanam and Madras (Chennai). After getting top ranking in the Financial Civil Service competitive Exam, he was appointed as Deputy Accountant general in Calcutta. At the time of his graduation, there were few opportunities for scientists in India. This forced him to accept a position with the Indian Civil Services as an Assistant Accountant General in Calcutta. While there, he was able to sustain his interest in science by working, in his remaining time, in the laboratories of the Indian Association for the Cultivation of Science. He studied the physics of stringed instruments and Indian drums.

In 1917, he was offered the professor of Physics at the Calcutta University, and he decided to accept this opportunity. After 15 years service at the Calcutta University, he left that job and shifted to Bangalore and became the Director of the Indian Institute of Science, where two years later he continued as a professor of physics. In 1947, the new Government of Independent India appointed him as the first National Professor. He also worked in the field of magnetic attraction and theory of musical instruments. He worked out the theory of transverse vibration of bowed strings, because of superposition velocities. This does a better job in explaining bowed string vibration over Helmholtzs approach.

Professor C V Raman was also the first to investigate the harmonic nature of the sound of the Indian drums such as the tabla and the mridanga. In 1930, for the first time in its history, an Indian scholar, educated entirely in India received highest honour in science, the 'Nobel Prize' in physics. In 1943, he founded 'Raman Research Institute', near Bangalore. His discovery of the 'Raman Effect' made a very distinctive contribution to Physics. He was also conferred the hishest title of 'Bharat Ratna' in 1954. The 'Raman Effect' was a demonstration of the 'Collision' effect of light bullets (Photons) passing through a transparent medium, whether solid, liquid or gaseous. Raman was also awarded the 'Lenin Peace Prize' in 1957. India celebrates National Science day on 28th February every year to commemorate Raman's discovery.

Death

He retired from the Indian Institute in 1948 and after one year, he established the Raman Research Institute in Bangalore, served as its director and remained active there until his death, at the age of eighty-two. Sir Venkata Raman died on Nevember 21, 1970 at Bangalore, India. We should proud on him.

3

Sarvepalli Radhakrishnan

Sarvepalli Radhakrishnan was born in Tirutani on September 5, 1888 into a poor brahmin family. His father Sarvepalli Veeraswami was employed on a meagre salary in the zamindari. His mother's name was Sitamma. It was difficult for Radhakrishnan's father to educate him with a meagre income and a large family to take care of.

Radhakrishnan went through most of his education on scholarships. He initially went to school in Tirutani and then to the Lutheran Mission School in Tirupati for his high school. He joined the Voorhee's College in Vellore but switched to the Madras Christian College at the age of 17. He chose philosophy as his major and attained a B.A. and M.A. He was afraid that his M.A. thesis, "The Ethics of the Vedanta" would offend his philosophy professor, Dr. A.G. Hogg. Instead, Dr. Hogg commended Radhakrishnan on doing an excellent job. Radhakrishnan's M.A. thesis was published when he was only 20

Radhakrishnan was married to Sivakamuamma at the

age of 16 while still in Vellore. Radhakrishnan accepted an Assistant Lectureship at the Madras Presidency College in 1909. While at the College, he mastered the classics of Hindu philosophy, namely the Upanishads, Bhagvad Gita, Brahmasutra, and commentaries of Sankara, Ramunuja and Madhava. He also acquainted himself with Buddhist and Jain philosophy. At the same time he read philosophical commentaries of Plato, Plotinus, Kant, Bradley, and Bergson. Later on in his life, he studied Marxism and Existentialism.

In 1914, in a strange twist of fate, Radhakrishnan met Srinivasa Ramanujan, the mathematical genius. Srinivasa was leaving for Cambridge for studies and had come to seek Radhakrishnan's blessings because a goddess came in his dream and told him to do so before undertaking the trip. The two never met again.

Academic Career

In 1918, Radhakrishnan was selected as Professor of Philosophy by the University of Mysore. By the time, Radhakrishnan had written many articles for journals of repute like The Quest, Journal of Philosophy and the International Journal of Ethics. He completed his first book "The Philosophy of Rabindranath Tagore." He believed Tagore's philosophy to be the "genuine manifestation of the Indian spirit." Radhakrishnan's second book, "The Reign of Religion in Contemporary Philosophy" was published in 1920.

Radhakrishnan's books and articles, drew the attention of Ashutosh Mookerjee, Vice Chancellor of Calcutta University. He nominated Radhakrishnan to the prestigious George V Professor of Philosophy at the Calcutta University, 1921. In 1923, Dr. Radhakrishnan's "Indian Philosophy" was published. The book was in response to the request made by Prof. J. H. Muirhead, to write a book on Indian philosophy for the Library of Philosophy. Radhakrishnan accomplished this mammoth task by producing a systematic and readable account of Indian philosophy. The book was hailed as a "philosophical classic and a literary masterpiece."

Radhakrishnan was called to Oxford University, England, to deliver the prestigious "Upton Lectures" on "The Hindu View of Life." The lectures were followed by an invitation to head the Department of Comparative Religion at Oxford. A philanthropist, Spalding, created a professorship for Radhakrishnan to teach Religion and Ethics at Oxford.

Radhakrishnan used his lectures as a platform to further India's cause for freedom. He thundered, "India is not a subject to be administered but a nation seeking its soul." He would graphically describe the "shame of subjection and the lines of sorrow" apparent on every Indian's face.

In 1931, Radhakrishnan was elected Vice Chancellor of the Andhra University. The University was in a state of stagnation. Radhakrishnan restructured the Honors and Post-Graduate teaching in Humanities and Languages, and Science and Technology Departments from scratch. By the time he left in 1936, he had transformed the University into a robust and well-recognized institution.

In 1939, Radhakrishnan became the Vice Chancellor of the Benaras Hindu University, Uttar Pradesh, founded by Pt. Madan Mohan Malaviya. The University was under pressure from the Governor, Sir Maurice Hallet, to turn the campus into a war hospital in response to the Quit India Movement launched by Gandhiji and the Congress. Radhakrishnan rushed to Delhi and successfully persuaded the Viceroy, Lord Linlithgow, to halt the Governor's action. The Governor instead suspended financial support to the University. Radhakrishnan went on "a Begging Pilgrimage," to collect funds from sympathizers and philanthropists. When Malaviyaji retired from University work completely, the Benaras Hindu University requested Radhakrishnan's services for an indefinite period which Radhakrishnan acquiesced to.

Political Career

After independence on August 15, 1947, Radhakrishnan was requested to Chair the University Education Commission in 1948. The Radhakrishnan Committee's suggestions helped mould the education system for India's needs.

In 1949, Dr. Radhakrishnan was appointed ambassador to the Soviet Union. The appointment raised many eyebrows because people wondered what kind of an impression Radhakrishnan, a student of idealist philosophy, would make on Joseph Stalin, an ardent communist. In 1950, Radhakrishnan was called to the Kremlin to meet with the Premier. This was rather irregular. Radhakrishnan was accompanied by Indian Embassy Minister, Rajeshwar Dayal and Soviet Foreign Minister Andrei Vyshinsky and interpreter Pavlov. Radhakrishnan told Stalin, "We had an emperor in India who, after bloody victory, renounced war and became a monk. You have waded your way to power through force. Who knows that might happen to you also." Radhakrishnan was referring to Stalin's infamous "bloody" purges. Stalin smiled and replied, "Yes, miracles do happen sometimes. I was in a theological seminary for five years!"

On April 5, 1952, a few days before Radhakrishnan's departure for India, Stalin called on Radhakrishnan. Radhakrishnan records Stalin's face being bloated. Radhakrishnan patted him on the cheek and on the back. Stalin said, "You are the first person to treat me as a human being and not as a monster. You are leaving us and I am sad. I want you to live long. I have not long to live." Stalin died six months later. Radhakrishnan's legacy in Moscow was a firm and friendly understanding between India and the Soviet Union. A relationship which has flourished over the years and has become even stronger.

Radhakrishnan was elected Vice-President of India in 1952. The Vice-President presides over the Rajya Sabha (Upper House) sessions, much like the Speaker does in the Lok Sabha (Lower House). Often, during a heated debate, Radhakrishnan would intervene with slokas from the sanskrit classics or quotations from the Bible to calm the charged atmosphere. Nehru commented later, "By the way in which

Radhakrishnan conducted the proceedings of the Rajya Sabha, he had made the meetings of the House look like family gatherings!"

Dr. Radhakrishnan was honored with the Bharat Ratna in 1954. Around the same time, an 883-page compilation titled "The Philosophy of Dr. Sarvepalli Radhakrishnan" was released in America.

In 1956, Radhakrishnan's devoted wife, Sivakamuamma, passed away after sharing 50 years of married life. The couple had five daughters and a son.

After serving two terms as Vice-President, Radhakrishnan was elected President of India in 1962. Radhakrishnan's tenure as President was marked by the disastrous Indo-China war of 1962, his state visit to the United States in 1963, the end of the Nehru-era with Nehru's death in 1964, and India's victorious performance against Pakistan in 1965 under Lal Bahadur Shastri. Radhakrishnan guided each of the Prime Ministers wisely and helped see India through those trying years safely.

At the age of 79, Dr. Radhakrishnan returned to Madras in May 1967 to a warm homecoming. He spent his last years at his house "Girija" in Mylapore, Madras.

Death

Dr. Radhakrishnan died on April 17, 1975.

4

Bhagwan Das

Bhagwan Das (January 12, 1869 – September 18, 1958) was an Indian Theosophist and public figure. For a time he served in the Central Legislative Assembly of British India. He became allied with the Hindustani Culture Society and was active in opposing rioting as a form of protest. As an advocate for national freedom from the British rule, he was often in danger of reprisals from the Colonial government. He was awarded Bharat Ratna in 1955. He was the fourth recipient of India's highest civilian award.

Life

Born in Varanasi, India, he graduated school to became a deputy in the collections bureau, and later left to continue his academic pursuits. Das joined the Theosophical Society in 1894 inspired by a speech by Annie Besant. After the 1895 split, he sided with the Theosophical Society Adyar. Within that society, he was an opponent of Jiddu Krishnamurti and his Order of the Star in the East organisation. Das joined the Indian National Congress during the Non-cooperation movement and was honoured with the Bharat Ratna in 1955.

With Besant he formed a professional collaboration which led to the founding of the Central Hindu College, which became Benaras Hindu University. Das would later found the Kashi Vidya Peeth, a national university where he served as headmaster. Das was a scholar of Sanskrit, from which he added to the body of Hindi language. He wrote approximately 30 books, many of these in Sanskrit and Hindi.

A prominent road in New Delhi is named after him and a colony is also named after his name in Sigra area of Varanasi 'Dr. Bhagwan Das Nagar.'

Works

- *A concordance dictionary to The yoga-sutras of Patanjali.* Kaashai, Benares 1938.
- *A few Truths about Theosophy.* in *The Theosophist,* Adyar September 1889.
- *Ancient solutions of modern problems.* Theosophical Publishing House, Adyar 1933.
- *Ancient versus modern "scientific socialism", or, Theosophy and capitalism, fascism, communism.* Theosophical Publishing House, Adyar 1934.
- *Annie Besant and the changing world.* Theosophical Publishing House, Adyar 1934.
- *Communalism and its cure by theosophy, Or spiritual health, the only sure basis of material wealth.* Theosophical Publishing House, Adyar 1934.
- *Eugenics, Ethics and Metaphysics.* Theosophical Publishing House, Adyar 1930.
- *Indian ideals of women's education.* Current Thought Press, Madras 1929.
- *Krishna, a study in the theory of Avataras.* Theosophical Publishing House, Adyar 1924.
- *My picture of free India.* Indian Book Shop, Benares et al. 1944.
- *The central Hindu college and Mrs. Besant, the rise*

of the Alcyone cult. Divine Life Press, London 1913.

- *The dawn of another Renaissance*. Theosophical Publishing House, Adyar 1931.
- *The Essential Unity of all Religions*. Theosophical Press, Wheaton 1939.
- *The Ethico-Psychological Crux in Political Science and Art, or, Who Should be Legislators?*. Theosophical Publishing House, Adyar 1931.
- *The fundamental idea of theosophy*. Theosophist Office, Madras 1912.
- *The metaphysics and psychology of Theosophy*. in *The Theosophist*, Adyar 1916. und
- *The philosophy of non-co-operation and of spiritual-political swaraj*. Tagore & Co., Madras 1922.
- *The psychology of conversion*. Theosophical Publishing House, Adyar 1917.
- *The religion of theosophy*. Theosophist Office, Madras 1911.
- *The science of peace, an attempt at an exposition of the first principles of the science of the self*. Theosophical Publishing House, Benares et al. 1904.
- *The science of religion, or, Sanatana vaidika dharma, an attempt at an exposition of principles*. Indian Book Shop, Benares 1948.
- *The Science Of Social Organization, or, The Laws Of Manu In The Light Of Atma Vidya*. Theosophical Publishing House, Adyar 1935.
- *The science of social organisation, or, The laws of Manu in the light of Theosophy*. Theosophist Office, Adyar 1910.
- *The science of the emotions*. Theosophical Publishing House, Benares et al. 1908.
- *The spiritualisation of the science of politics by Brahma-vidya*. Theosophical Publishing House, Adyar 1919.
- *The superphysics of the Great War*. Theosophical Publishing House, Adyar 1916.

5

Sir Mokshagundam Visvesvaraya

Sir Mokshagundam Visvesvaraya KCIE (popularly known as **Sir MV**; 15 September 1860 – 14 April 1962 was a notable Indian engineer, scholar, statesman and the Diwan of Mysore during 1912 to 1918. He was a recipient of the Indian Republic's highest honour, the Bharat Ratna, in 1955. He was knighted as a Knight Commander of the Indian Empire (KCIE) by King George V for his contributions to the public good. Every year, 15 September is celebrated as Engineer's Day in India in his memory. He is held in high regard as a pre-eminent engineer of India. He was the chief designer of the flood protection system for the city of Hyderabad in Andhra Pradesh, as well as the chief engineer responsible for the construction of the Krishna Raja Sagara dam in Mandya.

Early years

Sir Mokshagundam Visvesvaraya was born in 1860 September 15, in a Telugu Brahmin family to Mokshagundam Srinivasa Shastry and Venkatalakshmamma in Muddenahalli village, 40 miles from Bangalore, Mysore State (now Karnataka), India. Mokshagundam is a village in Prakasam

District's Cumbum Tahasil (then Kurnool District) of Andhra Pradesh where the ancestors of Visvesvarayya emigrated from. Visvesvaraya lost his father at the age of 15. He enrolled for kannada medium primary school in Chikballapur and attended high school in Bangalore. He earned his Bachelor of Arts from Central College, Bangalore affiliated to Madras University in 1881 and later studied civil engineering at the prestigious College of Engineering, Pune, popularly known as COEP.

Career as an engineer

Upon graduating as an engineer, Visvesvaraya took up a job with the Public Works Department (PWD) of Mumbai and was later invited to join the Indian Irrigation Commission. He implemented an extremely intricate system of irrigation in the Deccan area. He also designed and patented a system of automatic weir water floodgates that were first installed in 1903 at the Khadakvasla Reservoir near Pune. These gates were employed to raise the flood supply level of storage in the reservoir to the highest level likely to be attained by a flood without causing any damage to the dam. Based on the success of these gates, the same system was installed at the Tigra Dam in Gwalior and the Krishna Raja Sagara (KRS) Dam in Mandya/ Mysore,Karnataka. In 1906–07, the Government of India sent him to Eden, Africa to study water supply and drainage system and the project prepared by him was implemented in Eden successfully. Visvesvaraya achieved celebrity status when he designed a flood protection system for the city of Hyderabad. He was instrumental in developing a system to protect Visakhapatnam port from sea erosion. Visvesvaraya supervised the construction of the KRS Dam across the Kaveri River from concept to inauguration. This dam created the biggest reservoir in Asia when it was built. He was rightly called the "Father of modern Mysore state" (now Karnataka): During his period of service with the Government of Mysore state, he was responsible for the founding of, (under the Patronage of Mysore Government), the Mysore Soap Factory, the Parasitoide Laboratory, the Mysore Iron & Steel Works (now known as Visvesvaraya Iron and Steel Limited) in Bhadravathi, the Sri Jayachamarajendra Polytechnic Institute, the Bangalore Agricultural University, the State Bank of Mysore, The Century Club, Mysore Chambers of Commerce and numerous other industrial ventures. He encouraged private investment in industry during his tenure as Diwan of Mysore. He was instrumental in charting out the plan for road construction between Tirumala and Tirupati. He was known for sincerity, time management and dedication to a cause.

Career In Brief

- Joined service as Assistant Engineer in Bombay, 1884; served in Nasik, Khandesh and Poona;
- Services lent to Municipality of Sukkur in Sind, 1894: designed and carried out the water works of that Municipality, 1895;
- Executive Engineer, Surat, 1896;
- Assistant Superintending Engineer, Poona, 1897–99; visited China and Japan, 1898;
- Executive Engineer for Irrigation, Poona, 1899;
- Sanitary Engineer, Bombay, and Member, Sanitary Board, 1901; gave evidence before the Indian Irrigation Commission, 1901;
- Designed and constructed Automatic Gates patented by him at Lake Fife Storage Reservoir; introduced a new system of irrigation known as the "Block System", 1903; represented the Bombay Government at the Simla Irrigation Commission, 1904; on special duty, 1905;
- Superintending Engineer, 1907; visited Egypt, Canada. United States of America and Russia, 1908;
- Services lent as Special Consulting Engineer,

Hyderabad, to supervise and carry out Engineering works in connection with the Musi floods, 1909;

- Retired from British service, 1909;
- Chief Engineer and Secretary to the Government of Mysore, 1909;
- Dewan of Mysore, P. W. and Railway Department, 1913.

Diwan of Mysore

After opting for voluntary retirement in 1908, he took a foreign tour to study industrialised nations and after, for a short period he worked for the Nizam of Hyderabad, India. He suggested flood relief measures for Hyderabad town, which was under constant threat of floods by Musi river. Later, during November 1909, Visvesvaraya was appointed as Chief Engineer of Mysore State. Further, during the year, 1912, he was appointed as Diwan (First Minister) of the princely state of Mysore. He was Diwan for 7 years.

With the support of Krishnaraja Wodeyar IV, Maharaja of Mysore, Visvesvaraya made good contribution as Diwan to the all-round development of Mysore state. Not only the achievements listed above, but many other industries and public works owe their inception or active nurturing to him. He was instrumental in the founding of the Government Engineering College at Bangalore in 1917, one of the first engineering institutes in India. This institution was later named the University Visvesvaraya College of Engineering after its founder. He also commissioned several new railway lines in Mysore state.

Awards and honours

Visvesvaraya was appointed a Companion of the Order of the Indian Empire (CIE) in 1911. In 1915, while he was the Diwan of Mysore, Visvesvaraya was knighted as a Knight Commander of the Order of the Indian Empire (KCIE) by the

British for his myriad contributions to the public good. After India attained independence, he was awarded with the nation's highest honour, the Bharat Ratna, in 1955. He was feted with honorary membership of the international Institution of Civil Engineers (based in London) and a fellowship of the Indian Institute of Science (based in Bangalore). He was awarded several honorary doctoral degrees like D.Sc., LL.D., D.Litt. from eight universities in India. He was president of the 1923 Session of the Indian Science Congress. Sir M.V. was awarded honorary Membership of London Institution of Civil Engineers for an unbroken 50 years. He was the most popular person from Karnataka, in a newspaper survey conducted by Prajavani.

Recognition

Visvesvaraya has received recognition in various fields, most notably the education sector and the engineering sector. Visvesvaraya Technological University which is based in Belgaum, the University to which most engineering colleges in Karnataka are affiliated to, has been named in his honour, as well as prominent colleges like University Visvesvaraya College of Engineering, Bangalore, Sir M. Visvesvaraya Institute of Technology, Bangalore and Visvesvaraya National Institute of Technology, Nagpur. College of Engineering, Pune, his alma mater, has erected a statue in his honour. The Visvesvaraya Industrial and Technological Museum, a museum in Bangalore is named in his honour.

Memorial at Muddenahalli

The Visvesvaraya National Memorial Trust manages a memorial of Visvesvaraya at his birthplace Muddenahalli. The memorial exhibits his awards, titles and personal belongings, including his living room, spectacles, cups, his copy of the Webster's dictionary, and a block with which his visiting cards were printed. Models of the Krishna Raja Sagar dam, which Visvesvaraya designed and supervised the construction of, are also exhibited. The memorial is located adjacent to his house, which was refurnished and regarded as a temple by the locals.

Works

- Visvesvaraya, M (1920), *Reconstructing India*, P. S. King & son, ltd, OCLC 2430680
- Visvesvaraya, M (1936), *Planned economy for India*, Bangalore: Bangalore Press, OCLC 19373044
- Visvesvaraya, M (1951), *Memories of my working life*, Bangalore, OCLC 6459729
- Visvesvaraya, M (1932), *Unemployment in India; its causes and cure*, Bangalore: The Bangalore Press, OCLC 14348788
- Visvesvaraya, M (1917), *Speeches*, Bangalore: Govt. Press, OCLC 6258388
- A Brief Memoir of my complete working life, Government Press, Bangalore, 1959

6

Govind Ballabh Pant

Govind Ballabh Pant was born on August 30, 1887 in Shyahi Devi hills in Almora. His mother's name was Govindi. His father, Manorath Pant, was constantly on the road. Govind was brought up by his grandfather, Bandri Dutt Joshi, who played a prominent part in molding the youngster's views. Govind greatly respected his grandfather's firm belief in honesty and tried to inculcate them into his own life.

Education

As a child, Govind was mediocre. He loved playing "gilli danda" and football. He was always late to school. In fact he was never on time most of his young life. All of his interests were those of a layman and did not indicate the shrill and extraordinary individual that he was going to transform into.

In later years of his school he showed a remarkable and impressive growth. He excelled in studies, especially Mathematics and was a leader amongst his classmates. After finishing school, Govind made plans to go to Allahabad to further his education but was discouraged by his relatives on account of Govind's delicate health. The incentive to obtain further education was far grater then his concern towards his health. He said farewell to his relatives and left for Allahabad in 1905. Govind enrolled at the Muir Centeral College where his ingenious and radiant personality was quickly recognized by his professors. He excelled in the fields of Mathematics, Literature and Politics. Even though his health continued to suffer throughout his College career, his avid ambition led him to attain a degree from one of the finest universities in India at the time.

Political Career

His first opportunity to support the Congress came in December 1905 when he served as a swayamsewak at the Congress session at Allahabad. He was greatly impressed by Gopalkrishna Gokhale and Madan Mohan Malaviya's views. Just two years later a kumbh mela took place where Govind, along with Hargovind Pant, a friend, worked as swayamsewaks. Here he made a thundering speech with a distinct nationalist color. The speech was reported to the college Principal, who as punishment, forbade Govind from taking the B.A. examination. Govind was stunned by the action. His main goal to come to Allahabad was to receive a degree and now that was in jeopardy. Pt. Mandan Mohan Malaviya threatened the principal with legal action. Finally the principal succumbed to pressure and allowed Govind to take the examination.

Govind decided to study law in 1907, following his B.A. degree. In 1909 he was awarded the Lumsden award when he scored highest in the Bar examination.

Govind Pant began to practice in Almora in 1910. Then he moved to Ranikhet and eventually to Kashipur, a flourishing and affluent city, in 1912. During his booming practice in Kashipur, he established an organization called Perm Sabha. The main focus of the organization was to integrate social and literary works of India. The Sabha stopped the British from shutting down one of the Kashipur schools by generating enough funds to pay the school taxes.

A law at the time required the local people to carry the luggage of travelling British officials, without payment. The Parishad, under the guidance of Pant, demonstrated and successfully abolished the practice of coolie beggar. The Parishad also fought against illiteracy, hunger and for preservation of forests.

Pant delved into politics in December of 1921. Greatly impressed by Gandhiji's concept of a non-violent freedom struggle, Pant devoted himself to the non-cooperation movement.

Pant was elected to the United Province (renamed Uttar Pradesh by Pant himself) Legislative Assembly as a Swarajist candidate from Nainital. He made a strong impression on the congressmen present in the U.P. Legislative Assembly by giving a remarkable speech on the subject of eroding hills. Pant focused on rapidly passing bills concerning social as well as political reforms badly needed at the time under British Raj. Thus internal reforms became an integral part of Pant's agenda. Many issues such as zamindari, forest preservation, amongst others were addressed in the Legislative Assembly.

In 1925, a few freedom fighters stopped a train and looted government money near Lucknow. The British began to indiscriminantly arrest freedom fighters. Pant tried relentlessly to defend the arrested freedom fighters in court, but the administration had dictated their sentences well before the trial. Three of the men were convicted and hanged while others were given life sentences.

Congress voted to boycott the Simon Commission on account of its all-white panel. The Commission landed in Lahore on October 11, 1928. In a demonstration Lala Lajpat Rai was struck down by lathis and Pant was severely injured (the physical impact would incapacitate him rest of his life) in a procession in Lucknow

After Gandhiji's Salt Satyagraha in March of 1930, Pant

organized a massive salt movement in the United Provinces. In May of 1930 he was arrested and held at Dehra Dun jail. After his release he worked relentlessly against the zamindars and government to protect farmers from high rents. His pleas for lower rents went unanswered and eventually a major famine struck the region.

Pant was arrested for a period of seven months because he attended provincial Congress session in Uttar Pradesh when the Government banned it. Pant joined the U.P. Legislative Council in 1935 when the Government of India Act allowed a provincial government.

In the U.P. ministry, Pant saw the problem of untouchability that had concerned Gandhiji for many years. Pant tried to reach the root of untouchability, which was in prevalence in remote areas where Gandhiji's preachings had not yet reached. Pant reformed many areas during his post. Education, labor's plight and farmers' fight against zamindars were some of the social reforms he focused on.

While the world was submerged in the second World War, India saw a rift develop between the extremist and moderate wings of the Congress. The moderates supported Gandhiji in assisting the British Crown in the war efforts, and the other believed in Subash Chandra Bose's ideology of taking advantage of the situation and toppling the British Raj from India through all means possible. Pant was called to act as a peacemaker, and urged the Congress to support Gandhiji.

In 1940 Pant was arrested on the charge of helping in the satyagraha movement and was sent to Almora prison. On launching "Quit India" resolution in 1942, all the prominent Indian leaders, including Pant, were arrested. Pant was sent to Ahmednagar Jail. From jail he wrote to his children and kept busy writing on political matters. Pant's health continued to deteriorate and finally Nehru had to plead for his release. Pant was released in March of 1945.

After Independence, Pant was nominated Chief Minister

of Uttar Pradesh. During his office, the state faced numerous problems; poverty, black-marketing and unemployment being some of them. The state witnessed many insurgent riots, following partition. Pant traveled to inflicted areas to calm the people. He abolished the zamindari system and worked on many other bills to help farmers. He saw that Harijans were treated fairly, and concentrated on developing the education, medical and industrial (mainly cottage) sectors.

Upon the death of Sardar Patel, Nehru called on Pant to take the position of Home Minister. The most renowned work that he accomplished as Home Minister was to make Hindi the official language of India. In 1957, the Government of India honored Pant with the Bharat Ratna award.

Death

In 1960 Pant suffered a heart attack. In February of 1961, he fell ill while still in office and died on March 7, 1961 after slipping into a coma for several days.

7

Jawaharlal Nehru

Jawaharlal Nehru, also known as Pandit Jawaharlal Nehru, was one of the foremost leaders of Indian freedom struggle. He was the favourite disciple of Mahatma Gandhi and later on went on to become the first Prime Minister of India. Jawahar Lal Nehru is widely regarded as the architect of modern India. He was very fond of children and children used to affectionately call him Chacha Nehru.

Life and Education

Jawahar Lal Nehru was born on November 14, 1889. His father Motilal Nehru was a famous Allahabad based barrister. Jawaharlal Nehru's mother's name was Swaroop Rani. Jawaharlal Nehru was the only son of Motilal Nehru. Motilal Nehru has three daughters apart from Jawaharlal Nehru. Nehrus were Saraswat Brahmin of Kashmiri lineage.

Jawaharlal Nehru received education in some of the finest schools and universities of the world. He did his schooling from Harrow and completed his Law degree from Trinity College, Cambridge. The seven years he spent in England widened his horizons and he acquired a rational and skeptical outlook and sampled Fabian socialism and Irish nationalism, which added to his own patriotic dedication.

Political Career

Jawaharlal Nehru returned to India in 1912 and started legal practice. He married Kamala Nehru in 1916. Jawahar Lal Nehru joined Home Rule League in 1917. His real initiation into politics came two years later when he came in contact with Mahatma Gandhi in 1919. At that time Mahatma Gandhi had launched a campaign against Rowlatt Act. Nehru was instantly attracted to Gandhi's commitment for active but peaceful, civil disobedience. Gandhi himself saw promise and India's future in the young Jawaharlal Nehru.

Nehru family changed its family according to Mahatma Gandhi's teachings. Jawaharlal and Motilal Nehru abandoned western clothes and tastes for expensive possessions and pastimes. They now wore a Khadi Kurta and Gandhi cap. Jawaharlal Nehru took active part in the Non- Cooperation Movement 1920-1922) and was arrested for the first time during the movement. He was released after few months.

Jawaharlal Nehru was elected President of the Allahabad Municipal Corporation in 1924, and served for two years as the city's chief executive. This proved to be a valuable administrative experience for stood him in good stead later on when he became the prime minister of the country. He used his tenure to expand public education, health care and sanitation. He resigned in 1926 citing lack of cooperation from civil servants and obstruction from British authorities.

From 1926 to 1928, Jawaharlal served as the General Secretary of the All India Congress Committee. In 1928-29, the Congress's annual session under President Motilal Nehru was held. During that session Jawaharlal Nehru and Subhas Chandra Bose backed a call for full political independence, while Motilal Nehru and others wanted dominion status within the British Empire. To resolve the point, Gandhi said that the British would be given two years to grant India dominion status. If they did not, the Congress would launch a national struggle for full, political independence. Nehru and Bose reduced the time of opportunity to one year. The British did not respond.

In December 1929, Congress's annual session was held in Lahore and Jawaharlal Nehru was elected as the President of the Congress Party. During that sessions a resolution demanding India's independence was passed and on January 26, 1930 in Lahore, Jawaharlal Nehru unfurled free India's flag. Gandhiji gave a call for Civil Disobedience Movement in 1930. The movement was a great success and forced British Government to acknowledge the need for major political reforms.

When the British promulgated the Government of India Act 1935, the Congress Party decided to contest elections. Nehru stayed out of the elections, but campaigned vigorously nationwide for the party. The Congress formed governments in almost every province, and won the largest number of seats in the Central Assembly. Nehru was elected to the Congress presidency in 1936, 1937, and 1946, and came to occupy a position in the nationalist movement second only to that of Gandhi. Jawaharlal Nehru was arrested in 1942 during Quit India Movement. Released in 1945, he took a leading part in the negotiations that culminated in the emergence of the dominions of India and Pakistan in August 1947.

Nehru as a Nation Builder

In 1947, he became the first Prime Minister of independent India. He effectively coped with the formidable challenges of those times: the disorders and mass exodus of minorities across the new border with Pakistan, the integration of 500-odd princely states into the Indian Union, the framing of a new constitution, and the establishment of the political and administrative infrastructure for a parliamentary democracy.

Jawaharlal Nehru played a key role in building modern India. He set up a Planning Commission, encouraged development of science and technology, and launched three successive five-year plans. His policies led to a sizable growth in agricultural and industrial production. Nehru also played a major role in developing independent India's foreign policy. He called for liquidation of colonialism in Asia and Africa and along with Tito and Nasser, was one of the chief architects of the nonaligned movement. He played a constructive, mediatory role in bringing the Korean War to an end and in resolving other international crises, such as those over the Suez Canal and the Congo, offering India's services for conciliation and international policing. He contributed behind the scenes toward the solution of several other explosive issues, such as those of West Berlin, Austria, and Laos.

Death

But Jawahar Lal Nehru couldn't improve India's relations with Pakistan and China. The Kashmir issue proved a stumbling block in reaching an accord with Pakistan, and the border dispute prevented a resolution with China. The Chinese invasion in 1962, which Nehru failed to anticipate, came as a great blow to him and probably hastened his death. Jawaharlal Nehru died of a heart attack on May 27, 1964.

8

Dhondo Keshav Karve

During the 19th and the early part of the 20th century, India was in the dark grip of casteism and ritualism. Naturally, those who were at the lower end of the social scale suffered the most and amongst them, women bore the brunt all the more, since they were not treated as equal as men. Widows, especially, had a harrowing time as they were considered to be a curse. Because child marriage was widely prevalent, the fate of child widows was particularly pathetic. Touched by the plight of such women and inspired by the works of social reformers, Dhondo Keshav Karve decided to dedicate his life for their cause. Throughout his life, he established numerous institutions that were dedicated towards pulling out women from darkness. He recognized that the main reason for such apathy towards women was that they were bereft of education and so worked towards closing that chasm. It is a testimony to his life that his admirers and well wishers addressed him affectionately as Annasheb, which means elder brother. If women and widows get more respect today, if women are more outgoing and preparing to challenge what was once the bastion of men then it is all because of the selfless and dedicated service of one man, Dhondo Keshav Karve.

Early Life

Dhondo Keshav Karve, affectionately known as Annasheb Karve, was born in the year 1858 in a lower middle-class Chitpavan Brahmin family, in Maharashtra, to Keshav Bapunna Karve. He completed his intermediate from Wilson College in Mumbai and wanted to enter the public service examination but was denied as the authorities thought that he looked too young. So, he studied mathematics at Elphinstone College in Mumbai. In 1891, he joined Fergusson College in Pune as a faculty of mathematics and taught there until 1914. Karve's move to dedicate his life towards the cause of female education and welfare was inspired by the work of Pandita Ramabai, the renowned social reformer. He was also inspired to work for the upliftment of widows, who at those times were looked on with disdain and were considered as social outcasts, by the works of Vishnushastri and Pandit Iswar Chandra Vidyasagar. He also considered the writings of Herbert Spencer to have had a major influence on him.

Social Work

To encourage widow remarriage Karve set up the Widhawa Wiwahottejak Mandali in 1893. Apart from working towards widow remarriages, the organization also worked towards helping the needy children of widows. Two years later, the institute was renamed Widhawa Wiwaha Pratibandh-Niwarak Mandali (Society to Remove Obstacles to Marriages of Widows). Continuing his work on uplifting the status of women in society, he founded a Hindu Widows' Home Association in 1896 in a village called Hingane on the outskirts of Pune. The reason for setting up the institution in such an area was because the Brahmin community opposed his reformist activities. They ostracized him as he was also from the Brahmin community. Not the one to lose hope or be bowed down, he instead re-affirmed his belief all the more and set up a Mahilashram in the same village. This ashram was not only for widows but served as a shelter and school for all women, as educational institutions for women during those days were very scarce. In 1907, Karve started the Mahila Vidyalaya, an educational society for women. To train workers for the Widows Home Association and the Mahila Vidyalaya, he established Nishkam Karma Math (Social Service Society) the following year. In subsequent years as the Widows Home Association flourished, it was renamed Maharshi Karve Stree Shikshan Samstha in honor of its founder.

Since Karve still taught mathematics at the Fergusson College, he would travel daily from the Hingane village to the college. While at the city he would collect donations from sympathizers and also spread awareness about the plight of the widows, and women in general. After reading about the Japan Women's University, Karve was inspired to set up the first women university in India in Pune in the year 1916. The University started with just five students. The University expanded rapidly when in 1920 an industrialist and philanthropist, Sir Vithaldas Thackersey, donated 1.5 million rupees. The university was then renamed Shreemati Nathibai Damodar Thackersey (SNDT) Indian Women's University in honor of the mother of the benefactor. In 1931 the University established the first college in Mumbai. Thereafter, in 1936 the University was shifted to Mumbai from Pune and in 1949 the Government of India recognized it as a statutory university. After setting up the university, he established a Training College for Primary School Teachers the next year and Kanya Shala, a school for girls. Realizing the lack of primary schools in villages, he established in 1936 the Maharashtra Village Primary Education Society whose main goal was to set up schools in villages where there were none. Through this education society, he also sought to promote reading habits among adults. By 1944, he began working towards fostering human equality among his fellow beings. With this aim in view he founded the Samata Sangh (Association for the Promotion of Human Equality).

World Tour

In 1929, on a tour of Europe for a period of six months,

from March to August, Karve attended the Primary Teachers' Conference at Malvern in England. He also attended a meeting of the East India Association at Caxton Hall in London where he delivered a lecture on "Education of Women in India". After England, he toured Geneva and attended an educational conference where he spoke on "The Indian Experiment in Higher Education for Women". He also attended an international meeting of educators set up under the auspices of the New Education Fellowship. He then left for a tour of America visiting various forums and lecturing on women's education and social reforms in India. Subsequently, he went to Tokyo and visited the Women's University and returned to India in April 1930. However, by December of the same year he left for Africa on a fifteen month tour visiting Mombasa, Kenya, Uganda, Tanganyika, Zanzibar, Portuguese East Africa, and South Africa and spreading information about his work on uplifting of the status of women in India.

Awards And Recognition

In 1955, the Government of India honoured Karve with the Padma Vibhushan and in 1958 with the Bharat Ratna for his contributions to social work. In addition, he was awarded the Doctor of Letters by the Banaras Hindu University, Pune University, SNDT University and Mumbai University in 1942, 1951, 1954 and 1957 respectively. The Maharshi Karve Road in Mumbai is named in his honour.

Personal Life

When Karve was fourteen, his parents married him off to an eight year old girl called Radhabai. She passed away in 1891 at the age of twenty-seven due to complications at childbirth. However, their son Raghunath Karve survived who later on became a renowned social reformer. In 1928, Karve published an autobiographical work in Marathi titled 'Atmawrutta' and in 1936 he published another autobiographical work, this time in English titled 'Looking Back'. After the death of his first wife, he married for the second time two years later, a 23 year old widow called Godubai. This act of marrying a widow was against the social mores of that time, which forbade widow remarriage and so he had to face considerable opposition. His reformatory thoughts were supported by his wife who also displayed revolutionary zeal. She had been widowed at the age of eight and in her twenties became the first widow student. With his second wife he had three children, Shankar, Dinkar, and Bhaskar.

Death

The great social reformer Dhondo Keshav Karve passed away on 9th November, 1962 at the age of 105.

9

Dr Bidhan Chandra Roy

Dr Bidhan Chandra Roy, one of the very few people who are talented enough to acquire both the M.R.C.P. and F.R.C.S. degrees, was an eminent physician, one of the most important freedom fighters for India and also the second Chief Minister of West Bengal. Bidhan Chandra Roy led a very eventful life during which he excelled in each profession he had taken up. In addition, Dr Bidhan Chandra Roy also laid the foundation stone of cities Bidhannagar and Kalyani in West Bengal. After his flourishing terms as a part of the alumni of the Calcutta Medical College and as the Vice Chancellor of Calcutta University, Bidhan Chandra Roy entered into active politics and subsequently was elected the Chief Minister of West Bengal, a post that he held till his death. Dr Bidhan Chandra Roy is fondly remembered through the celebration of the National Doctor's Day on July 1 (his birth and death day) every year.

Childhood and Education

Bidhan Chandra Roy was born on July 1, 1882 in the Bankipore region of Patna, Bihar. He was the youngest of the five children of his parents. Bidhan Chandra Roy's mother died when he was 14 years of age and it was his father who took over the reins of the family. Since his father had to remain outdoors for his work as an excise inspector, the five siblings had to share responsibility of all household work. From a very young age, Bidhan Chandra Roy realized the importance of learning domestic work and lending a helping hand even to people who he was not directly related to, lessons which his father instilled in Bidhan Chandra Roy's heart. Bidhan Chandra Roy completed his I.A. from Presidency College, Calcutta and his B.A. from Patna College, Bihar.

After completing his graduation in Mathematics, Bidhan Chandra Roy applied for admission in both Bengal Engineering College and Calcutta Medical College. Being academically competent, he successfully qualified both but chose to pursue medical studies. Bidhan Chandra Roy left Patna in June 1901 to start his medical studies at the Calcutta Medical College. Life at the Calcutta Medical College was very difficult for the future physician. Not only was there the pressure of studies, he also had to earn enough money to support himself in the city as his father was no longer in service. Bidhan Chandra Roy earned scholarships to bear the cost of his studies and books, while completely ignoring personal health. It was during his study years at the Calcutta Medical College that the Partition of Bengal was announced. Though the freedom fighter in Bidhan Chandra Roy wanted to be a part of the state's struggle, he convinced himself that studies were more important than any other activity at that point of time in life.

Career

Dr Bidhan Chandra Roy joined the Provincial Health Service after his studies at Calcutta Medical College were over. While he was appointed as a doctor, B. C. Roy also lent a helping hand as a nurse whenever he had the time. Additionally, he even established a private practice to earn extra money. In February 1909, Bidhan Chandra Roy left for

England to continue further medical studies at St Bartholomew's Hospital in London. But the Dean at the hospital did not want to accept the application of an Asian. Unwilling to return defeated, Bidhan Chandra Roy submitted the same application thirty times, before the authorities at St Bartholomew's Hospital finally relented and allowed him to take admission. By the year 1911, Bidhan Chandra Roy had completed both his M.R.C.P. and F.R.C.S. degrees in a span of only two years and three months, a rare achievement. He returned to India in the year 1911 to join as faculty of Calcutta Medical College, subsequently shifting to the Campbell Medical School and then the Carmichael Medical College.

Right from his childhood days, Bidhan Chandra Roy had learnt about social service from his father. Therefore as a doctor too, he worked for the common man by donating large sums of money towards the establishment of medical colleges which would provide both medical education and medical aid to people. Several medical institutions in Calcutta, like the Jadavpur T.B. Hospital, the R.G. Kar Medical College, the Chittaranjan Seva Sadan, the Chittaranjan Cancer Hospital, the Victoria Institution and the Kamala Nehru Hospital were set up by Bidhan Chandra Roy. Bidhan Chandra Roy entered politics in the year 1925. He contested elections from Barrackpore constituency of the Bengal Legislative Council and won against popular opponent Surendranath Banerjee. The same year Bidhan Chandra Roy tabled a resolution to study the causes, effects and prevention of pollution in the Hooghly district.

In the year 1928, Bidhan Chandra Roy was elected to the All India Congress Committee. He became the leader of the Civil Disobedience Movement in Bengal in the year 1929 when he coaxed Pandit Motilal Nehru to nominate him a member of the CWC. In the year 1930, when the Civil Disobedience Movement was still on, Bidhan Chandra Roy and many other members of the CWC were arrested when the CWC was declared an unlawful body. The August 26 arrest landed Dr B C Roy in Alipore Jail. Bidhan Chandra Roy's involvement with the CWC brought improvements in education, introduced free medical services and led to the establishment of grant in aid hospitals, charitable dispensaries, good roads and better water and electricity supply.

After being elected to the All India Congress Committee, Dr Bidhan Chandra Roy became a good friend of Mahatma Gandhi's. When Gandhi had taken ill during the Quit India Movement of 1942, it was Dr B C Roy who treated him after convincing Gandhi to consume medicines, even though they were not made in India. In the year 1942, Bidhan Chandra Roy was elected as the Vice Chancellor of the University of Calcutta. It was during his term that the Japanese bombings in Rangoon took place, leading to a revolution in Calcutta too. Bidhan Chandra Roy was of the belief that education should not suffer as the more educated the youth, the better they can serve their country. Keeping this principle in mind, B C Roy made special air-raid shelters for students and teachers for classes to be held even at a time of war. He also conducted relief activities for the suffering. It was in recognition of his services that he received the Doctorate of Science degree in 1944.

Chief Minister

Dr Bidhan Chandra Roy's name was proposed by the Congress for the post of the Chief Minister of West Bengal. However, Bidhan Chandra Roy himself never wanted to assume office as the Bengal CM as he wanted to remain dedicated to his profession as a physician, a position he thought would be jeopardized if he assumes such an important office in politics. It was on the insistence of Mahatma Gandhi that Bidhan Chandra Roy agreed to become the Chief Minister of West Bengal and was elected to the position on January 23, 1948. His 14 years as the second West Bengal CM was immensely successful. Bidhan Chandra Roy was instrumental in seeing the end to violence and food and job shortages in the state following the creation of East Pakistan. The Congress also benefited by Bidhan Chandra Roy's association with the party. He was a much loved man among the common people of Bengal and the country as a whole. Though he entered into active politics, Bidhan Chandra Roy never forgot the value of education in one's life. According to him, only education could pave the way to a good and resourceful human being. He made this sentiment clear at a convocation address that he made on December 15, 1956 at the University of Lucknow.

Death

Dr Bidhan Chandra Roy died on July 1, 1962 a little while after he had completed his daily activities of treating patients who visited him during early hours of the morning and also going over political matters of West Bengal.

Honors

In recognition of his immense services to the society, Dr Bidhan Chandra Roy was awarded the highest civilian award, the Bharat Ratna by the government of India on February 4, 1961. Dr Bidhan Chandra Roy's residence was converted into a nursing home named after his mother Aghorkamini Devi. The government of India set up the Dr B C Roy Memorial Library and Reading Room for Children in the Children's Book Trust in New Delhi in the year 1967. The B C Roy National Award was also started in the year 1976 to celebrate the contributions of individuals in the fields of medicine, politics, science, philosophy, arts and literature.

10

Purushottam Das Tandon

Purushottam Das Tandon, the Punjabi Khatri from pre-independent Uttar Pradesh in India, was one of the most popular advocates of freedom for the country from British rule. Purushottam Das Tandon worked in association with the Congress party and took part in several events to show his protests against the British rulers. He was dedicated to the well being of his country even after independence and thus, remained attached with politics after August 1947. However, his years within the folds of the Congress were not free of controversies, largely because of his deteriorating relationship with Jawaharlal Nehru after India's independence. Purushottam Das Tandon is best remembered for his contribution towards helping to make Hindi the official language of India and for his participation in party meetings held at the Lok Sabha in spite of the fact that he was the Speaker and was expected to remain neutral and impartial in his opinions and views.

Early Life

Purushottam Das Tandon was born on August 1, 1882 in the city of Allahabad in Uttar Pradesh in British-dominated India. After completing school, Purushottam Das Tandon obtained a degree in Law and another masters degree in History before setting on a professional life. The year 1906 was his first year in law practice after which Purushottam Das Tandon joined the bar of the Allahabad High Court. In the year 1908, he joined as a junior to prominent lawyer Tej Bahadur Sapru. For the next few years Purushottam Das Tandon practiced law before finally quitting in the year 1921 to concentrate on politics and freedom struggle.

Role in Freedom Struggle

Purushottam Das Tandon was dedicated towards achieving freedom for India since his student days. Even while he was studying, he became a member of the Congress party in the year 1899 and found time to be a part of some activities undertaken by the party for the welfare of India. In 1906, when Purushottam Das Tandon also started practicing law, he represented his native Allahabad at the All India Congress Committee. He was also involved in the workings of the Lok Sevak Sangh and the committee instituted for studying the Jallianwala Bagh incident of 1919.

After he left law practice in 1921, Purushottam Das Tandon courted arrest because of his involvement in the Non Cooperation Movement of the 1920s and the Satyagraha incident of the 1930s. Purushottam Das Tandon was elected the president of the Provincial Kisan Sabha in Bihar in the year 1934 and it was during his term and leadership that several farmers' movements started in pre independent India. Purushottam Das Tandon was elected to the Constituent Assembly of India in the year 1946 and remained in office of the Speaker of the Legislative Assembly of Uttar Pradesh for a period of 13 years, spanning pre and post independence times from July 31, 1937 to August 10, 1950.

After Independence Politics

Purushottam Das Tandon contested for the post of President of the Congress party in the year 1948 but lost to Pattabhi Sitaramayya. However he was successful in securing the same position after two years in 1950 defeating Acharya Kriplani to head the Nagpur session of Congress the same year. Purushottam Das Tandon became a member of the Lok Sabha in the year 1952 and joined the Rajya Sabha in 1956. After 1956, Purushottam Das Tandon gradually became ill and had to quit from active politics to take care of his health.

Controversies and Contradictions

As mentioned earlier, the career of Purushottam Das Tandon was marked with many a controversy. Firstly, though it was the freedom fighter himself who spoke about the similarities between the Hindus and the Muslims, his actions showed that Purushottam Das Tandon was inclined towards the Hindus, a fact which also resulted in securing for him the name of 'soft Hindu nationalist'. He was associated with the Radha Soami cult and always tried to incorporate Hindu religious ideals in politics. Purushottam Das Tandon was one politician who spoke out vehemently against the concept of religious conversion, even voicing his thoughts in the constituent assembly of the country.

Purushottam Das Tandon also spoke out against the partition of India after independence. He was one of the rare members of the AICC who protested before ratifying the resolution that would lead to partition. However many people were of the opinion that his unwillingness to share power with the Muslim League after the 1937 elections actually led to the partition of India after 1947. The relationship between Jawaharlal Nehru and Purushottam Das Tandon was good as long as the former commended the latter on his 'No Tax' campaign. It was during the 1940s that the first signs of dissent began to appear. Purushottam Das Tandon's success in bagging the post of president of the Congress party against favorite Acharya Kriplani annoyed Jawaharlal Nehru more and destroyed their relationship further.

Advocating the Hindi Language

Purushottam Das Tandon worked furtively with the Hindi Prachar Sabhas to bring the Hindi language at the forefront and establish it as the official language of the country. However, in his efforts to promote Hindi, Purushottam Das Tandon completely ignored other Indian languages and was labeled a chauvinist. While leaders like Mahatma Gandhi voted for Hindustani, a mixture of Hindi and Urdu to be declared the national language, Purushottam Das Tandon spoke against the Urdu script, voting for the Devanagari script instead. This was a further cause for the deterioration of his relationship with Jawaharlal Nehru. Purushottam Das Tandon was for the Sanskritisation of the Hindi language and his argument while promoting the Hindi language in the constituent assembly was that the mother tongue should be used as the medium of instruction. It was largely due to Purushottam Das Tandon's efforts that Hindi became the national language of India.

Anecdotes on Purushottam Das Tandon

Purushottam Das Tandon was always different from the other freedom fighters during his time in terms of his pattern of work and attitude. Here are some popular anecdotes which made the rounds on Purushottam Das Tandon:

- He was a staunch believer of ahimsa or non violence and therefore used only rubber chappals instead of leather ones.
- While Speakers used to avoid party meetings in order to maintain their stance of impartiality, Purushottam Das Tandon attended all of them and also said that he would resign from his position as Speaker if the house lacks confidence in his actions. No members of the house dared speak about this issue.

- Purushottam Das Tandon was also known for his philanthropic nature. He often asked a clerk responsible for handling the salaries of the members of parliament to drop his cheques to a public service fund. His argument was that he got enough money from his seven sons, all of whom were earning and all of whom sent him one hundred rupees per month. Therefore he did not require his own salary and could thus use it for the welfare of the needy. His complete disinterest in money and possessions earned him the title of 'Rajarshi'.

Awards and Recognition

- Purushottam Das Tandon earned the tile 'Rajarshi' which means 'Royal Saint' in Sanskrit for his giving and unselfish nature.
- He was presented the Bharat Ratna, the highest civilian award of India in the year 1961, just a year before his death.

11

Dr. Rajendra Prasad

Dr. Rajendra Prasad was the first President of independent India. He was the President of the Constituent Assembly that drafted the Constitution. He had also served as a Cabinet Minister briefly in the first Government of independent India. Dr. Rajendra Prasad was one of the foremost disciples of Gandhiji and he played a crucial role in Indian freedom struggle.

Dr. Rajendra Prasad was born on December 3, 1884 in Ziradei village in Siwan district of Bihar. His father's name was Mahadev Sahay and his mother's name was Kamleshwari Devi. Rajendra Prasad was youngest among his siblings. Mahadev Sahay was a Persian and Sanskrit language scholar. Dr. Rajendra Prasad was greatly attached to his mother and elder brother Mahendra.

Education

At the age of five Rajendra Prasad was, according to the practice in the community to which he belonged, put under a Maulavi who taught him Persian. Later, he was taught Hindi and arithmetic. At the age of 12, Rajendra Prasad was married to Rajvanshi Devi.

Dr. Rajendra Prasad was a brilliant student. He stood first in the entrance examination to the University of Calcutta, and was awarded a monthly scholarship of Rs.30. He joined the famous Calcutta Presidency College in 1902. Here his teachers included the great scientist Jagdish Chandra Bose and the highly respected Prafulla Chandra Roy. Later on he switched from Science to Arts and completed his M.A. and Masters in Law. Meanwhile, in 1905, Doctor, Rajendra Prasad was initiated into the Swadeshi Movement by his elder brother Mahendra. He also joined the Dawn Society run by Satish Chandra Mukherjee, and Sister Nivedita.

Gandhi and Rajendra Prasad

The arrival of Mahatma Gandhi on the Indian national scene greatly influenced Dr. Rajendra Prasad. While Gandhiji was on a fact-finding mission in Champaran district of Bihar, he called on Rajendra Prasad to come to Champaran with volunteers. Dr. Rajendra Prasad was greatly impressed by the dedication, conviction and courage that Gandhiji displayed. Gandhiji's influence greatly altered Dr. Rajendra Prasad's outlook. He sought ways to simplify his life and reduced the number of servants he had to one. He started doing his daily chores such as sweeping the floor, washing the utensils-the tasks he had all along assumed others would do for him.

After coming into contact with Gandhiji, Dr. Rajendra Prasad, immersed himself fully into the freedom struggle. He played a active role during Non-Cooperation Movement. Dr. Rajendra Prasad was arrested in 1930 while participating in Salt Satyagraha. He was in jail when on 15 January 1934 a devastating earthquake struck Bihar. Rajendra Prasad was released from the jail two days later and he immediately set himself for the task of raising funds and organizing relief. The Viceroy also raised a fund for the purpose. However, while Rajendra Prasad's fund collected over Rs.3.8million, the Viceroy could only manage one-third of that amount. The way the relief was organized, it amply demonstrated the administrative acumen of Dr. Rajendra Prasad. Soon after this Dr Rajendra Prasad was elected as the President of the Bombay session of the Indian National Congress. He was elected as Congress President again in 1939 in the following the resignation of Netaji Subash Chandra Bose.

In July 1946, when the Constituent Assembly was established to frame the Constitution of India, Dr. Rajendra Prasad was elected its President. Two and a half years after independence, on January 26, 1950, the Constitution of independent India was ratified and Dr. Rajendra Prasad was elected as India's first President. As a President, he used his moderating influence silently and unobtrusively and set a healthy precedent for others to follow. During his tenure as President he visited many countries on missions of goodwill and sought to establish and nourish new relationships.

In 1962, after 12 years as President, Dr. Rajendra Prasad retired, and was subsequently awarded the Bharat Ratna, the nation's highest civilian award.

Death

He spent the last few months of his life in retirement at the Sadaqat Ashram in Patna. Dr. Rajendra Prasad died on February 28, 1963.

12

Dr Zakir Hussain

Dr Zakir Hussain is best known for his two year stint at the office of the President of India spanning from May 13, 1967 to May 3, 1969. He was the third President of independent India. However, it is not only his career in the President's office which makes him one of the greatest heroes that India has seen. Dr Zakir Hussain was one of the biggest exponents of education in India and it was under his leadership that the National Muslim University was founded. Till today, the National Muslim University exists under the name of Jamia Milia Islamia, a central university in New Delhi, and continues to flourish, producing some of the best students each year. Dr Zakir Hussain had served as the Governor of Bihar and had also taken oath as the Vice President of the country before ending his political career as the third President of India.

Childhood & Early Life

Zakir Hussain was born in the Kaimganj district of Farrukhabad in Uttar Pradesh. Though he was born an Indian, his family history can be traced back to the Pushtun tribes that occupied the border areas between Pakistan and Afghanistan. It is said that his ancestors migrated to Uttar Pradesh during the 18th century. His father and mother passed away when he was only 10 and 14 years old respectively, leaving young Zakir to complete his school education from the Islamia High School in Etawah. He, later, attended the Anglo-Muhammadan Oriental College in Aligarh (today known as the Aligarh Muslim University), the place which saw the beginning of his career as a reformist politician.

Middle Years

Zakir Hussain had already gained recognition throughout India as the leader of the student union during his years of study at the Anglo-Muhammadan Oriental College. However, it was not only politics that interested him. After completing his formal education, Zakir Hussain became the leader of a young group of students who together founded the National Muslim University in Aligarh on October 29, 1920. (The university then shifted base to Karol Bagh, New Delhi in 1925. Ten year later it yet again shifted base this time permanently to Jamia Nagar, New Delhi and was named it Jamia Millia Islamia). He was merely 23 years old when he established the educational institution

Zakir's keen interest and dedication towards education more than politics became evident when he went to Germany to pursue a PhD in Economics. It was in the University of Berlin that Zakir Hussain brought out an anthology of some of the best works of Urdu poet Mirza Khan Ghalib. The chief motive of Zakir Hussain was to use education as the chief tool to help India during the period of freedom struggle against the British. In fact, Zakir Hussain was so dedicated in his goal towards dissemination of education in India, that he was also successful in winning the attention of his adversary, Mohammed Ali Jinnah, in the field of politics.

Return To India

Though Dr. Zakir Hussain visited Germany for his

education, he returned soon after to provide academic and administrative leadership to Jamia Milia Islamia. The university was on the verge of being shut down in the year 1927 and it was due to the efforts of Dr Zakir Hussain that the educational institution has managed to stay afloat. He continued to lend his support, providing academic and managerial leadership to the institution for twenty one years. It was due to his efforts that the university immensely contributed in India's struggle for freedom from the British Rule. As a teacher, Dr Zakir Hussain propagated the learnings of Mahatma Gandhi and Hakim Ajmal Khan. He was an active member of several educational reform movements in the country in the mid 1930s.

Dr Zakir Hussain was elected the Vice Chancellor of the Aligarh Muslim University (his alma mater previously known as Anglo-Muhammadan Oriental College) in independent India. During his stint as Vice Chancellor, Dr Zakir Hussain was able to avert several teachers within the institution from lending their support in creating a separate state of Pakistan. Dr. Zakir Hussain was awarded Padma Vibhushan in 1954. With the end of his term as Vice Chancellor of Aligarh Muslim University, Dr Zakir Hussain was nominated to the Rajya Sabha and thus, became a member of the Indian Parliament in 1956. However, he held this position only for a year after which he became the Governor of Bihar, a post he occupied for five years from 1957 - 1962.

Zakir was honored with the Bharat Ratna award in 1963. He was also the recipient of D.Litt. (Honoris Causa) by the Universities of Delhi, Calcutta, Aligarh, Allahabad and Cairo. With the end of his term as Governor, Dr Zakir Hussain soon succeeded to the office of Vice President of India, becoming the second Vice President of the country for a period of five years. It was on May 13, 1967 that Dr Zakir Hussain created history by being the first Muslim President of India to be elected for such a prestigious position. He was also the third politician to occupy the office of the Indian President, after Dr Rajendra Prasad, Sarvepalli Radhakrishnan.

Death

Dr Zakir Hussain passed away on the 3rd of May, 1969, two years after he was sworn in as President of India. His death also made him the first President to die while still in office. He was buried on the campus of the Jamia Millia Islamia (or Central University) in New Delhi.

13

Dr. Pandurang Vaman Kane

Some of the greatest writings on social reforms of India came from this man, Dr. Pandurang Vaman Kane. He was conferred with an honorary degree of doctor of law at a special convocation ceremony. He was an indologist, i.e., a person who excels at languages and literature, and could converse easily in both Sanskrit and English. He authored several books, especially on religious and civil law. In these books, he compiled the scriptures of ancient and medieval India. Being a scholar, this great person was revered all over the country. The book 'History of Dharmasastra', penned by Dr. Kane is, by far, one of the most inspiring books written about the social reforms of ancient India. The title 'Mahamahopadhyaya' (the greatest teacher of all teachers) was bestowed upon him in his later days and in 1963, he was given the highest civilian award of India, the Bharat Ratna.

Early Life

Dr. Kane was born in the Ratnagiri district of Maharashtra to a very conservative Chitpavan Brahmin family. Not much is known about his background or his family history. Dr.

Kane graduated from the University of Mumbai and worked there as a historian and Vice Chancellor. He also helped in establishing the Kurukshetra University in Indic studies.

Career

In 1930, Dr. Kane's best known work, 'History of Dharmasastra' - which was under the subtitle 'Ancient and Medieval Religions and Civil Law in India' - was published. This book's launch was announced by Dr. Radhakrishnan and it has been a significant landmark in the history of India. The book was a true combination of conception and execution and has nearly 6500 pages of information, such as several texts and manuscripts, all compiled in one. It is also known to contain certain information on the Mahabharat, Puranas and Kautilya in Sanskrit. Dr. Kane's basic idea behind writing the book was to make the public aware of the ancient social laws and customs in India and also to study the social processes that were prevalent in ancient India. The last publication was on November 17th 1962. He was said to have used reliable resources like the Asiatic Society of Bombay and the Bhandarkar Oriental Research Institute.

His next work as an author was a book called 'Vyavaharamayukha'. An introductory paragraph on the history of Dharmasastra was included in this book so that the reader got a fair idea of the subject, apart from the contents of the book itself. This became one of his major works and was translated into English and Marathi, apart from being written in Sanskrit. It was made up of nearly 15000 pages.

An additional part of Dr. Kane's career was spent in debating the Indian constitution. He believed that these set of rules and regulations were a break from traditional ideas that were widespread in India. He further implied that people residing in this country have rights but no obligations.

Several issues were brought to light due to the nature of his work and writings. During the reign of the Atal Bihari Vajpayee in India, there was a discussion whether the ancient Indian ate beef. For answers, they reverted to Dr. Kane's works to prove that Hindus respected and worshipped the Cow and eating beef was not allowed. Another example was the issue of whether girls in India were allowed to wear the sacred thread. But, it was found out, through his books, that it was restricted only to men.

Death

The exact date and cause of Dr. Kane's death remain unknown. However, it is confirmed that it happened in the year 1972 when he was 92 years old.

Awards And Accolades

He was the Mahamahopadhyaya for his excellence in writings. Therefore, his name is always prefixed with an MM.

He was awarded the prestigious, Sahiya Akademi Award in 1956 for 'History of Dharmasastra, Vol IV' under the category of Sanskrit translation.

Dr. Kane was also an esteemed honorary member of the Bhartiya Vidya Bhavan where he achieved new heights of greatness.

Becoming a part of the Rajya Sabha as a Member of Parliament (MP) was also under his list of achievements and he was there for having a distinguished record in the field of academics.

Last but not least, he was conferred with the highest civilian accolade of India, the Bharat Ratna, in 1963.

Legacy

In 1974, for his study on Religious and Civil Law, the town hall of the Asiatic Society of Bombay (where he conducted his research) commemorated him with an institute called the MM P. V. Kane Institute for Post Graduate Studies and Research.

His legacy is furthered by the fact that a P. V. Kane Gold Medal is given to scholars for their outstanding contribution in the study of Vedic, Dharmasastra or Alankara Literature.

14

Lal Bahadur Shastri

Lal Bahadur Shastri was the second Prime Minister of independent India. Though diminutive in physical stature he was a man of great courage and will. He successfully led country during the 1965 war with Pakistan. To mobilize the support of country during the war he coined the slogan of "Jai Jawan Jai Kisan". Lal Bahadur Sastri also played a key role in India's freedom struggle. He led his life with great simplicity and honesty and was a great source of inspiration for all the countrymen.

Early Life

Lal Bahadur Shastri was born on October 2, 1904 at Mughalsarai, Uttar Pradesh. His parents were Sharada Prasad and Ramdulari Devi. Lal Bahadur's surname was Srivastava but he dropped it as he did not want to indicate his caste. Lal Bahadur's father was a school teacher and later on he became a clerk in the Revenue Office at Allahabad. Though Sharada Prasad was poor, he lived a life of honesty and integrity. Lal Bahadur lost his father when he was only one. Ramdulari Devi raised Lal Bahadur and her two daughters at her father's house.

There is a very famous incident regarding Lal Bahadur Shastri's childhood which took place when he was six years old. One day, while returning from school, Lal Bahadur and his friends went to an orchard that was on the way to home. Lal Bahadur Shastri was standing below while his friends climbed the trees to pluck mangoes. Meanwhile, the gardener came and caught hold of Lalbahadur Shastri. He scolded Lal Bahadur Shastri and started beating him. Lal Bahadur Shastri pleaded to gardener to leave him as he was orphan. Taking pity on Lal Bahadur, the gardener said, "Because you are an orphan, it is all the more important that you must learn better behavior." These words left a deep imprint on Lal Bahadur Shastri and he swore to behave better in the future.

Political Career

Lal Bahadur stayed at his grandfather's house till he was ten. By that time he had passed the sixth standard examination. He went to Varanasi for higher education. In 1921 when Mahatma Gandhi launched the non-cooperation movement against British Government, Lal Bahadur Shastri, was only seventeen years old. When Mahatma Gandhi gave a call to the youth to come out of Government schools and colleges, offices and courts and to sacrifice everything for the sake of freedom, Lal Bahadur came out of his school. Though his mother and relatives advised him not to do so, he was firm in his decision. Lal Bahadur was arrested during the Non-cooperation movement but as he was too young he was let off.

After his release Lal Bahadur joined Kashi Vidya Peeth and for four years he studied philosophy. In 1926, Lal Bahadur earned the degree of "Shastri" After leaving Kashi Vidya Peeth, Lal Bahadur Shastri joined "The Servants of the People Society", which Lala Lajpat Rai had started in 1921. The aim of the Society was to train youths that were prepared to dedicate their lives in the service of the country. In 1927, Lal Bahadur Shastri married Lalitha Devi. The marriage ceremony was very simple and Shastriji took only a charkha (spinning wheel) and few yards of Khadi in dowry.

In 1930, Gandhiji gave the call for Civil Disobedience Movement. Lal Bahadur Shastri joined the movement and encouraged people not to pay land revenue and taxes to the government. He was arrested and put in jail for two and a half years. In jail Shastriji became familiar with the works of western philosophers, revolutionaries and social reformers. Lal Bahadur Shastri had great self respect. Once when he was in prison, one of his daughters fell seriously ill. The officers agreed to release him out for a short time but on condition that he should agree in writing not to take part in the freedom 'movement during this period. Lal Bahadur did not wish to participate in the freedom movement during his temporary release from prison; but he said that he would not give it in writing. He thought that it was against his self-respect to give it in writing.

After Second World War started in 1939, Congress launched "Individual Satyagraha" in 1940 to demand freedom. Lal Bahadur Shastri was arrested during Individual Satyagraha and released after one year. On August 8, 1942, Gandhiji gave the call for Quit India Movement. Lal Bahadur actively participated in the movement. He went underground but was later arrested. Lal Bahadur Shastri was released in 1945 along with other major leaders. He earned the praise of Pandit Govind Vallabh Pant by his hard work during the 1946 provincial elections. Lal Bahadur's administrative ability and organization skills came to the fore during this time. When Govind Vallabh Pant became the Chief Minister of Uttar Pradesh, he appointed Lal Bahadur Shastri as his Parliamentary Secretary. In 1947, Lal Bahadur Shastri became the Minister of Police and Transport in Pant's Cabinet.

Lal Bahadur Sastri was the General Secretary of the Congress Party when the first general elections were held after India became Republic. Congress Party returned to power with a huge majority. In 1952, Jawahar Lal Nehru appointed Lal Bahadur Shastri as the Railways and Transport Minister in the Central Cabinet. Lal Bahadur Shastri's contribution in providing more facilities to travelers in third class compartments cannot be forgotten. He reduced the vast disparity between the first class and third class in the Railways. Lal Bahadur Shastri resigned from Railways in 1956, owning moral responsibility for a railway accident. Jawaharlal Nehru tried to persuade Shastriji but Lal Bahadur Shastri refused to budge from his stand. By his action Lal Bahadur Shastri set new standards of morality in public life.

In the next general elections when Congress returned to power, Lal Bahadur Shastri became the Minister for Transport and Communications and later the Minister for Commerce and Industry. He became the Home Minister in 1961, after the death of Govind Vallabh Pant. In the 1962 India-China war Shastriji played a key role in maintaining internal security of the country.

After the death of Jawaharlal Nehru in 1964, Lal Bahadur Shastri was unanimously elected as the Prime Minister of India. It was a difficult time and the country was facing huge challenges. There was food shortage in the country and on the security front Pakistan was creating problems. In 1965, Pakistan tried to take advantage of India's vulnerability and attacked India. Mild-mannered Lal Bahadur Shastri rose to the occasion and led the country ably. To enthuse soldiers and farmers he coined the slogan of "Jai Jawan, Jai Kisan". Pakistan lost the war and Shastriji's leadership was praised all over the world.

Death

In January 1966, to broker peace between India and Pakistan, Russia mediated a meeting between Lal Bahadur Shastri and Ayub Khan in Tashkent, Russia. India and Pakistan signed the joint declaration under Russian mediation. Under the treaty India agreed to return to Pakistan all the territories occupied by it during the war. The joint declaration was signed on January 10, 1966 and Lal Bahadur Shastri died of heart attack on the same night.

15

Indira 'Priyadarshini' Gandhi

Life

Indira 'Priyadarshini' Gandhi was born on 19 November, 1917, in Allahabad to Kamala and Jawaharlal Nehru. Indira's father was a well-educated lawyer and an active member of the Indian Independence Movement. Since the Nehru family was the centre of national political activity, Indira Gandhi was exposed to politics when she was a little child. A leader like Mahatma Gandhi was among the frequent visitors of the Nehru house in Allahabad. She passed her Metric from Pune University and went to Shantiniketan in West Bengal. Here, the students were made to lead a very strict and disciplined life. She later went on to study in Switzerland and Oxford University in London. Indira, then stayed few months in Switzerland with her ailing mother. In 1936, after Kamala Nehru finally succumbed to tuberculosis, she returned to India. At the time of Kamala's death, Jawaharlal Nehru, was languishing in the Indian jails.

After his return to the country, Indira showed an active participation in the national movement. She also became a member of the Indian National Congress. Here, she met Feroze Gandhi, a journalist and key member of the Youth Congress - the youth wing of the Congress Party. In 1941, despite his father's objections, she married Feroze Gandhi. In 1944, Indira gave birth to Rajiv Gandhi followed two years later by Sanjay Gandhi.

Post Independence

After the independence, Indira Gandhi's father Jawaharlal Nehru became the first Prime Minister of India. Indira Gandhi decided to shift to Delhi to assist his father. Her two sons remained with her but Feroze decided to stay back in Allahabad. He was working as an editor of The National Herald newspaper founded by Motilal Nehru.

During the 1951-52 Parliamentary Elections, Indira Gandhi handled the campaigns of her husband, Feroze, who was contesting from Rae Bareli, Uttar Pradesh. After being elected as MP, Feroze opted to live in a separate house in Delhi.

Feroze soon became a prominent force against the corruption in the Nehru led government. He exposed a major scandal involving prominent insurance companies and the Finance Minister T.T. Krishnamachari. The Finance Minister was considered to be a close aide of Prime Minister Jawaharlal Nehru. Feroze had developed as a noted figure in the country's political circle. He, with a small coterie of supporters and advisors continued to challenge the Central government. On 8 September 1960, Feroze died after a major cardiac arrest.

India as Congress President

In 1959, Indira Gandhi was elected as the President of the Indian National Congress Party. She was one of the political advisors of Jawaharlal Nehru. After the death of Jawaharlal Nehru on 27 May 1964, Indira Gandhi decided to contest elections and eventually elected. She was appointed as the in-charge of the Information and Broadcasting Ministry under Prime Minister Lal Bahadur Shastri

It was believed that Indira Gandhi was an adept at the art of politics and image-making. This is corroborated by an event happened during the Indo-Pakistani War of 1965. While the war was going, Indira Gandhi went on a holiday trip to Srinagar. Despite repeated warnings by the security forces that Pakistani insurgents had entered very close to the hotel, she was staying, Gandhi refused to move. The incident fetched her huge national and international media attention.

As Prime Minister

Following the death of Lal Bahadur Shastri on 11 January 1966, in Tashkent, the race to the coveted throne of Prime Minister began. The party faced a serious trouble, as, all the senior leaders of the Congress party desired to contest. Unable to reach at a consensus, the high-command picked Indira as their contender. The virtual reason behind Indira's selection was the thought that "Indira would, indirectly be run by the top leadership." But Indira Gandhi, showing extraordinary political skills elbowed the Congress stalwarts out of power.

In 1971, in order to stop the Bangladeshi refugees from flowing in into the country, Indira Gandhi supported the East Pakistan's struggle for freedom against West Pakistan. India provided logistical support and also sent troops to fight against West Pakistan. India's triumph in the war of 1971 against Pakistan enhanced the popularity of Indira Gandhi as a shrewd political leader.

Imposition of Emergency

In 1975, the Opposition parties and social activists staged regular demonstrations against the Indira Gandhi-led Central government over rising inflation, the poor state of economy and unchecked corruption. The same year, a ruling of Allahabad High Court that Indira Gandhi had used illegal practices during the last election helped in adding fuel to the existing political fire. The verdict ordered her to vacate her seat, immediately. The agitation and anger of the people intensified. Realizing the consequences, on 26 June, 1975, Indira Gandhi declared "an emergency, due to the turbulent political situation in the country".

During the state of emergency, her political foes were imprisoned, constitutional rights of the citizens were abrogated, and the press placed under strict censorship. The Gandhian socialist Jaya Prakash Narayan and his supporters sought to unify students, peasants and labour organizations in a 'Total non-violent Revolution' to transform Indian society. Narayan was later arrested and jailed.

Meanwhile, her younger son, Sanjay Gandhi, began to run the country with full-authority. Sanjay Gandhi had ordered the removal of slum dwellings, and in an attempt to curb India's growing population, initiated a highly resented program of forced sterilization.

In 1977, fearing military coup if the emergency continued further, Indira Gandhi called for elections. She was brutally thrashed by the emerging Janata Dal, led by Morarji Desai and Jai Prakash Narayan. Congress managed to win only 153 Lok Sabha seats, as compared to 350 seats it grabbed in the previous Lok Sabha.

With so little in common among the allies of the Janata Party, the members were busy in internal strife. In an effort to expel Indira Gandhi from the Parliament, the Janata government ordered to arrest her. However, the strategy failed disastrously and gained Indira Gandhi, a great sympathy from the people who had considered her as an autocrat just two years back.

In the next elections, Congress returned to power with a landslide majority. Experts viewed the victory of the Congress as a result of inefficient and ineffective "Janata Dal".

Operation Blue Star and her assassination

In September 1981, a Sikh militant group demanding "Khalistan" entered into the premises of the Golden Temple, Amritsar. Despite the presence of thousands of civilians in the Temple complex, Indira Gandhi ordered the Army to barge into the holy shrine. The operation was carried out with tanks and armored vehicles. The act was viewed as an unparalleled tragedy in the Indian political history. The impact of the onslaught increased the communal tensions in the country. Many Sikhs resigned from the armed and civil administrative office and also returned their government awards. On 31 October 1984, Indira Gandhi's bodyguards Satwant Singh and Beant Singh, as a revenge of the Golden Temple assault, assassinated the Prime Minister at her Safdarjung Road residence.

16

V.V. Giri

If the situation in the labor force of India is going from strength to strength, if workers in Indian industries and other sectors are able to exercise their rights today, then the only person responsible for this is the charismatic activist and social reformer V.V Giri. Thanks to him, the labour force found a new voice and it was only through his struggles and leadership, his sympathies and concern for the weaker class that ensured that the rights of workers were not trampled upon. V.V. Giri was built on the socialist mold, but at the same time, he was a pragmatist who believed in the practical and humane approach to all problems. His dream of a career in law was cut short when he came under the influence of Irish nationalists and a chance meeting with Gandhi made him decide to work for his country. He realized that if the labor force of India can be organized then not only can their condition be improved, but they can also become a potent force in the national struggle for freedom from the British rule. His commitment to his cause and his abiding empathy for the weak and the downtrodden had kept him in a league that is far different from any other politician nowadays.

Childhood & Early Life

Varahagiri Venkata Giri was born in a Telugu-speaking Brahmin family in Berhampur in the year 1894. His father, Varahagiri Venkata Jogaiah Pantulu, was an eminent and prosperous lawyer. The young lad completed his primary and secondary education in his hometown. In order to study law, V.V Giri went to the University College Dublin in 1913. The same year, he met Gandhi who influenced Giri deeply and finally made him realize that the freedom struggle is far more important than law. At college, Giri became involved with the Sinn Fein movement which led to his expulsion from Ireland in 1916, leaving him unable to complete his law degree. It was the freedom and workers movement of Ireland and the revolutionary ideas of people like De Valera, Collins, Pearee, Desmond Fitzgerald, MacNeil, and Connolly, whom he met personally, that influenced him further to participate in such movements in India. Subsequently, V.V Giri returned to India and started actively participating in the Labour Movement, later becoming the General Secretary. He was also very active in the Nationalist Movement.

Career

Pre-Independence

By 1922, Giri became a trusted aide of N.M. Joshi, who worked for the cause of the workers, and with the support of his mentor, Giri aligned himself with the organizations working for the cause of the working class. Later, because of his commitment to the Trade Union Movement, he was elected as the President of the All India Railwaymen's Federation. He also served as the President of the All India Trade Union Congress twice, once in 1926 and again in 1942. He was instrumental in propelling the various trade unions towards the nationalist movement. From 1931 to 1932, as a Worker's Representative, Giri attended the Second Round Table

Conference in London. In 1934 he was selected as a member of the Imperial Legislative Assembly. His tryst with politics began when he stood in 1936 General Elections as a Congress candidate. He won the election and the next year his party made him the Minister of Labor and Industries in the Madras Presidency. When the Congress Government resigned in 1942 to protest against the British rule, V.V. Giri returned to the Labour Movement to take part in the Quit India Movement. He was imprisoned and sent to jail. Again, after the General Election of 1946 he was given the labour ministry.

Post-Independence

After India got its independence, V.V. Giri was sent to Ceylon as the High Commissioner. After his tenure there, he returned to India and ran for Parliament in 1952, when he was elected for the 1st Lok Sabha and served till 1957. During this time, Giri was made a member of the Union Cabinet heading the Ministry of Labor and served from 1952 until his resignation in 1954. After his stint at the Lok Sabha, he headed a team of distinguished academicians and public men working towards promoting the study of labor and industrial relations. Their efforts bore fruit when in the year 1957 The Indian Society of Labor Economics was established. After union activism and politics, another era for this statesman began when he was appointed as the Governor of Uttar Pradesh, where he served from 1957 to 1960 and then as the Governor of Kerala from 1960 to 1965 and finally as the Governor of Mysore from 1965 to 1967.

From 1957, while still occupying the post of Governor, he worked as the President of the Indian Conference of Social Work. Then after a decade long spell of being the Governor of various Indian states, he was elected as the Vice-President of India in 1967. In 1969, when the then President Zakir Hussain passed away V.V Giri became the acting President. He, then, ran the election for the post of the president and after initial opposition from his party members whom he prevailed over he became the fourth President of India and served till 1974. The Government of India recognized his contributions and achievement when he was awarded the Bharat Ratna, India's highest civilian award in 1975. Throughout his life, V.V Giri was noted for his oratorical skills. He was also a prolific writer who has written books on "Industrial Relations" and "Labor problems in Indian industry".

Legacy

In 1974, the Government of India's Ministry of Labor established an autonomous institution for "research, training, education, publication and consultancy on labour related issues". This institution was, in 1995, renamed the V.V Giri National Labor Institute in his honor. An outspoken activist of labor rights, Giri will always be remembered for his work towards uplifting the workers and working towards preserving their rights.

Personal Life & Death

V.V Giri married early in life to Saraswati Bai. At the age of 85, Giri passed away in Chennai in the year 1980.

17

Kumarasami Kamaraj

Kumarasami Kamaraj , better known as **K. Kamaraj**, (15 July 1903 – 2 October 1975) was an Indian politician from Tamil Nadu widely acknowledged as the "Kingmaker" in Indian politics during the 1960s. He was the chief minister of Tamil Nadu during 1954–1963 and a Member of Parliament during 1952–1954 and 1969–1975. He was known for his simplicity and integrity.

He was involved in the Indian independence movement. As a high-ranking office bearer of the Indian National Congress, he was instrumental in bringing to power two Prime Ministers, Lal Bahadur Shastri in 1964 and Indira Gandhi in 1966. In Tamil Nadu, his home state, he is still remembered for bringing school education to millions of the rural poor by introducing free education and the free Midday Meal Scheme during his tenure as chief minister. He was awarded India's highest civilian honour, the Bharat Ratna, posthumously in 1976. The domestic terminal of the Chennai airport is named "Kamaraj Terminal", Chennai's Beach Road renamed "Kamarajar Salai", Bengaluru's North Parade Road as "K. Kamaraj Rd." and the Madurai Kamaraj University in his honour.

Early life

Kamaraj was born on 15 July 1903 to Kumarasamy Nadar and Sivakami Ammal at Virudhunagar in Tamil Nadu. His real name was Kamakshi and his mother affectionately called him Raja; later his name became Kamaraj (Kamatchi + Raja). His parents were from a trading family. His father Kumarasamy Nadar was a coconut merchant. In 1907, four years after the birth of Kamaraj, his sister Nagammal was born. At age 5 (1907), Kamaraj was admitted to a traditional school (called 'Thinnai Palli' in Tamil, a system of school available in the past) on the next day of "Saraswathy Pooja". In 1908 he was admitted to Yenadhi Narayana Vidhya Salai. In 1909 Kamaraj was admitted in Virudupatti High School—Kshatriya Vidhya Sala , which is the only high school in Virdhupatti. Kamaraj's father died when he was six years old and his mother was forced to support her family by selling her jewellery. In 1914 Kamaraj dropped out of school to support his family. After that he worked in his uncle's clothshop as a salesboy.

During this time he started joining processions and attending public meetings about the Indian Home Rule Movement and British Rule addressed by orators like Dr. Varadarajulu Naidu, V.Kalyana Sundara Mudaliar and George Joseph. Kamaraj developed an interest in prevailing political conditions by reading newspapers daily.

The Jallianwala Bagh massacre was the decisive turning point in his life, and at this point he decided his aim was to fight for national freedom and to bring an end to foreign rule. In 1920, at the age of 18, he became active as a political worker and joined Congress as a full-time worker. In 1921 Kamaraj was organising public meetings at Virudhunagar for Congress leaders. He was eager to meet Gandhi, and when Gandhi visited Madurai on 21 September 1921 Kamaraj attended Gandhi's public meeting and met him for the first time in person. He visited villages carrying Congress propaganda.

In 1922 Congress was boycotting the visit of the Prince of Wales as part of the Non-Cooperation Movement. He came to Madras and took part in this event. He participated in the famous Vaikom Satyagraha led by George Joseph against the atrocities of the higher caste Hindus against the Harijans. In 1923–25 Kamaraj participated in the Nagpur Flag Satyagraha . In 1927 Kamaraj started the Sword Satyagraha in Madras and was chosen to lead the Neil Statue Satyagraha, but this was given up later in view of the Simon Commission boycott. Kamaraj led almost all the agitation and demonstration against British rule.

Kamaraj was first jailed in June 1930 for two years in Alipore Jail, Calcutta, for participation in the "Salt Satyagraha" led by Rajagopalachari at Vedaranyam; he was released early in 1931 in consequence of the Gandhi-Irwin Pact before he could serve his full term imprisonment.

In 1932 Section 144 was imposed in Madras prohibiting the holding of meetings and organisation of processions against the arrest of Gandhi in Bombay. In Virdhunagar under Kamaraj's leadership processions and demonstrations happened every day. Kamaraj was arrested again in January 1932 and sentenced to 1 year's imprisonment.

In 1933 Kamaraj was falsely implicated in the Virudhunagar bomb case. Dr. Varadarajulu Naidu and George Joseph argued on Kamaraj's behalf and proved the charges to be baseless.

Kamaraj was conducting a vigorous campaign throughout the State asking people not to contribute to war funds when Sir Arthur Hope the Madras Governor was collecting contributions to funds for the Second World War. In December 1940 he was arrested again at Guntur under the 'Defence of India rules' for speeches opposing contributions to the war fund and sent to Vellore Central Prison while he was on his way to Wardha to get Gandhi's approval for a list of Satyagrahis. While in jail, he was elected as Municipal Councillor of Virudhunagar. He was released 9 months later in Nov 1941 and resigned from this post as he thought he had greater responsibility for the nation. His principle was "One should not accept any post to which one could not do full justice".

In 1942 Kamaraj attended the All India Congress Committee in Bombay and returned to spread propaganda material for the "Quit India Movement" called by Gandhi. The Police issued orders to all the leaders who attended this Bombay session. Kamaraj did not want to get arrested before he took the message to all district and local leaders. He decided not to go to Madras and decided to cut short his trip; he saw a large number of policemen waiting for the arrest of Congress leaders in Arakonam but managed to escape from the police and went to Ranipet, Tanjore, Trichy and Madurai to inform local leaders about the Programme. He reached Virdhunagar after finishing his work and sent a message to the local police that he was ready to be arrested. He was arrested in August, 1942. He was under detention for 3 years and was released in June, 1945. This was the last term of his prison life.

Kamaraj was imprisoned six times by the British for his pro-Independence activities, accumulating more than 3,000 days in jail.

Politics

On 13 April 1954, Kamaraj became the Chief Minister of Madras Province. To everyone's surprise, Kamaraj nominated C. Subramaniam and M. Bhakthavatsalam, who had contested his leadership, to the newly formed cabinet.

Education

As Chief Minister, Kamaraj removed the family vocation based Hereditary Education Policy introduced by Rajaji. The State made immense strides in education and trade. New schools were opened, so that poor rural students were to walk no more than 3 miles (4.8 km) to their nearest school. Better facilities were added to existing ones. No village remained without a primary school and no panchayat without a high school. Kamaraj strove to eradicate illiteracy by introducing free and compulsory education up to the eleventh standard. He introduced the Midday Meal Scheme to provide at least one meal per day to the lakhs of poor school children (for the first time in the world). He introduced free school uniforms to weed out caste, creed and class distinctions among young minds.

During the British regime the education rate was only 7 per cent. But in Kamaraj's period it reached 37% . Apart from increasing the number of schools, steps were taken to improve standards of education. To improve standards, the number of working days was increased from 180 to 200; unnecessary holidays were reduced; and syllabuses were prepared to give opportunity to various abilities. Kamaraj and Bishnuram Medhi (Governor) took efforts to establish IIT Madras in 1959.

Agriculture

Major irrigation schemes were planned in Kamaraj's period. Dams and irrigation canals were built across Lower Bhavani, Mani Muthar, Aarani, Vaigai, Amaravathi, Sathanur, Krishnagiri, Pullambadi, Parambikulam and Neyyaru among others. The Lower Bhavani Dam in Erode district brought 207,000 acres (840 km^2) of land under cultivation. 45,000 acres (180 km^2) of land benefited from canals constructed from the Mettur Dam. The Vaigai and Sathanur systems facilitated cultivation across thousands of acres of lands in Madurai and North Arcot districts respectively. Rs 30 crores were planned to be spent for Parambikulam River scheme, and 150 lakhs of acres of lands were brought under cultivation; one third of this (i.e. 56 lakhs of acres of land) received a permanent irrigation facility.

In 1957–61 1,628 tanks were de-silted under the Small Irrigation Scheme, and 2,000 wells were dug with outlets. Long term loans with 25% subsidy were given to farmers. In addition farmers who had dry lands were given oil engines and electric pump sets on an instalment basis.

18

Mother Teresa

Baptized on August 27, 1910, in Skopje, Macedonia, Mother Teresa taught in India for 17 years before she experienced her 1946 "call within a call" to devote herself to caring for the sick and poor. Her order established a hospice; centers for the blind, aged, and disabled; and a leper colony. She was summoned to Rome in 1968, and in 1979 received the Nobel Peace Prize for her humanitarian work.

Early Life

Catholic nun and missionary Mother Teresa was born circa August 26, 1910, in Skopje, the current capital of the Republic of Macedonia. On August 27, 1910, a date frequently cited as her birthday, she was baptized as Agnes Gonxha Bojaxhiu. Mother Teresa's parents, Nikola and Drana Bojaxhiu, were of Albanian descent; her father was an entrepreneur who worked as a construction contractor and a trader of medicines and other goods. The Bojaxhius were a devoutly Catholic family, and Nikola Bojaxhiu was deeply involved in the local church as well as in city politics as a vocal proponent of Albanian independence.

In 1919, when Mother Teresa was only 8 years old, her father suddenly fell ill and died. While the cause of his death remains unknown, many have speculated that political enemies poisoned him. In the aftermath of her father's death, Mother Teresa became extraordinarily close to her mother, a pious and compassionate woman who instilled in her daughter a deep commitment to charity.

Although by no means wealthy, Drana Bojaxhiu extended an open invitation to the city's destitute to dine with her family. "My child, never eat a single mouthful unless you are sharing it with others," she counseled her daughter. When Mother Teresa asked who the people eating with them were, her mother uniformly responded, "Some of them are our relations, but all of them are our people."

Religious Calling

Mother Teresa attended a convent-run primary school and then a state-run secondary school. As a girl, Mother Teresa sang in the local Sacred Heart choir and was often asked to sing solos. The congregation made an annual pilgrimage to the chapel of the Madonna of Letnice atop Black Mountain in Skopje, and it was on one such trip at the age of 12 that Mother Teresa first felt a calling to a religious life. Six years later, in 1928, an 18-year-old Agnes Bojaxhiu decided to become a nun and set off for Ireland to join the Loreto Sisters of Dublin. It was there that she took the name Sister Mary Teresa after Saint Thérèse of Lisieux.

A year later, Mother Teresa traveled on to Darjeeling, India for the novitiate period; in May 1931, Mother Teresa made her First Profession of Vows. Afterward she was sent to Calcutta, where she was assigned to teach at Saint Mary's High School for Girls, a school run by the Loreto Sisters and dedicated to teaching girls from the city's poorest Bengali families. Mother Teresa learned to speak both Bengali and Hindi fluently as she taught geography and history and dedicated herself to alleviating the girls' poverty through education.

On May 24, 1937, she took her Final Profession of Vows to a life of poverty, chastity and obedience. As was the custom for Loreto nuns, she took on the title of "mother" upon making her final vows and thus became known as Mother Teresa. Mother Teresa continued to teach at Saint Mary's, and in 1944 she became the school's principal. Through her kindness, generosity and unfailing commitment to her students' education, she sought to lead them to a life of devotion to Christ. "Give me the strength to be ever the light of their lives, so that I may lead them at last to you," she wrote in prayer.

A New Calling

However, on September 10, 1946, Mother Teresa experienced a second calling that would forever transform her life. She was riding a train from Calcutta to the Himalayan foothills for a retreat when Christ spoke to her and told her to abandon teaching to work in the slums of Calcutta aiding the city's poorest and sickest people. "I want Indian Nuns, Missionaries of Charity, who would be my fire of love amongst the poor, the sick, the dying and the little children," she heard Christ say to her on the train that day. "You are I know the most incapable person—weak and sinful but just because you are that—I want to use You for My glory. Wilt thou refuse?"

Since Mother Teresa had taken a vow of obedience, she could not leave her convent without official permission. After nearly a year and a half of lobbying, in January 1948 she finally received approval from the local Archbishop Ferdinand Périer to pursue this new calling. That August, wearing the blue and white sari that she would always wear in public for the rest of her life, she left the Loreto convent and wandered out into the city. After six months of basic medical training, she voyaged for the first time into Calcutta's slums with no more specific goal than to aid "the unwanted, the unloved, the uncared for."

The Missionaries of Charity

Mother Teresa quickly translated this somewhat vague calling into concrete actions to help the city's poor. She began an open-air school and established a home for the dying destitute in a dilapidated building she convinced the city government to donate to her cause. In October 1950, she won canonical recognition for a new congregation, the Missionaries of Charity, which she founded with only 12 members—most of them former teachers or pupils from St. Mary's School.

As the ranks of her congregation swelled and donations poured in from around India and across the globe, the scope of Mother Teresa's charitable activities expanded exponentially. Over the course of the 1950s and 1960s, she established a leper colony, an orphanage, a nursing home, a family clinic and a string of mobile health clinics.

In 1971, Mother Teresa traveled to New York City to open her first American-based house of charity, and in the summer of 1982, she secretly went to Beirut, Lebanon, where she crossed between Christian East Beirut and Muslim West Beirut to aid children of both faiths. In 1985, Mother Teresa returned to New York and spoke at the 40th anniversary of the United Nations General Assembly. While there, she also opened Gift of Love, a home to care for those infected with HIV/AIDS.

International Charity and Recognition

In February 1965, Pope Paul VI bestowed the Decree of Praise upon the Missionaries of Charity, which prompted Mother Teresa to begin expanding internationally. By the time of her death in 1997, the Missionaries of Charity numbered over 4,000—in addition to thousands more lay volunteers—with 610 foundations in 123 countries on all seven continents.

The Decree of Praise was just the beginning, as Mother Teresa received various honors for her tireless and effective charity. She was awarded the Jewel of India, the highest honor bestowed on Indian civilians, as well as the now-defunct Soviet Union's Gold Medal of the Soviet Peace Committee. And in 1979, Mother Teresa won her highest honor when she was awarded the Nobel Peace Prize in recognition of her work "in bringing help to suffering humanity."

Controversy

Despite this widespread praise, Mother Teresa's life and work have not gone without criticism. In particular, she has drawn criticism for her vocal endorsement of some of the Catholic Church's more controversial doctrines, such as opposition to contraception and abortion. "I feel the greatest destroyer of peace today is abortion," Mother Teresa said in her 1979 Nobel lecture.

In 1995, she publicly advocated a "no" vote in the Irish referendum to end the country's constitutional ban on divorce and remarriage. The most scathing criticism of Mother Teresa can be found in Christopher Hitchens' book *The Missionary Position: Mother Teresa in Theory and Practice*, in which Hitchens argued that Mother Teresa glorified poverty for her own ends and provided a justification for the preservation of institutions and beliefs that sustained widespread poverty.

Death and Legacy

After several years of deteriorating health in which she suffered from heart, lung and kidney problems, Mother Teresa died on September 5, 1997 at the age of 87. Since her death, Mother Teresa has remained in the public spotlight. In particular, the publication of her private correspondence in 2003 caused a wholesale re-evaluation of her life by revealing the crisis of faith she suffered for most of the last 50 years of her life.

In one despairing letter to a confidant, she wrote, "Where is my Faith—even deep down right in there is nothing, but emptiness & darkness—My God—how painful is this unknown pain—I have no Faith—I dare not utter the words & thoughts that crowd in my heart — & make me suffer untold agony." While such revelations are shocking considering her public image of perfect faith, they have also made Mother Teresa a more relatable and human figure to all those who experience doubt in their beliefs.

For her unwavering commitment to aiding those most in need, Mother Teresa stands out as one of the greatest humanitarians of the 20th century. She combined profound empathy and a fervent commitment to her cause with incredible organizational and managerial skills that allowed her to develop a vast and effective international organization of missionaries to help impoverished citizens all across the globe.

However, despite the enormous scale of her charitable activities and the millions of lives she touched, to her dying day she held only the most humble conception of her own achievements. Summing up her life in characteristically self-effacing fashion, Mother Teresa said, "By blood, I am Albanian. By citizenship, an Indian. By faith, I am a Catholic nun. As to my calling, I belong to the world. As to my heart, I belong entirely to the Heart of Jesus."

19

Vinayak Narahari "Vinoba" Bhave

Vinayak Narahari "Vinoba" Bhave was an Indian advocate of nonviolence and human rights. Often called *Acharya* (Sanskrit for teacher), he is best known for the Bhoodan Movement. He is considered as a *National Teacher of India* and the spiritual successor of Mohandas Gandhi.

Early life and Background

Vinoba was born into a pious Chitpavan Brahmin family on September 11, 1895 in Gagode in Kolaba district of Maharashtra. Vinayak Narahari Bhave was his childhood name and he was greatly influenced by his mother Rukmini Devi, a religious woman. He was highly inspired after reading the Bhagavad Gita, at a very young age.

A report in the newspapers about Gandhiji's speech at the newly founded Benaras Hindu University attracted Vinoba's attention. In 1916, on his way to Mumbai to appear for the intermediate examination, Vinoba Bhave put his school and college certificates into a fire. Vinoba took the decision after reading the piece of writing in the newspaper written by Mahatma Gandhi.

He wrote a letter to Gandhiji and after an exchange of letters, Gandhiji advised Vinoba to come for a personal meeting at Kochrab Ashram in Ahmedabad. Vinoba met Gandhiji on June 7, 1916 and subsequently abandoned his studies. Vinoba participated with keen interest in the activities at Gandhiji's ashram, like teaching, studying, spinning and improving the life of the community. His involvement with Gandhiji's constructive programmes related to Khadi, village industries, new education (Nai Talim), sanitation and hygiene also kept on increasing.

Vinoba went to Wardha on April 8, 1921 to take charge of the Ashram as desired by Gandhiji. In 1923, he brought out 'Maharashtra Dharma', a Marathi monthly which had his essays on the Upanishads. Later on, this monthly became a weekly and continued for three years. In 1925, he was sent by Gandhiji to Vaikom, Kerala to supervise the entry of the Harijans to the temple.

Vinoba was arrested several times during the 1920s and '30s and served a five-year jail sentence in the '40s for leading non-violent resistance to British rule. The jails for Vinoba had become the places of reading and writing. He wrote Ishavasyavritti and Sthitaprajna Darshan jail. He also learnt four South Indian languages and created the script of Lok Nagari at Vellore jail. In the jails, he gave a series of talks on Bhagavad Gita in Marathi, to his fellow prisoners. Bhave participated in the nationwide civil disobedience periodically conducted against the British, and was imprisoned with other nationalists. Despite these many activities, he was not well known to the public. He gained national prominence when Gandhi chose him as the first participant in a new nonviolent campaign in 1940.

Career

Freedom struggle

Vinoba Kutir at Sabarmati Ashram

He was associated with Mahatma Gandhi in the Indian independence movement. He stayed for some time at Gandhi's Sabarmati ashram in a cottage that was named after him,

'Vinoba Kutir'. In 1932 he was sent to jail by the British colonial government because of his activism against British rule. There he gave a series of talks on the Gita, in his native language Marathi, to his fellow prisoners.

These highly inspiring talks were later published as the book "Talks on the Gita", and it has been translated into many languages both in India and elsewhere. Vinoba felt that the source of these talks was something from above and he believed that its influence will endure even if his other works were forgotten.

In 1940 he was chosen by Gandhi to be the first individual Satyagrahi (an individual standing up for Truth instead of a collective action) against the British rule. It is said that Gandhi envied and respected Bhave's celibacy, a vow he made in his adolescence, in fitting with his belief in the Brahmacharya principle. Bhave also participated in the Quit India Movement.

Religious and social work

Gandhi and Vinoba

Vinoba's religious outlook was very broad and it synthesized the truths of many religions. This can be seen in one of his hymns "Om Tat Sat" which contains symbols of many religions.

Vinoba observed the life of the average Indian living in a village and tried to find solutions for the problems he faced with a firm spiritual foundation. This formed the core of his *Sarvoda movement*. Another example of this is the Bhoodan (land gift) movement started at Pochampally on 18 April 1951, after interacting with 80 Harijan families. He walked all across India asking people with land to consider him as one of their sons and so give him one sixth of their land which he then distributed to landless poor. Non-violence and compassion being a hallmark of his philosophy, he also campaigned against the slaughtering of cows.

Vinoba said, "I have walked all over India for 13 years. In the backdrop of enduring perpetuity of my life's work, I have established 6 ashrams.

Brahma Vidya Mandir

The Brahma Vidya Mandir is one of the ashrams that Bhave created. It is a small community for women that was created in order for them to become self-sufficient and non-violent in a community. This group farms to get their own food, but uses Gandhi's beliefs about food production, which include sustainability and social justice, as a guide. This community, like Gandhi and Bhave, has been influenced greatly by the *Bhagavad-Gita* and that is also used to determine their practices. The community perform prayers as a group every day, reciting from the Isha Upanishad at dawn, the Vishnu Sahasranama at mid-morning, and the *Bhagavad-Gita* in the evening. As of today, there are around 25 women who are members of the community and several men have also been allowed to join in the community.

Literary Career

Vinoba Bhave was a scholar, thinker, and writer who produced numerous books. He was a translator who made Sanskrit texts accessible to the common man. He was also an orator and linguist who had an excellent command of several languages (Marathi, Gujarati, Hindi, Urdu, English, Sanskrit). Vinoba Bhave was an innovative social reformer. Shri Vinoba Bhave called Nagari script the "Queen of World Scripts". He wrote brief introductions to, and criticisms of, several religious and philosophical works like the Bhagavad Gita, works of Adi Shankaracharya, the Bible and Quran. His criticism of Dnyaneshwar's poetry and works by other Marathi saints is quite brilliant and a testimony to the breadth of his intellect.

Vinoba Bhave had translated the Bhagavad Gita into Marathi. He was deeply influenced by the Gita and attempted to imbibe its teachings into his life, often stating that "The Gita is my life's breath".

Some of his works are:

- The essence of Quran
- The essence of Christian teachings
- Thoughts on education
- Swarajya Sastra

A University has been named after him, Vinoba Bhave University, which is located in Hazaribagh district in the State of Jharkhand.

Vinobha Bhave and Land Donation Movement

In 1951 Vinoba Bhave started his land donation movement, the Bhoodan Movement. He took donated land from land owner Indians and gave it away to the poor and landless, for them to cultivate. Then after 1954, he started to ask for donations of whole villages in a programme he called Gramdan. He got more than 1000 villages by way of donation. Out of these, he obtained 175 donated villages in Tamil Nadu alone. Noted Gandhian and atheist Lavanam was the interpreter of Vinoba Bhave during his land reform movement in Andhra Pradesh and parts of Orissa

Later Life and Death

Vinoba spent the later part of his life at his Brahma Vidya Mandir ashram in Paunar, Maharashtra. He died on 15 November 1982 after refusing food and medicine for a few days. The then prime minister of India, Indira Gandhi, who was visiting Moscow to attend the funeral of Soviet leader Leonid Brezhnev, cut short her visit to be at the funeral of Vinoba.

Criticism

V.S. Naipaul has given scathing criticism of Bhave in his collection of essays citing his lack of connection with rationality and excessive imitation of Gandhi. Even some of his admirers find fault with the extent of his devotion to Gandhi. Much more controversial was his support, ranging from covert to open, to Congress Party's government under Indira Gandhi, which was fast becoming unpopular. He controversially backed the Indian Emergency imposed by Prime Minister Indira Gandhi, calling it *Anushasana Parva* (*Time for Discipline*). Congress party opponents at that time had coined the derogatory term "Sarkari Sant (Government Saint)" to describe him. Noted Marathi writer Purushottam Laxman Deshpande publicly criticized him and mocked him by writing article titled as "Vanaroba" which is disambiguation of name "Vinoba" and literally means monkey.

However, in his end days he was very much against Prime Minister Indira Gandhi as she had ordered a shootout of the Sant Samaj who had undertaken a gherao of Parliament against cow slaughter. The criticism has been considered objectionable and unfounded later. By Anushasan Parva - Time for Discipline - he meant everyone to follow the rule including the rulers of that time.

At a later stage he called Intelligentsia to chart a path for the ruling community and public in general. During anushasn Parva - the king has to take the permission of the great men of his time - by that he meant to put the government under the guidance of the learned. The identified persons included Late Shrimannarayan- former Governor of Gujarat and a great Gandhian of his time. They had suggested lifting of emergency. Yet the erstwhile government did not pay heed to the advice which had Vinoba Bhave's blessings and initiative.

Awards

In 1958 Vinoba was the first recipient of the international Ramon Magsaysay Award for Community Leadership. He was awarded the Bharat Ratna posthumously in 1983.

20

Khân Abdul Ghaffâr Khân

Khân Abdul Ghaffâr Khân (6 February 1890 – 20 January 1988) also known as **Fakhr-e Afghân**, and **Bâchâ Khân**, **Pâchâ Khân** or **Bâdshâh Khân**, was an independence activist of Pashtun descent. He was a political and spiritual leader known for his nonviolent opposition to the British Rule in the Subcontinent, and a lifelong pacifist and devout Muslim. A close friend of Mahatma Gandhi, Bacha Khan has been nicknamed **Frontier Gandhi**. In 1910, Bacha Khan opened a mosque school at his hometown Utmanzai, and in 1911 joined the freedom movement of Haji Sahib of Turangzai. However in 1915, the British authorities banned his mosque school. Having witnessed the repeated failure of revolts against the British Raj, Bacha Khan decided that social activism and reform would be more beneficial for the Pashtuns. This led to the formation of *Anjuman-e Islâh al-Afghân* ("Afghan Reform Society") in 1921, and the youth movement *Paxtûn Jirga* ("Pashtun Assembly") in 1927. After Bacha Khan's return from the Hajj in May 1928, he founded the Pashto language monthly political journal *Paxtûn*. Finally, in November 1929, Bacha Khan founded the Khudai Khidmatgar ("Servants of God") movement, whose success triggered a harsh crackdown by the British Empire against him and his supporters and they suffered some of the most severe repression of the Indian independence movement. In 1962, Bacha Khan was named the Amnesty International Prisoner of Conscience of the Year. In 1987, he became the first non-Indian to be awarded Bharat Ratna, India's highest civilian award. Bacha Khan is a Pashtun national hero and a key figure of Pashtun nationalism.

Bacha Khan strongly opposed the All-India Muslim League's demand for the partition of India. When the Indian National Congress declared its acceptance of the partition plan without consulting the Khudai Khidmatgar leaders, he felt very sad and told the Congress "you have thrown us to the wolves." After partition, Bacha Khan pledged allegiance to Pakistan and demanded an autonomous "Pashtunistan" administrative unit within the country, but he was frequently arrested by Pakistani government between 1948 and 1954, and in 1956 for his opposition to the One Unit scheme under which the government announced to merge the former provinces of West Punjab, Sindh, North-West Frontier Province and Baluchistan into one administrative unit of West Pakistan. Bacha Khan also spent much of the 1960s and 1970s either in jail or in exile. Upon his death in 1988 in Peshawar under house arrest, following his will, he was buried in his house at Jalalabad, Afghanistan. Tens of thousands of mourners attended his funeral, marching through the Khyber Pass from Peshawar to Jalalabad, although it was marred by two bomb explosions killing 15 people. Despite the heavy fighting at the time, both sides of the Soviet war in Afghanistan, the communist army and the mujahideen, declared a ceasefire to allow his burial.

Early years

Ghaffar Khan was born into a generally peaceful and prosperous family from Utmanzai in the Peshawar Valley of British India. His father, Bahram Khan, was a land owner in the area commonly referred to as Hashtnaggar. Ghaffar was the second son of Bahram to attend the British run Edward's mission school since this was the only fully functioning school because it was run by missionaries. At school the young Ghaffar did well in his studies and was inspired by his mentor Reverend Wigram to see the importance of education in service to the community. In his 10th and final year of high school he was offered a highly prestigious commission in The Guides, an elite corp of Pashtun soldiers of the British Raj. Young Ghaffar refused the commission after realising even Guide officers were still second-class citizens in their own country. He resumed his intention of University study and Reverend Wigram offered him the opportunity to follow his brother, Dr. Khan Sahib, to study in London. An alumnus of Aligarh Muslim University, he eventually received the permission of his father, Ghaffar's mother wasn't willing to lose another son to London—and their own culture and religion. So Ghaffar began working on his father's lands while attempting to discern what more he might do with his life.

Ghaffar "Badshah" Khan

In response to his inability to continue his own education, Ghaffar Khan turned to helping others start theirs. Like many such regions of the world, the strategic importance of the newly formed North-West Frontier Province (now Khyber Pakhtunkhwa, Pakistan) as a buffer for the British Raj from Russian influence was of little benefit to its residents. The oppression of the British, the repression of the mullahs, and an ancient culture of violence and vendetta prompted Ghaffar to want to serve and uplift his fellow men and women by means of education. At 20 years of age, Ghaffar opened his first school in Utmanzai. It was an instant success and he was soon invited into a larger circle of progressively minded reformers.

While he faced much opposition and personal difficulties, Ghaffar Khan worked tirelessly to organize and raise the consciousness of his fellow Pushtuns. Between 1915 and 1918 he visited 500 villages in all part of the settled districts of Khyber-Pakhtunkhwa. It was in this frenzied activity that he had come to be known as *Badshah (Bacha) Khan* (King of Chiefs).

Being a secular Muslim he did not believe in religious divisions, he supported his niece(daughter of Doctor Khan sahib) marriage Sikh army officer named as Colonel Jaswant Singh. He married his first wife Meharqanda in 1912; she was a daughter of Yar Mohammad Khan of the Kinankhel clan of the Mohammadzai tribe of Razzar, a village adjacent to Utmanzai. They had a son in 1913, Abdul Ghani Khan, who would become a noted artist and poet. Subsequently, they had another son, Abdul Wali Khan (17 January 1917–), and daughter, Sardaro. Meharqanda died during the 1918 influenza epidemic. In 1920, Abdul Ghaffar Khan remarried; his new wife, Nambata, was a cousin of his first wife and the daughter of Sultan Mohammad Khan of Razzar. She bore him a daughter, Mehar Taj (25 May 1921 – 29 April 2012), and a son, Abdul Ali Khan (20 August 1922 – 19 February 1997). Tragically, in 1926 Nambata died early as well from a fall down the stairs of the apartment they were staying at in Jerusalem.

Khudai Khidmatgar

In time, Ghaffar Khan's goal came to be the formulation of a united, independent, secular India. To achieve this end, he founded the *Khudai Khidmatgar* ("Servants of God"), commonly known as the "Red Shirts" (*Surkh Posh*), during the 1920s.

The *Khudai Khidmatgar* was founded on a belief in the power of Gandhi's notion of Satyagraha, a form of active non-violence as captured in an oath. He told its members:

"I am going to give you such a weapon that the police and the army will not be able to stand against it. It is the weapon of the Prophet, but you are not aware of it. That weapon is patience and righteousness. No power on earth can stand against it."

The organization recruited over 100,000 members and became legendary in opposing (and dying at the hands of) the British-controlled police and army. Through strikes, political organisation and non-violent opposition, the *Khudai Khidmatgar* were able to achieve some success and came to dominate the politics of Khyber-Pakhtunkhwa. His brother, Dr. Khan Abdul Jabbar Khan (known as Dr. Khan Sahib), led the political wing of the movement, and was the Chief Minister of the province (from the late 1920s until 1947 when his government was dismissed by Mohammad Ali Jinnah of the Muslim League).

Ghaffar Khan and the Indian National Congress

Ghaffar Khan forged a close, spiritual, and uninhibited friendship with Mahatma Gandhi, the pioneer of non-violent mass civil disobedience in India. The two had a deep admiration towards each other and worked together closely till 1947.

Khudai Khidmatgar (servants of god) agitated and worked cohesively with the Indian National Congress, the leading national organization fighting for freedom, of which Ghaffar Khan was a senior and respected member. On several occasions when the Congress seemed to disagree with Gandhi on policy, Ghaffar Khan remained his staunchest ally. In 1931 the Congress offered him the presidency of the party, but he refused saying, "I am a simple soldier and Khudai Khidmatgar, and I only want to serve." He remained a member of the Congress Working Committee for many years, resigning only in 1939 because of his differences with the Party's War Policy. He rejoined the Congress Party when the War Policy was revised.

On April 23, 1930, Ghaffar Khan was arrested during protests arising out of the Salt Satyagraha. A crowd of Khudai Khidmatgar gathered in Peshawar's Kissa Khwani (Storytellers) Bazaar. The British ordered troops to open fire with machine guns on the unarmed crowd, killing an estimated 200–250. The Khudai Khidmatgar members acted in accord with their training in non-violence under Ghaffar Khan, facing bullets as the troops fired on them. Two platoons of the The

Garhwal Rifles regiment refused to fire on the non-violent crowd. They were later court-martialled with heavy punishment, including life imprisonment.

Ghaffar Khan was a champion of women's rights and nonviolence. He became a hero in a society dominated by violence; notwithstanding his liberal views, his unswerving faith and obvious bravery led to immense respect. Throughout his life, he never lost faith in his non-violent methods or in the compatibility of Islam and nonviolence. He viewed his struggle as a jihad with only the enemy holding swords. He was closely identified with Gandhi because of his non-violence principles and he is known in India as the 'Frontier Gandhi'. One of his Congress associates was Pandit Amir Chand Bombwal of Peshawar.

"O Pathans! Your house has fallen into ruin. Arise and rebuild it, and remember to what race you belong." – Ghaffar Khan

The Partition

Ghaffar Khan strongly opposed the partition of India.[While many Pashtuns (particularly the Red Shirts) were willing to work with Indian politicians, many other Pashtuns were sympathetic to the idea of a separate homeland for India's Muslims following the departure of the British. Targeted with being Anti-Muslim, Ghaffar Khan was attacked in 1946, leading to his hospitalization in Peshawar.

The Congress party refused last-ditch compromises to prevent the partition, like the Cabinet Mission plan and Gandhi's suggestion to offer the Prime Ministership to Jinnah. As a result, Ghaffar Khan and his followers felt a sense of betrayal by both Pakistan and India. Ghaffar Khan's last words to Gandhi and his erstwhile allies in the Congress party were: "You have thrown us to the wolves."

When the referendum over accession to Pakistan was held, Ghaffar Khan and the Indian National Congress Party boycotted the referendum. As a result, in 1947 the accession of Khyber-Pakhtunkhwa to Pakistan was made possible by a majority. A *loya jirga* in the Tribal Areas also garnered a similar result as most preferred to become part of Pakistan. Ghaffar Khan and his Khudai Khidmatgars, however, chose to boycott the polls along with other nationalistic Pakhtuns. Some have argued that a segment of the population voted was barred from voting.

Arrest and exile

Ghaffar Khan took the oath of allegiance to the new nation of Pakistan on 23 February 1948 at the first session of the Pakistan Constituent Assembly.

He pledged full support to the government and attempted to reconcile with the founder of the new state Muhammad Ali Jinnah. Initial overtures led to a successful meeting in Karachi, however a follow-up meeting in the Khudai Khidmatgar headquarters never materialised, allegedly due to the role of Khyber-Pakhtunkhwa Chief Minister, Abdul Qayyum Khan who warned Jinnah that Ghaffar Khan was plotting his assassination.

Following this, Ghaffar Khan formed Pakistan's first National opposition party, on 8 May 1948, the Pakistan Azad Party. The party pledged to play the role of constructive opposition and would be non-communal in its philosophy.

However, suspicions of his allegiance persisted and under the new Pakistani government, Ghaffar Khan was placed under house arrest without charge from 1948 till 1954. Released from prison, he gave a speech again on the floor of the constituent assembly, this time condemning the massacre of his supporters at Babrra.

"I had to go to prison many a time in the days of the Britishers. Although we were at loggerheads with them, yet their treatment was to some extent tolerant and polite. But the treatment which was meted out to me in this Islamic state of ours was such that I would not even like to mention it to you."

He was arrested several times between late 1948 and in 1956 for his opposition to the One Unit scheme. The government attempted in 1958 to reconcile with him and offered him a Ministry in the government, after the assassination of his brother, he however refused. He remained in prison till 1957 only to be re-arrested in 1958 until an illness in 1964 allowed for his release.

In 1962, Abdul Ghaffar Khan was named an "Amnesty International Prisoner of the Year". Amnesty's statement about him said, "His example symbolizes the suffering of upward of a million people all over the world who are prisoners of conscience."

In September 1964, the Pakistani authorities allowed him to go to United Kingdom for treatment. During winter his doctor advised him to go to United States. He then went into exile to Afghanistan, he returned from exile in December 1972 to a popular response, following the establishment of National Awami Party provincial government in Khyber-Pakhtunkhwa and Balochistan.

He was arrested by Prime Minister Zulfiqar Ali Bhutto's government at Multan in November 1973 and described Bhuttos government as "the worst kind of dictatorship".

In 1984, increasingly withdrawing from politics he was nominated for the Nobel Peace Prize. He visited India and participated in the centennial celebrations of the Indian National Congress in 1985; he was awarded the Jawaharlal Nehru Award for International Understanding in 1967 and later Bharat Ratna, India's highest civilian award, in 1987.

His final major political challenge was against the Kalabagh dam project, fearing that the project would damage the Peshawar valley, his hostility to it would eventually lead to the project being shelved after his death.

Ghaffar Khan died in Peshawar under house arrest in 1988 and was buried in his house at Jalalabad, Afghanistan, and over 200,000 mourners attended the funeral, including the Afghan president Mohammad Najibullah. This was a symbolic move by Ghaffar Khan, as this would allow his dream of Pashtun unification to live even after his death. The then Indian Prime Minister Rajiv Gandhi had gone to Peshawar, to pay his tributes to Khan Abdul Ghaffar Khan in spite of the fact that General Zia-ul-Haq had tried to stall his attendance citing security reasons, also the Indian government declared a five-day period of mourning in his honour.

Although he had been repeatedly imprisoned and persecuted, tens of thousands of mourners attended his funeral, described by one commentator as *a caravan of peace, carrying a message of love* from Pashtuns east of the Khyber to those on the west, marching through the historic Khyber Pass from Peshawar to Jalalabad. A cease-fire was announced in the Afghan Civil War to allow the funeral to take place, even though it was marred by bomb explosions killing 15.

Political Legacy

His third son Khan Abdul Ali Khan was non-political and a distinguished educator, and served as Vice-Chancellor of University of Peshawar. Ali Khan was also the head of Aitchison College, Lahore and Fazle Haq college, Mardan.

Mohammed Yahya Education Minister of Khyber Pukhtunkhwa, was the only son in law of Khan Abdul Ghaffar Khan.

Asfandyar Wali Khan is the grandson of Khan Abdul Gaffar Khan, and leader of the Awami National Party. The party was in power from 2008-2013.

Salma Ataullahjan is the great grand niece of Khan Abdul Gaffar Khan and a member of the Senate of Canada.

Abdul Ghaffar Khan's political legacy is mixed he is renowned amongst Pashtuns, Indians and internationally as a leader of a non-violent movement. He is credited with his tireless advocacy of peace in the region he belonged to.

However, within Pakistan, there is a large section of society which still has not come to grips with his siding with the All India Congress over the Muslim League as well as his opposition to Mr. M. A. Jinnah who is revered in Pakistan as the father of the nation. In particular people have questioned Ghaffar Khan's patriotism following his insistence that he be buried in Afghanistan after his death and not Pakistan. However, this view is opposed by the fact that he is an ethnic Pashtun, with there being officially no boundary between ancient northwest India and Afghanistan, hence being buried in the 'land of Pashtuns' (literal translation from Old Farsi) is a significant sign of his patriotism towards his ethnic roots as a Pashtun. Others ask how one's choice of burial place is an indication of one's Patriotism since a better indicator is one's actions while living and even though Khan Abdul Ghaffar Khan spent half of his 98 year life in jail most of it in Pakistani jails doing hard labor he continued to reside in Pakistan.

Film, Literature and Society

In 2008, a documentary, titled *The Frontier Gandhi: Badshah Khan, a Torch for Peace*, by filmmaker and writer T.C. McLuhan, premiered in New York. The film received the 2009 award for Best Documentary Film at the Middle East International Film Festival.

In Richard Attenborough's 1982 epic *Gandhi*, Khan Abdul Ghaffar Khan was portrayed by Dilsher Singh.

Ghaffar Khan was listed as one of 26 men who changed the world in a recent children's book published in the United States. He also wrote an autobiography (1969), and has been the subject of biographies by Eknath Easwaran (see article) and Rajmohan Gandhi. His philosophy of Islamic pacificism was recognised by US Secretary of State Hillary Clinton, in a speech to American Muslims.

In the Indian city of Delhi, the popular Khan Market is named in honour of Khan Abdul Ghaffar Khan, and another market in the Karol Bagh of New Delhi is named after him called Ghaffar Market.

Vibhu Puri is reportedly making a Bollywood Biopic on the life of Khan Abdul Ghaffar Khan titled Chenab Gandhi.

Peshawar International Airport was renamed as Bacha Khan International Airport in 2012 due to importance as a major opposition leader from Pakistan Azad Party and a respect to Pashtun Nationalism by Government of Pakistan.The largest flyover of Pakistan in Karachi was named as the Bacha Khan flyover by the Government of Sindh. In addition, Bacha Khan University Charsada, Bacha Khan Medical College Mardan and Bacha Khan Medical Complex, Swabi have been established in 2010 by the Awami National Party Government. Moreover, the busiest chowks of Karachi, Peshawr, Quetta, Loralai, Khyber Agency, Mardan have been renamed as Bacha Khan Chowk out of respect to the freedom fighter and Pashtun (Pathan) nationalist leader.

21

Marudhur Gopalan Ramachandran

Marudhur Gopalan Ramachandran, popularly known by his initials **MGR**, was an Indian film actor, director, producer, and politician who also served as the Chief Minister of Tamil Nadu successively for three terms.

In his youth, MGR and his elder brother, M.G. Chakrapani became members of a drama troupe to support their family. Influenced by Gandhian ideals, MGR joined the Indian National Congress. After a few years of acting in plays, he made his film debut in the 1936 film *Sathi Leelavathi* in a supporting role. In the late 1940s he graduated to leading roles and for the next three decades dominated the Tamil film industry. He became a member of the Dravida Munnetra Kazhagam (DMK) and rose rapidly through its ranks. He successfully used his popularity as a film hero to build a large political base. In 1972, he left the DMK to form his own party the Anna Dravida Munnetra Kazhagam (ADMK). In 1977 he became the chief minister of Tamil Nadu - the first film actor in India to become the chief minister of a state. He remained as chief minister till his death in 1987.

Early Life and Career

MGR was born in Nawalapitiya near Kandy, Sri Lanka, to Melakkath Gopala Menon and Maruthur Satyabhama. Melakkath Gopala Menon was staying in Vadavannur, in Palakkad District, Kerala before he was excommunicated in 1903, regarding an allegation that dealt with an illicit relationship with a widowed woman; he left his family and married Maruthur Satyabhama.

In his early days, MGR was a devout Hindu and a devotee of Murugan, as is the common practice for Hindus in Sri Lanka. Later, when he joined the DMK, a pro-rationalist party, he followed the rationalist ideology, though not appearing very aggressively atheistic. In later days after he founded his own party following his expulsion from the DMK, he seems to have shown some leaning towards religious faith. He had asked his followers to pray for the success of his AIADMK party.

His followers prayed for him when it was determined that he had a kidney illness. After his demise, his wife opened up a temple in his name.

After his father's death, he joined a drama company called "Madurai Original Boys company". Later, he entered the world of cinema, becoming an actor, director, producer, and editor. MGR married Bargavi also known as Thangamani who died early due to illness. He later married Sathanandavathhi who died soon due to tuberculosis. M.G.R. married V. N. Janaki a former Tamil film actress. Janaki divorced her husband, Ganapati Bhatt, to marry MGR.

Acting Career

He made his film debut in 1936, in the film *Sathi Leelavathi*, directed by Ellis Dungan, an American-born film director. Generally starring in romance or action films, MGR got his big breakthrough in the 1947 film *Manthiri Kumari*, written by M. Karunanidhi. Soon he rose to superstardom in the 1954 blockbuster Malaikallan. He acted as hero in the Tamil film industry's first ever colour movie, the 1955 blockbuster *Alibabavum 40 Thirudargalum*. He rose to become the heart throb of millions of Indians with movies such as *Thirudadhe, Enga Veettu Pillai, Aayirathil Oruvan, Anbe Vaa, Mahadevi, Panam Padaithavan, Ulagam Sutrum Vaalibhan, Adimai Penn*, etc. He won the National Film Award for Best Actor for the film *Rickshawkaran* in 1972. His film *Nadodi Mannan*, released in 1958, was a Tamil version of the interpretation of the *Prisoner of Zenda*, produced and directed by himself and released in 1956, ran to full houses. He began to act in many movies that appealed to the direct sentiments of the common man and the rich as well. His 1973 blockbuster *Ulagam Sutrum Vaalibhan* broke previous box office records. It was one of the few movies filmed abroad in those days. It was shot in Singapore, Malaysia, Thailand, Hong Kong and Japan. The DMK unsuccessfully tried to curtail that movie. His acting career ended in 1984 with his last film, *Ullagam Suthi Paru*, which he acted when he was diagnosed with kidney failure.

Political Career

MGR was a member of the Congress Party till 1953, and he used to wear khâdî. In 1953 MGR joined the Dravida Munnetra Kazhagam (DMK) attracted by founder C.N.Annadurai. He became a vocal Tamil and Dravidian nationalist and prominent member of the DMK ("Dravida Munnetra Kazhagam" aka Dravidian Progressive Federation). He added glamour to the Dravidian movement which was sweeping Tamil Nadu. MGR became a member of the state Legislative Council in 1962. He was first elected to the Tamil Nadu Legislative Assembly in 1967. After the death of his mentor, Annadurai, MGR became the treasurer of DMK in 1969 after Muthuvel Karunanidhi became the chief minister.

M.R. Radha and MGR had worked in 25 films together. On 12 January 1967 M.R. Radha with a producer visited MGR to talk about a future project. During the conversation

M.R. Radha stood up and shot MGR in his left ear twice and then pretended to shoot himself. MGR drove to the hospital by himself and spoke to the doctor with his own voice for the last time. After the operation his voice changed. Since he had been shot in his ear MGR lost hearing in his left ear and had ringing in the ear problems but never complained until he had kidney problems in the early 1983. When Sinnappa Devar paid his first visit to see MGR at the hospital after the shooting incident he paid an advance for the next MGR's movie. So after getting released from the hospital and finishing *Arasakattalai* MGR acted in Devar's movie *Vivasaayee* against doctors' advice. When finishing the movie *Kaavalkaaran* MGR's speaking parts were reduced. This was the only movie MGR spoke with old and new voices between scenes: When MGR was acting in *Kaavalkaran* in 1967 opposite J. Jayalalithaa the shooting happened.

Petralthaan Pillaya was the last movie of MGR-MR Radha together. Shooting ended just few days before MGR was shot at. The bullet was permanently lodged in his neck and his voice damaged. Within hours of the shooting, some 50,000 fans had gathered at the hospital where MGR had been taken. People cried in the streets. For six weeks, he lay in the hospital as fans awaited each report of his health. He was visited by a steady stream of commoners and luminaries of film industry, polity and bureaucracy. From his hospital bed, he conducted his campaign for Madras Legislative Assembly. He won twice the number of votes polled by his Congress rival and the largest vote polled by any candidate for the Assembly.

In 1972, DMK leader Karunanidhi started to project his first son M.K. Muthu in a big way in film and politics. Understanding the tactics played by Karunanidhi to corner him, MGR started to claim that corruption had grown in the party after the demise of Annadurai and in a public meeting asked for the financial details of the party to be publicised, which enraged the leadership of DMK. Consequently, MGR was expelled from the party as per Karunanidhi's plan. He forcefully floated a new party named Anna Dravida Munnetra Kazhagam (ADMK), later renamed All India Anna Dravida Munnetra Kazhagam (AIADMK), the only powerful opponent of the DMK. He mobilised between 1972 and 1977 to spread and preach his party ambition with films like *Netru Indru Naalai* (1974), *Idhayakani* (1975), *Indru Pol Endrum Vazhga* (1977), etc.

He became Chief Minister of Tamil Nadu on 30 June 1977, remaining in office till his death in 1987. In 1979, members of his party Satyavani Muthu and Aravinda Bala Pajanor became the first non-Congress politicians from Tamil Nadu to be ministers in the Union Cabinet. The AIADMK won every state assembly election as long as MGR was alive. Although Anna Durai and Karunanidhi had acted in stage plays in trivial roles, in their younger days, before becoming chief minister, MGR was the first popular film actor to be a Chief Minister in India. Though the Congress won by a small margin of votes with the DMK in the 1980 parliamentary elections, the AIADMK under MGR won the state elections the same year. This made the Congress to ally with the AIADMK in the 1984 elections. MGR ended his acting career in 1977.

Once he became Chief Minister of Tamil Nadu, he placed great emphasis on social development, especially education. One of his most successful policies was the conversion of the "Midday Meal Scheme" introduced by the popular Congress Chief Minister and kingmaker K Kamaraj, which already was encouraging underprivileged children to attend school, into "MGR's Nutritious Meal Scheme" in the government-run and -aided schools in Tamil Nadu by adding *saththurundai* — a nutritious sugary flour dumpling. This scheme was at a cost of Rs.100 crore and was imposed in 1982. A little more than 120,000 children of the state were benefited. He also introduced Women's Special buses. He introduced a liquor ban in the state and preservation of old temples and historical monuments, ultimately increasing the state's tourist income. He set up a free school for the cinema technicians children in Kodambakkam called MGR Primary & Higher Secondary School which provided free mid-day meals in the 1950s. He led the ADMK to victory in the 1984 assembly elections despite not taking part in the campaigning. At that time he was undergoing medical treatment in America and his images were broadcast in Tamil Nadu through cinema halls. This was an effective campaign tactic and ADMK won the elections claiming around 56% of assembly seats, indicating the depth of his popular support. He won his seat in a double landslide victory in 1984. He still holds the record of being the chief minister with the highest consistent longevity of more than a decade.

Karunanidhi claimed on 1 April 2009 and again on 13 May 2012 that MGR was ready for the merger of his party with the DMK in 1979, with Biju Patnaik acting as the mediator. The plan failed, because Panruti Ramachandran, who was close to MGR acted as a spoiler and MGR changed his mind.

Bharat Ratna

After his death in 1988, he became the third Chief Minister from the state of Tamil Nadu to receive the Bharat Ratna. The timing of the award was controversial, due to the fact that it was given so quickly after his death and he was elected as Chief Minister only 11 years before the award. Many opponents, mostly outside Tamil Nadu, criticized the current ruling party INC, under Rajiv Gandhi to have influenced the selection committee to give the award in order to help win the upcoming 1989 Lok Sabha election. The ruling party forming a coalition with Jayalalithaa, successor to MGR at that time were able to sweep Tamil Nadu winning 38 out of 39 seats, INC were however unable to win nationally.

Awards

- Filmfare Best Actor Award for *Enga Veettu Pillai*
- Filmfare Best Film Award for *Adimai Penn*

- National Film Award for Best Actor for the film *Rickshawkaran* in 1971.
- Honorary doctorate received from University of Madras and The World University (Arizona).
- Bharat Ratna was conferred by the Government of India (posthumously) in 1988 for his reformation activities and support from Tamil Nadu.

Philanthropy

He personally offered relief in disasters and calamities like fire, flood, drought, and cyclones. He was the first donor during the war with China in 1962, donating Rs. 75,000 to the war fund. He was the founder and editor of *Thai* weekly magazine and *Anna* daily newspaper in Tamil. He was the owner of Sathya Studios and Emgeeyar Pictures (willed to charity) which produced many of the films he acted in. He had gifted a golden sword weighing half a Kilogram to Mookambika temple in Kollur, Udupi district.

Illness and Death

In October 1984, MGR was diagnosed with kidney failure, which was further complicated by diabetes, a mild heart attack and a massive stroke. He was rushed to the Downstate Medical Center, Brooklyn, United States for treatment, undergoing a kidney transplant. He returned to Chennai on 4 February 1985. He was sworn in as chief minister of Tamil Nadu for the third consecutive term on 10 February 1985. The next 2 years and 10 months were spent in frequent trips to the United States for treatment.

MGR never fully recovered from his illness and died on 24 December 1987 at 3:30 am in Chennai Apollo Hospital after his prolonged illness. He was almost 71. His death sparked off a frenzy of looting and rioting all over the state. Shops, movie theatres, buses and other public and private property became the target of violence let loose. The police had to resort issuing shoot-at-sight orders. Tamilians from

Bangalore rushed to Madras in trains to see the mortal remains of MGR. Government had announced free train facility for this visit. The violence during the funeral alone left 29 people dead and 47 police personnel badly wounded.

This state of affairs continued for almost a month across Tamil Nadu. Around one million people followed his remains, around 30 followers committed suicide and people had their heads tonsured. After his death, his political party, the All India Anna Dravida Munnetra Kazhagam, split between his wife Janaki Ramachandran and J. Jayalalithaa; they merged in 1988.

In 1989 Dr. M. G. R. Home and Higher Secondary School for the Speech and Hearing Impaired was established in the erstwhile residence MGR Gardens, Ramapuram, in accordance with his will dated 17 January 1986. His official residence at 27, Arcot Street, T.Nagar is now MGR Memorial House and is open for public viewing. His film studio, Sathya Studios, has been converted into a women's college.

22

Dr B R Ambedkar

Dr B R Ambedkar, popularly known as Babasaheb Ambedkar, was one of the architects of the Indian Constitution. He was a well-known politician and an eminent jurist. Ambedkar's efforts to eradicate the social evils like untouchablity and caste restrictions were remarkable. The leader, throughout his life, fought for the rights of the dalits and other socially backward classes. Ambedkar was appointed as the nation's first Law Minister in the Cabinet of Jawaharlal Nehru. He was posthumously awarded the Bharat Ratna, India's highest civilian honor in 1990.

His Life

Bhimrao Ambedkar was born to Bhimabai Sakpal and Ramji on 14 April 1891 in Madhya Pradesh. He was the fourteenth child of his parents. Ambedkar's father was a Subedar in the Indian Army and posted at Mhow cantonment, MP. After the retirement of his father in 1894, the family moved to Satara. Shortly after, his mother passed away. Four years later, his father remarried and the family shifted to Bombay, where he cleared his matriculation in 1908. His father Bhimabai Sakpal died in Bombay, in 1912.

Ambedkar was a victim of caste discrimination. His parents hailed from the Hindu Mahar caste, which was viewed as "untouchable" by the upper class. Due to this, Ambedkar had to face severe discriminations from every corners of the society. The discrimination and humiliation haunted Ambedkar even at the Army school, run by British government. Fearing social outcry, the teachers would segregate the students of lower class from that of Brahmins and other upper classes. The untouchable students were often asked by the teacher to sit outside the class. After shifting to Satara, he was admitted to a local school but the change of school did not change the fate of young Bhimrao. Discrimination followed wherever he went. In 1908, Ambedkar got the opportunity to study at the Elphinstone College. Besides clearing all the exams successfully Ambedkar also obtained a scholarship of twenty five rupees a month from the Gayakwad ruler of Baroda, Sahyaji Rao III. Political Science and Economics were the subjects in which he graduated from the Bombay University in 1912. Ambedkar decided to use the money for higher studies in the USA.

After coming back from the US, Ambedkar was appointed as the Defence secretary to the King of Baroda. Even, there also he had to face the humiliation for being an 'Untouchable'. With the help of the former Bombay Governor Lord Sydenham, Ambedkar obtained the job as a professor of political economy at the Sydenham College of Commerce and Economics in Bombay. In order to continue his further studies, in 1920 he went to England at his own expenses. There he was awarded honour of D.Sc by the London University. Ambedkar also spent few months at the University of Bonn, Germany, to study economics. On 8 June, 1927, he was awarded a Doctorate by the University of Columbia.

Dalit Movement

After returning to India, Bhimrao Ambedkar decided to fight against the caste discrimination that almost fragmented the nation. Ambedkar opined that there should be separate electoral system for the untouchables and lower caste people. He also favored the concept of providing reservations for Dalits and other religious communities.

Ambedkar began to find ways to reach to the people and make them understand the drawbacks of the prevailing social evils. He launched a newspaper called "Mooknayaka" (leader of the silent). It was believed that, one day, after hearing his speech at a rally, Shahu IV, an influential ruler of Kolhapur dined with the leader. The incident also created a huge uproar in the socio-political arena of the country.

Political career

In 1936, Ambedkar founded the Independent Labor Party. In the 1937 elections to the Central Legislative Assembly his party won 15 seats. Ambedkar oversaw the transformation of his political party into the All India Scheduled Castes Federation, although it performed poorly in the elections held in 1946 for the Constituent Assembly of India.

Ambedkar objected to the decision of Congress and Mahatma Gandhi to call the untouchable community as Harijans. He would say that even the members of untouchable community are same as the other members of the society. Ambedkar was appointed on the Defence Advisory Committee and the Viceroy's Executive Council as Minister for Labor. His reputation as a scholar led to his appointment as free India's first, Law Minister and chairman of the committee responsible to draft a constitution.

Framer of Constitution

Bhimrao Ambedkar was appointed as the chairman of the constitution drafting committee. He was also a noted scholar and eminent jurist. Ambedkar emphasized on the construction of a virtual bridge between the classes of the society. According to him, it would be difficult to maintain the unity of the country if the difference among the classes were not met.

Conversion to Buddhism

In 1950, Ambedkar traveled to Sri Lanka to attend a convention of Buddhist scholars and monks. After his return he decided to write a book on Buddhism and soon, converted himself to Buddhism. In his speeches, Ambedkar lambasted the Hindu rituals and caste division. Ambedkar founded the Bharatiya Bauddha Mahasabha In 1955. His book "The Buddha and His Dhamma" was published posthumously.

On October 14, 1956 Ambedkar organized a public ceremony to convert around five lakh of his supporters into Buddhism. Ambedkar traveled to Kathmandu to attend the Fourth World Buddhist Conference. He completed his final manuscript, "The Buddha or Karl Marx" on December 2, 1956.

Death

Since 1954-55 Ambedkar was suffering from serious health problems including diabetes and weak eyesight. On 6 December, 1956 he died at his home in Delhi. Since, Ambedkar adopted the Buddhism as his religion, a Buddhist-style cremation was organized for him. The ceremony was attended by hundreds of thousands of supporters, activists and admirers.

23

Rolihlahla Mandela

Rolihlahla Mandela was born into the Madiba clan in Mvezo, Transkei, on July 18, 1918, to Nonqaphi Nosekeni and Nkosi Mphakanyiswa Gadla Mandela, principal counsellor to the Acting King of the Thembu people, Jongintaba Dalindyebo.

His father died when he was 12 years old (1930) and the young Rolihlahla became a ward of Jongintaba at the Great Place in Mqhekezweni.*

Hearing the elder's stories of his ancestor's valour during the wars of resistance, he dreamed also of making his own contribution to the freedom struggle of his people.

Education

He attended primary school in Qunu where his teacher Miss Mdingane gave him the name Nelson, in accordance with the custom to give all school children "Christian" names.

He completed his Junior Certificate at Clarkebury Boarding Institute and went on to Healdtown, a Wesleyan secondary school of some repute, where he matriculated.

Nelson Mandela began his studies for a Bachelor of Arts degree at the University College of Fort Hare but did not complete the degree there as he was expelled for joining in a student protest.

He completed his BA through the University of South Africa and went back to Fort Hare for his graduation in 1943.

On his return to the Great Place at Mqhekezweni the King was furious and said if he didn't return to Fort Hare he would arrange wives for him and his cousin Justice. They ran away to Johannesburg instead, arriving there in 1941. There he worked as a mine security officer and after meeting Walter Sisulu, an estate agent, who introduced him to Lazer Sidelsky. He then did his articles through a firm of attorneys, Witkin Eidelman and Sidelsky.

Meanwhile he began studying for an LLB at the University of the Witwatersrand. By his own admission he was a poor student and left the university in 1952 without graduating. He only started studying again through the University of London after his imprisonment in 1962 but also did not complete that degree.

In 1989, while in the last months of his imprisonment, he obtained an LLB through the University of South Africa. He graduated in absentia at a ceremony in Cape Town.

Political Career

Nelson Mandela, while increasingly politically involved from 1942, only joined the African National Congress in 1944 when he helped to form the ANC Youth League.

In 1944 he married Walter Sisulu's cousin Evelyn Mase, a nurse. They had two sons, Madiba Thembekile 'Thembi' and Makgatho and two daughters both called Makaziwe, the first of whom died in infancy. They effectively separated in 1955 and divorced in 1958.

Nelson Mandela rose through the ranks of the ANCYL and through its work, in 1949 the ANC adopted a more radical mass-based policy, the Programme of Action.

In 1952 he was chosen at the National Volunteer-in-Chief of the Defiance Campaign with Maulvi Cachalia as his deputy. This campaign of civil disobedience against six unjust laws was a joint programme between the ANC and the South African Indian Congress. He and 19 others were charged under the Suppression of Communism Act for their part in the campaign and sentenced to nine months hard labour, suspended for two years.

A two-year diploma in law on top of his BA allowed Nelson Mandela to practice law, and in August 1952 he and Oliver Tambo established South Africa's first black law firm, Mandela and Tambo.

At the end of 1952 he was banned for the first time. As a restricted person he was only permitted to watch in secret as the Freedom Charter was adopted in Kliptown on 26 June 1955.

Nelson Mandela was arrested in a countrywide police swoop on 5 December 1955, which led to the 1956 Treason Trial. Men and women of all races found themselves in the dock in the marathon trial that only ended when the last 28 accused, including Mr Mandela were acquitted on 29 March 1961.

On 21 March 1960 police killed 69 unarmed people in a protest against the pass laws held at Sharpeville. This led to the country's first state of emergency and the banning of the ANC and the Pan Africanist Congress on 8 April. Nelson Mandela and his colleagues in the Treason Trial were among thousands detained during the state of emergency.

During the trial on 14 June 1958 Nelson Mandela married a social worker, Winnie Madikizela. They had two daughters, Zenani and Zindziswa. The couple divorced in 1996.

Days before the end of the Treason Trial Nelson Mandela travelled to Pietermaritzburg to speak at the All-in Africa Conference, which resolved that he should write to Prime Minister Verwoerd requesting a non-racial national convention, and to warn that should he not agree there would be a national strike against South Africa becoming a republic. As soon as he and his colleagues were acquitted in the Treason Trial Nelson Mandela went underground and began planning a national strike for 29, 30 and 31 March. In the face of massive mobilisation of state security the strike was called off early. In June 1961 he was asked to lead the armed struggle and helped to establish Umkhonto weSizwe (Spear of the Nation).

On 11 January 1962, using the adopted name David Motsamayi, Nelson Mandela secretly left South Africa. He travelled around Africa and visited England to gain support for the armed struggle. He received military training in Morocco and Ethiopia and returned to South Africa in July 1962. He was arrested in a police roadblock outside Howick on 5 August while returning from KwaZulu-Natal where he briefed ANC President Chief Albert Luthuli about his trip.

He was charged with leaving the country illegally and inciting workers to strike. He was convicted and sentenced to five years' imprisonment which he began serving in the Pretoria Local Prison. On 27 May 1963 he was transferred to Robben Island and returned to Pretoria on 12 June. Within a month police raided a secret hide-out in Rivonia used by ANC and Communist Party activists, and several of his comrades were arrested.

On 9 October 1963 Nelson Mandela joined ten others on trial for sabotage in what became known as the Rivonia Trial. While facing the death penalty his words to the court at the end of his famous 'Speech from the Dock' on 20 April 1964 became immortalised:

"I have fought against white domination, and I have fought against black domination. I have cherished the ideal of a democratic and free society in which all persons live together in harmony and with equal opportunities. It is an ideal which I hope to live for and to achieve. But if needs be, it is an ideal for which I am prepared to die."

On 11 June 1964 Nelson Mandela and seven other accused: Walter Sisulu, Ahmed Kathrada, Govan Mbeki, Raymond Mhlaba, Denis Goldberg, Elias Motsoaledi and Andrew Mlangeni were convicted and the next day were sentenced to life imprisonment. Denis Goldberg was sent to Pretoria Prison because he was white, while the others went to Robben Island.

Nelson Mandela's mother died in 1968 and his eldest son Thembi in 1969. He was not allowed to attend their funerals.

On 31 March 1982 Nelson Mandela was transferred to Pollsmoor Prison in Cape Town with Sisulu, Mhlaba and Mlangeni. Kathrada joined them in October. When he returned to the prison in November 1985 after prostate surgery Nelson Mandela was held alone. Justice Minister Kobie Coetsee visited him in hospital. Later Nelson Mandela initiated talks about an ultimate meeting between the apartheid government and the ANC.

On 12 August 1988 he was taken to hospital where he was diagnosed with tuberculosis. After more than three months in two hospitals he was transferred on 7 December 1988 to a house at Victor Verster Prison near Paarl where he spent his last 14 months of imprisonment. He was released from its gates on Sunday 11 February 1990, nine days after the unbanning of the ANC and the PAC and nearly four months after the release of his remaining Rivonia comrades. Throughout his imprisonment he had rejected at least three conditional offers of release.

Nelson Mandela immersed himself in official talks to end white minority rule and in 1991 was elected ANC President to replace his ailing friend Oliver Tambo. In 1993 he and President FW de Klerk jointly won the Nobel Peace Prize and on 27 April 1994 he voted for the first time in his life.

On 10 May 1994 he was inaugurated South Africa's first democratically elected President. On his 80th birthday in 1998 he married Graça Machel, his third wife.

True to his promise Nelson Mandela stepped down in

1999 after one term as President. He continued to work with the Nelson Mandela Children's Fund he set up in 1995 and established the Nelson Mandela Foundation and The Mandela Rhodes Foundation.

In April 2007 his grandson Mandla Mandela became head of the Mvezo Traditional Council at a ceremony at the Mvezo Great Place.

Nelson Mandela never wavered in his devotion to democracy, equality and learning. Despite terrible provocation, he never answered racism with racism. His life has been an inspiration to all who are oppressed and deprived; to all who are opposed to oppression and deprivation.

He died at his home in Johannesburg on 5 December 2013.

*Nelson Mandela's father died in 1930 when Mr Mandela was 12 and his mother died in 1968 when he was in prison. While the autobiography *Long Walk to Freedom* places Madiba's father's death in 1927, historical evidence shows it must have been later, most likely 1930. In fact, the original *Long Walk to Freedom* manuscript (written on Robben Island) states the year as 1930.

24

Rajiv Ratna Gandhi

Rajiv Ratna Gandhi 20 August 1944 – 21 May 1991) was the sixth Prime Minister of India, serving from 1984 to 1989. He took office after the 1984 assassination of Prime Minister Indira Gandhi, his mother, to become the youngest Indian premier.

A scion of the politically powerful Nehru–Gandhi family associated with the Indian National Congress party, for much of Rajiv's childhood his grandfather Jawaharlal Nehru was prime minister. For his college education, he went to Britain where he met and began dating Antonia Maino, an Italian waitress. Rajiv returned to India in 1966 and became a professional pilot for the state-owned Indian Airlines. In 1968, he married Maino—who changed her name to Sonia Gandhi—and the couple settled down in Delhi to a domestic life with their children Rahul and Priyanka. Although for much of the 1970s his mother was prime minister, and his brother Sanjay wielded significant unofficial power, Rajiv remained apolitical. After Sanjay's death in a plane crash in 1980, Rajiv reluctantly entered politics at the behest of Indira. The following year he won his brother's Amethi seat and became a member of the Lok

Sabha (the lower house of Parliament). As part of his political grooming, Rajiv was made a general secretary of the Congress and given significant responsibility in organising the 1982 Asian Games.

On the morning of 31 October 1984, his mother was assassinated by her Sikh bodyguards to avenge Operation Blue Star; later that day, Rajiv Gandhi was appointed Prime Minister. His leadership was put to the test over the next few days as organised mobs rioted against the Sikh community, resulting in the death of thousands in Delhi alone. Nevertheless, that December, a nationwide sympathy vote for Rajiv's Congress party helped it win the greatest Lok Sabha majority (411 seats out of 542) in history.

Rajiv Gandhi was also mired in many controversies: the 1984 anti-Sikh riots, Bhopal disaster and Shah Bano case. In 1988, Gandhi reversed the coup in Maldives antagonising militant Tamil groups such as PLOTE. He was also responsible for first intervening and then sending Indian Peace Keeping Force troops for peace efforts in Sri Lanka in 1987, which soon ended in open conflict with the Liberation Tigers of Tamil Eelam (LTTE). In mid-1987, the Bofors scandal damaged his honest, corruption-free image and resulted in a major defeat for his party in the 1989 elections.

Rajiv Gandhi remained Congress President until the elections in 1991. While campaigning for the elections, he was assassinated by a suicide bomber from the LTTE. His widow Sonia became the president of Congress party in 1998, and led the party to victory in the 2004 and 2009 parliament elections. His son Rahul is a Member of Parliament and Vice President of the Congress. Rajiv Gandhi was posthumously awarded the highest civilian award by the government of India, Bharat Ratna in 1991.

Early Life and Career

Rajiv Gandhi was born into India's most famous political family. His maternal grandfather was the Indian independence leader Jawaharlal Nehru, who was India's first Prime Minister after independence. His father, Feroze, was one of the younger members of the Indian National Congress party, and had befriended the young Indira, and also her mother Kamala Nehru, while working on party affairs at Allahabad. Subsequently, Indira and Feroze grew closer to each other while in England, and they married, despite initial objections from Jawaharlal due to his religion (Zoroastrianism).[1]

He was born in 1944 in Mumbai, during a time when both his parents were in and out of British prisons. In August 1947, Jawaharlal Nehru became the prime minister of independent India, and the family settled in Allahabad, and then at Lucknow, where Feroze became the editor of the *National Herald* newspaper (founded by Motilal Nehru). The marriage was faltering and, in 1949, Indira and the two sons moved to Delhi to live with Nehru, ostensibly so that Indira could assist her father in his duties, acting as official hostess, and helping run the huge residence. Meanwhile, Feroze continued alone in Lucknow. Relations were strained further when Feroze challenged corruption within the Congress leadership over the Haridas Mundhra scandal. After Feroze Gandhi had a heart attack in 1958, the family reconciled briefly before Feroze died from a second heart attack in 1960.

Rajiv first studied at Welham Boys' School in Dehra Dun, and then went on to the Doon School. He was sent to London in 1961 to study his A-levels. In 1962, he was offered a place at Trinity College, Cambridge, to study engineering. Rajiv stayed at Cambridge until 1965, but did not finish his degree.[2] In 1966, he was offered and took up a place at Imperial College London, but after a year left that course without a degree.

Rajiv began working for Indian Airlines as a professional pilot while his mother became Prime Minister in 1966. He exhibited no interest in politics. He married a waitress at a Greek restaurant Albina Màino who later became known as Sonia Gandhi. In 1970, his wife gave birth to their first child

Rahul, and in 1972, to Priyanka, their second.

Political Career

Following his younger brother Sanjay Gandhi's death in 1980, Gandhi was pressured by Congress politicians and his mother to enter politics. He and Sonia were both opposed to the idea, and he even publicly stated that he would not contest for his brother's seat. Nevertheless, he eventually announced his candidacy for Parliament. His entry was criticized by many in the press, public and political opposition. Rajiv also became a member of the Asian Games Organizing Committee in 1982 with his close friend and then sports minister Sardar Buta Singh as president of the committee. He fought his first election from Sanjay's erstwhile Amethi Lok Sabha seat, a Nehru–Gandhi bastion, and defeated Sharad Yadav. It was widely perceived that Indira Gandhi was grooming Rajiv for the prime minister's job, and he soon became the president of the Indian Youth Congress, the Congress party's youth wing.

Prime Minister of India

Rajiv Gandhi was in West Bengal when his mother, Prime Minister Indira Gandhi was assassinated on 31 October 1984 by two of her Sikh bodyguards, Satwant Singh and Beant Singh, to avenge the military attack on the Golden Temple during Operation Blue Star. Sardar Buta Singh, as well as President Zail Singh pressed Rajiv to become India's prime minister, within hours of his mother's assassination. Commenting on the anti-Sikh riots in Delhi, Rajiv Gandhi said, "When a giant tree falls, the earth below shakes"; a statement for which he was widely criticized. Many Congress politicians were accused of orchestrating the violence. Soon after assuming office, Rajiv asked President Zail Singh to dissolve Parliament and hold fresh elections, as the Lok Sabha completed its five-year term. Rajiv Gandhi also officially became the President of the Congress party. The Congress party won a landslide victory with the largest majority in history of Indian Parliament—giving Gandhi absolute control of government. He also benefited from his youth and a general perception of being free of a background in corrupt politics.

Economic Policy

He increased government support for science and technology and associated industries, and reduced import quotas, taxes and tariffs on technology-based industries, especially computers, airlines, defence and telecommunications. In 1986, he announced a National Policy on Education to modernise and expand higher education programs across India. He founded the Jawahar Navodaya Vidyalaya System in 1986 which is a Central government based institution that concentrates on the upliftment of the rural section of the society providing them free residential education from 6th till 12 grade. His efforts created MTNL in 1986, and his public call offices, better known as PCOs, helped spread telephones in rural areas. He introduced measures significantly reducing the *Licence Raj*, in post-1990 period, allowing businesses and individuals to purchase capital, consumer goods and import without bureaucratic restrictions.

Foreign Policy

Rajiv Gandhi began leading in a direction significantly different from his mother's socialism. He improved bilateral relations with the United States – long strained owing to Indira's socialism and friendship with the USSR — and expanded economic and scientific cooperation. During his state visit to the Soviet Union he met with Premier Nikolai Tikhonov, Andrey Gromyko of the Ministry of Foreign Affairs and Mikhail Gorbachev.

Security Policy

Rajiv Gandhi (left) congratulates Indian Army explorers for reaching the South Pole.

Rajiv authorised an extensive police and army campaign to contain terrorism in Punjab. A state of martial law existed in the Punjab state, and civil liberties, commerce and tourism were greatly disrupted. There are many accusations of human rights violations by police officials as well as by the militants during this period. It is alleged that even as the situation in Punjab came under control, the Indian government was offering arms and training to the LTTE rebels fighting the government of Sri Lanka. The Indo-Sri Lanka Peace Accord was signed by Rajiv Gandhi and the Sri Lankan President J. R. Jayewardene, in Colombo on 29 July 1987. The very next day, on 30 July 1987, Rajiv Gandhi was assaulted on the head with a rifle butt by a young Sinhalese naval cadet named Vijayamunige Rohana de Silva, while receiving the honour guard. The intended assault on the back of Rajiv Gandhi's head glanced off his shoulder and it was captured in news crew photographs and video.

With his speech while addressing the Joint Session of the US Congress and India, he said, "India is an old country, but a young nation; and like the young everywhere, we are impatient. I am young and I too have a dream. I dream of an India,strong, independent, self-reliant and in the forefront of the front ranks of the nations of the world in the service of mankind."

25

Vallabhbhai Jhaverbhai Patel

Vallabhbhai Jhaverbhai Patel (Hindi pronunciation) (31 October 1875 – 15 December 1950) was an Indian barrister and statesman, one of the leaders of the Indian National Congress and one of the founding fathers of the Republic of India. He was a social leader who played a leading role in the country's struggle for independence and guided its integration into a united, independent nation. In India and elsewhere, he was often addressed as **Sardar**, which means *Chief* in Hindi, Urdu and Persian.

He was raised in the countryside of Gujarat. Vallabhbhai Patel was employed in successful practice as a lawyer. Patel subsequently organised peasants from Kheda, Borsad, and Bardoli in Gujarat in non-violent civil disobedience against oppressive policies imposed by the British Raj; in this role, he became one of the most influential leaders in Gujarat. He rose to the leadership of the Indian National Congress and was at the forefront of rebellions and political events, organising the party for elections in 1934 and 1937, and promoting the Quit India movement.

As the first Home Minister and Deputy Prime Minister of India, Patel organised relief for refugees in Punjab and Delhi, and led efforts to restore peace across the nation. Patel took charge of the task to forge a united India from the British colonial provinces allocated to India and more than five hundred self-governing princely states, released from British suzerainty by the Indian Independence Act 1947. Using frank diplomacy, backed with the option and use of military force, Patel's leadership persuaded almost every princely state. Often known as the "Iron Man of India" or "Bismarck of India", he is also remembered as the "Patron Saint" of India's civil servants for establishing modern all-India services.

Early Life and Education

Sardar Vallabhbhai Patel's native place was **Karamsad**. His actual date of birth was never officially recorded — Patel entered 31 October as his date of birth on his matriculation examination papers. They lived in the village of Karamsad, Bombay Presidency, where Jhaverbhai owned a homestead. Somabhai, Narsibhai and Vithalbhai Patel (also a future political leader) were his elder brothers. He had a younger brother, Kashibhai and a sister, Dahiba. As a young boy, Patel helped his father in the fields and twice a month kept a day-long fast, abstaining from food and water — a Hindu cultural observance that helped him to develop physical toughness. When he was eighteen years old, Patel's marriage was arranged with Jhaverba, a young girl of twelve or thirteen years from a nearby village. According to custom, the young bride would continue to live with her parents until her husband started earning and could establish their household.

Patel travelled to attend schools in Nadiad, Petlad and Borsad, living self-sufficiently with other boys. He reputedly cultivated a stoic character — a popular anecdote recounts how he lanced his own painful boil without hesitation, even as the barber supposed to do it trembled. Patel passed his matriculation at the late age of 22; at this point, he was generally regarded by his elders as an unambitious man destined for a commonplace job. Patel himself harboured a plan to study to become a lawyer, work and save funds, travel to England and study to become a barrister. Patel spent years away from his family, studying on his own with books borrowed from other lawyers and passed examinations within two years. Fetching Jhaverba from her parents' home, Patel set up his household in Godhra and was called to the bar. During the many years it took him to save money, Patel — now an advocate — earned a reputation as a fierce and skilled lawyer. The couple had a daughter, Maniben, in 1904, and a son, Dahyabhai, in 1906. Patel also cared for a friend suffering from Bubonic plague when it swept across Gujarat. When Patel himself came down with the disease, he immediately sent his family to safety, left his home and moved into an isolated house in Nadiad (by other accounts, Patel spent this time in a dilapidated temple); there, he recovered slowly.

Patel practised law in Godhra, Borsad and Anand while taking on the financial burdens of his homestead in Karamsad.Patel was also the first chairman and founder of the E.M.H.S. "Edward Memorial High School" Borsad which is at presently known as Jhaverbhai Dajibhai Patel High School. When he had saved enough for England and applied for a pass and a ticket, they arrived in the name of "V. J. Patel," at Vithalbhai's home, who bore the same initials. Having harboured his own plans to study in England, Vithalbhai remonstrated to his younger brother that it would be disreputable for an older brother to follow his younger brother. In keeping with concerns for his family's honour, Patel allowed Vithalbhai to go in his place. He also financed his brother's stay and began saving again for his own goals.

In 1909, Patel's wife Jhaverba was hospitalised in Bombay (now Mumbai) to undergo a major surgical operation for cancer. Her health suddenly worsened and despite successful emergency surgery, she died in the hospital. Patel was given a note informing him of his wife's demise as he was cross-examining a witness in court. According to others who witnessed, Patel read the note, pocketed it and continued to intensely cross-examine the witness and won the case. He broke the news to others only after the proceedings had ended. Patel decided against marrying again. He raised his children with the help of his family and sent them to English-medium schools in Mumbai. At the age of 36, he journeyed to England and enrolled at the Middle Temple Inn in London. Finishing a 36-month course in 30 months, Patel topped his class despite having no previous college background. Returning to India, Patel settled in the city of Ahmedabad and became one of the city's most successful barristers. Wearing European-style clothes and urbane mannerisms, he also became a skilled bridge player. Patel nurtured ambitions to expand his practice and accumulate great wealth and to provide his children with modern education. He had also made a pact with his brother Vithalbhai to support his entry into politics in the Bombay Presidency, while Patel himself would remain in Ahmedabad and provide for the family. He was a vegetarian.

Leading India

Governor General Chakravarti Rajagopalachari, Nehru and Patel formed the *triumvirate* which ruled India from 1948 to 1950. Prime Minister Nehru was intensely popular with the masses, but Patel enjoyed the loyalty and the faith of rank and file Congressmen, state leaders and India's civil services. Patel was a senior leader in the Constituent Assembly of India and was responsible in a large measure for shaping India's constitution. He is also known as the "Bismarck of India" Patel was a key force behind the appointment of Dr. Bhimrao Ramji Ambedkar as the chairman of the drafting committee, and the inclusion of leaders from a diverse political spectrum in the process of writing the constitution.

Patel was the chairman of the committees responsible for minorities, tribal and excluded areas, fundamental rights and provincial constitutions. Patel piloted a model constitution for the provinces in the Assembly, which contained limited powers for the state governor, who would defer to the President—he clarified it was not the intention to let the governor exercise power which could impede an elected government. He worked closely with Muslim leaders to end separate electorates and the more potent demand for reservation of seats for minorities. Patel would hold personal dialogues with leaders of other minorities on the question, and was responsible for the measure that allows the President to appoint Anglo-Indians to Parliament. His intervention was key to the passage of two articles that protected civil servants from political involvement and guaranteed their terms and privileges. He was also instrumental in the founding the Indian Administrative Service and the Indian Police Service, and for his defence of Indian civil servants from political attack, he is known as the "patron saint" of India's services. When a delegation of Gujarati farmers came to him citing their inability to send their milk production to the markets without being fleeced by intermediaries, Patel exhorted them to organise the processing and sale of milk by themselves, and guided them to create the Kaira District Co-operative Milk Producers' Union Limited, which preceded the Amul milk products brand. Patel also pledged the reconstruction of the ancient but dilapidated Somnath Temple in Saurashtra—he oversaw the creation of a public trust and restoration work, and pledged to dedicate the temple upon the completion of work (the work was completed after Patel's death, and the temple was inaugurated by the first President of India, Dr. Rajendra Prasad).

When the Pakistani invasion of Kashmir began in September 1947, Patel immediately wanted to send troops into Kashmir. But agreeing with Nehru and Mountbatten, he waited till Kashmir's monarch had acceded to India. Patel then oversaw India's military operations to secure Srinagar, the Baramulla Pass and the forces retrieved much territory from the invaders. Patel, along with Defence Minister Baldev Singh administered the entire military effort, arranging for troops from different parts of India to be rushed to Kashmir and for a major military road connecting Srinagar to Pathankot be built in 6 months. Patel strongly advised Nehru against going for arbitration to the United Nations, insisting that Pakistan had been wrong to support the invasion and the accession to India was valid. He did not want foreign interference in a bilateral affair. Patel opposed the release of Rs. 55 crores to the Government of Pakistan, convinced that the money would go to finance the war against India in Kashmir. The Cabinet had approved his point but it was reversed when Gandhi, who feared an intensifying rivalry and further communal violence, went on a fast-unto-death to obtain the release. Patel, though not estranged from Gandhi, was deeply hurt at the rejection of his counsel and a Cabinet decision.

In 1949, a crisis arose when the number of Hindu refugees entering West Bengal, Assam and Tripura from East Pakistan climbed over 800,000. The refugees in many cases were being forcibly evicted by Pakistani authorities, and were victims of intimidation and violence.[57] Nehru invited Liaquat Ali Khan, Prime Minister of Pakistan to find a peaceful solution. Despite his aversion, Patel reluctantly met Khan and discussed the matters. Patel strongly criticised, however, Nehru's intention to sign a pact that would create minority commissions in both countries and pledge both India and Pakistan to a commitment to protect each other's minorities. Syama Prasad Mookerjee and K.C. Neogy, two Bengali ministers resigned and Nehru was intensely criticised in West Bengal for allegedly appeasing Pakistan. The pact was immediately in jeopardy. Patel however, publicly came out to Nehru's aid. He gave emotional speeches to members of Parliament, and the people of West Bengal, and spoke with scores of delegations of Congressmen, Hindus, Muslims and other public interest groups, persuading them to give peace a final effort.

Gandhi's death and relations with Nehru

Patel was intensely loyal to Gandhi and both he and Nehru looked to him to arbitrate disputes. However, Nehru and Patel sparred over national issues. When Nehru asserted control over Kashmir policy, Patel objected to Nehru's sidelining his home ministry's officials. Nehru was offended by Patel's decision-making regarding the states' integration, having neither consulted him nor the cabinet. Patel asked Gandhi to relieve him of his obligation to serve, believing that an open political battle would hurt India. After much personal deliberation and contrary to Patel's prediction, Gandhi on 30 January 1948 told Patel not to leave the government. A free India, according to Gandhi, needed both Patel and Nehru. Patel was the last man to privately talk with Gandhi, who was assassinated just minutes after Patel's departure. At Gandhi's wake, Nehru and Patel embraced each other and addressed the nation together. Patel gave solace to many associates and friends and immediately moved to forestall any possible violence. Within two months of Gandhi's death, Patel suffered a major heart attack; the timely action of his daughter, his secretary and nurse saved Patel's life. Speaking later, Patel attributed the attack to the "grief bottled up" due to Gandhi's death.

Criticism arose from the media and other politicians that Patel's home ministry had failed to protect Gandhi. Emotionally exhausted, Patel tendered a letter of resignation, offering to leave the government. Patel's secretary persuaded him to withhold the letter, seeing it as fodder for Patel's political enemies and political conflict in India. However, Nehru sent Patel a letter dismissing any question of personal differences and his desire for Patel's ouster. He reminded Patel of their 30-year partnership in the freedom struggle and asserted that after Gandhi's death, it was especially wrong for them to quarrel. Nehru, Rajagopalachari and other Congressmen publicly defended Patel. Moved, Patel publicly endorsed Nehru's leadership and refuted any suggestion of discord. Patel publicly dispelled any notion that he sought to be prime minister. Though the two committed themselves to joint leadership and non-interference in Congress party affairs, they would criticise each other in matters of policy, clashing on the issues of Hyderabad's integration and UN mediation in Kashmir. Nehru declined Patel's counsel on sending assistance to Tibet after its 1950 invasion by the People's Republic of China and ejecting the Portuguese from Goa by military force.

When Nehru pressured Dr. Rajendra Prasad to decline a nomination to become the first President of India in 1950 in favour of Rajagopalachari, he thus angered the party, which felt Nehru was attempting to impose his will. Nehru sought Patel's help in winning the party over, but Patel declined and Prasad was duly elected. Nehru opposed the 1950 Congress presidential candidate Purushottam Das Tandon, a conservative Hindu leader, endorsing Jivatram Kripalani instead and threatening to resign if Tandon was elected. Patel rejected Nehru's views and endorsed Tandon in Gujarat, where Kripalani received not one vote despite hailing from that state himself. Patel believed Nehru had to understand that his will was not law with the Congress, but he personally discouraged Nehru from resigning after the latter felt that the party had no confidence in him.

On 29 March 1949, authorities lost radio contact with a plane carrying Patel, his daughter Maniben and the Maharaja of Patiala. Engine failure caused the pilot to make an emergency landing in a desert area in Rajasthan. With all passengers safe, Patel and others tracked down a nearby village and local officials. When Patel returned to Delhi, thousands of Congressmen gave him a resounding welcome. In Parliament, MPs gave a long, standing ovation to Patel, stopping proceedings for half an hour. In his twilight years, Patel was honoured by members of Parliament and awarded honorary doctorates of law by the Punjab University and Osmania University.

Death

Patel's health declined rapidly through the summer of 1950. He later began coughing blood, whereupon Maniben began limiting his meetings and working hours and arranged for a personalised medical staff to begin attending to Patel. The Chief Minister of West Bengal and doctor Bidhan Roy heard Patel make jokes about his impending end, and in a private meeting Patel frankly admitted to his ministerial colleague N. V. Gadgil that he was not going to live much longer. Patel's health worsened after 2 November, when he began losing consciousness frequently and was confined to his bed. He was flown to Mumbai on 12 December on advice from Dr Roy, to recuperate as his condition deemed critical. Nehru, Rajagopalchari, Rajendra Prasad and Menon all came to see him off at the airport in Delhi. Patel was extremely weak and had to be carried onto the aircraft in a chair. In Bombay, large crowds gathered at Santacruz Airport to greet him, to spare him from this stress, the aircraft landed at Juhu Aerodrome, where Chief Minister B.G. Kher and Morarji Desai were present to receive him with a car belonging to the Governor of Bombay, that took Vallabhbhai to Birla House. After suffering a massive heart attack (his second), he died on 15 December 1950 at Birla House in Bombay. In an unprecedented and unrepeated gesture, on the day after his death more than 1,500 officers of India's civil and police services congregated to mourn at Patel's residence in Delhi and pledged "complete loyalty and unremitting zeal" in India's service. His cremation was planned at Girgaum Chowpatty, however this was changed to Sonapur (Now Marine Lines) when his daughter conveyed that it was his wish to be cremated like a common man in the same place as his wife and brother were earlier cremated. His cremation in Sonapur in Bombay, was attended by a 10 lakh strong crowd including Prime Minister Nehru, Rajagopalachari, and President Rajendra Prasad.

26

Morarji Desai

Morarji Desai (29 Feb 1896 – 10 April 1995), was a notable Indian independence activist and the fourth Prime Minister of India from 1977 - 1979. He was also the first Prime Minister to head India's first non-Congress Government. He held many important posts in the Government of India such as: Chief Minister of Bombay State, Home Minister, Finance Minister and Deputy Prime Minister of India. At foreign fronts, Desai holds international fame for his peace activism and made notable efforts to initiate peace between two-rival South Asian states, Pakistan and India. After India's first nuclear explosion in 1974, Desai helped restore friendly relations with China and Pakistan, and vowed to avoid armed conflict such as Indo-Pakistani war of 1971. Desai has the credible distinction of being the only Indian national to be conferred with Pakistan's highest civilian award, *Nishan-e-Pakistan*, which was conferred on him by President Ghulam Ishaq Khan in 1990 in a colorful ceremony. Domestically, he played crucial role in Indian nuclear program after it was targeted by major nuclear powers after conducting a surprise test in 1974. Later, his policies promoted social, health and administrative reforms in the country.

Early Life

Morarji Desai was born into an Anavil Brahmin family in Bhadeli, Valsad in Bombay Presidency (now in Gujarat). He underwent his primary schooling in Saurashtra The Kundla School, Savarkundla now called J.V. Modi school and later joined Bai Ava Bai High School, Valsad. After graduating from Wilson College, Mumbai, he joined the civil service in Gujarat. Desai resigned as deputy collector of Godhra in May 1930 after being found guilty of going soft on Hindus during the riots of 1927-28 there. Desai then joined the freedom struggle under Mahatma Gandhi and joined the civil disobedience movement against British rule in India. He spent many years in jail during the freedom struggle and owing to his sharp leadership skills and tough spirit, he became a favourite amongst freedom-fighters and an important leader of the Indian National Congress in Gujarat. When provincial elections were held in 1934 and 1937, Desai was elected and served as the Revenue Minister and Home Minister of the Bombay Presidency.

In Government

Before the independence of India, he became Bombay's Home Minister and later was elected as Chief Minister of Bombay State in 1952. The state was a bi-lingual state, home to Gujarati-speaking and Marathi-speaking people. Since the 1956, Samyukta Maharashtra Samiti led a movement for a Marathi-only speaking state of Maharashtra. A staunch nationalist himself, Morarji Desai was opposed to such movements including the Mahagujarat Movement led by Indulal Yagnik demanding a new state of Gujarat. He proposed that the metropolitan Mumbai (as coined by earlier Koli inhabitants), be made into a union territory or a separate development region to suit its cosmopolitan nature, due to its long-settled citizens from diverse settings across various linguistic, cultural, and religious backgrounds spanning several generations. In opposition to his alleged Gandhian thoughts, he ordered police to fire on a mob of demonstrators by the Mumbai-unit of Samyukta Maharashtra Samiti at Flora Fountain when there was heavy damage caused to public property and commercial offices by the rampaging rioters in the vicinity of Bombay Stock Exchange, considered the primary trading hub and financial capital of the nation. Morarji ordered firing which killed 105 rioters during the entire incident. This escalated the issue and justice was done by creating two separate states based on language as formulated after independence. After the subsequent formation of the present State of Maharashtra, Mumbai became its state capital. Flora Fountain was renamed as "Hutatma Chowk" (Martyrs' Square) to commemorate the 105 men killed in the firing. Later Desai moved to Delhi as he got appointed in the cabinet.

As Home Minister, Desai outlawed any portrayals of indecency (which included "kissing" scenes) in films and theatrical productions. Being a staunch Gandhian, Desai was socially conservative, pro-business, and in favour of free enterprise reforms, as opposed to Prime Minister Jawaharlal Nehru's socialistic policies.

Rising in Congress leadership, as a fierce nationalistic and anti-corruption leanings, Desai was at odds with Prime Minister Nehru and his allies, and with Nehru's age and health failing, he was considered as a possible contender for the position of Prime Minister. Outflanked in the leadership contest after Nehru's death in 1964 by the Nehruvian Lal Bahadur Shastri, Desai remained content to build support within the ranks.

In early 1966, the unexpected passing away of Prime Minister Lal Bahadur Shastri after only 18 months in power, made Morarji Desai once again a contender for the top position. However, he was defeated by Nehru's daughter, Indira Gandhi in the Congress party leadership election by a narrow margin. Desai served as Deputy Prime Minister and Finance minister of India in the Indira Gandhi government until 1969 when Prime Minister Mrs Gandhi without consulting him took away the finance portfolio from him. at the same time, she also nationalised the fourteen biggest banks in India. These acts compelled Morarji Desai resign from the Gandhi cabinet. In the subsequent split of the Congress party, Morarji joined the Indian National Congress (Organisation) faction of the party, whereas Mrs. Gandhi's formed a new faction named Indian National Congress (Ruling). The 1971 general elections to the Indian parliament were won by Indira Gandhi's Indicate faction in a landslide. Morarji Desai, however, was elected as a member of the Lok Sabha or lower house of Parliament. Morarji Desai again went on indefinite hunger strike on 12 March 1975 to support Nav Nirman movement.

Allegations by Mrs. Indira Gandhi's opponents of her using Government civil servants and equipment during campaigning in the 1971 elections led to Mrs Gandhi's conviction of electoral fraud by the Allahbad High Court in 1975. During the subsequent Emergency rule in 1975–76, Morarji-bhai and other opposition leaders were put in jail by the Indira Gandhi government.

The popular anti-corruption movement led by Jayaprakash Narayan and the anti-Emergency wave in 1977 led to the complete routing of the Congress party in Northern India and a landslide victory for the opposition Janata alliance in the National elections held in March 1977. Morarji Desai was selected by the Janata alliance, later Janata Party as their parliamentary leader, and thus became the first non-Congress Prime Minister of India.

Prime Minister of India (1977-79) Premiership of Morarji Desai

After Indira Gandhi decided to lift The Emergency, general elections were held. Janata Party registered a landslide victory in the election and Morarji Desai became the Prime Minister. Desai worked to improve relations with neighbour and arch-rival Pakistan and restored normal relations with China, for the first time since the 1962 war. He communicated with Zia-ul-Haq and established friendly relations. Diplomatic relations were also re-established with China. His government undid many amendments made to the constitution during emergency and made it difficult for any future government to impose national emergency. However, the Janata Party coalition, was full of personal and policy friction and thus failed to achieve much owing to continuous in-wrangling and much controversy. With no party in leadership of the coalition, rival groups vied to unseat Desai. Controversial trials of prominent Congress leaders, including Indira Gandhi over Emergency-era abuses worsened the fortunes of his administration.

Since India's first nuclear test in 1974, Desai kept India's nuclear reactors stating "they will never be used for atomic bombs, and I will see to it if I can help it". In 1977, the Carter administration sold India, heavy water and uranium for its nuclear reactors but required American on-site inspection of nuclear materials. Desai declined, seeing the American stance as contradictory, in light of its own nuclear arsenal.

Retirement and Death

In 1979, Raj Narain and Charan Singh pulled out of the Janata Party, forcing Desai to resign from office and retire from politics at the age of 83. The chief reason for the collapse was the demand by the duo and other left leaning members like Madhu Limaye, Krishan Kant and George Fernandes that no member of the Janata party could simultaneously be a member of an alternative social or political organisation. This attack on *dual membership* was directed specifically at members of the Janata party who had been members of the Jan Sangh, and continued to be members of Rashtriya Swayamsevak Sangh, the Jan Sangh's ideological parent.

Desai campaigned for Janata Party in 1980 General Election as a senior politician but did not contest the election himself. , In retirement, he lived in Mumbai, and died at the age of 99. He had been honoured much in his last years as a freedom-fighter of his generation.

Morarji Desai was a strict follower of Mahatma Gandhi's principles and a moralist. He was a vegetarian "both by birth and by conviction."

Feud with R&AW

Morarji Desai had described the Research and Analysis Wing (R&AW), India's external intelligence agency, as the praetorian guard of Indira Gandhi and had promised to stop all activities of the R&AW after becoming prime minister. He closed down much of the agency, and reduced its budget and operations. B. Raman, the former head of the Counter-Terrorism Division of R&AW and noted security analyst, reveals that, in an unguarded moment, Morarji Desai indiscreetly told Pakistan's Chief Martial Law Administrator General Zia ul-Haq that his government was well aware of Pakistan's nuclear development which prompted the Pakistani government in removing all spies from around its nuclear research facilities and thus finally being successful in its nuclear dream.

Social Service

Morarji Desai was a Gandhian follower, social worker, institution builder and a great reformer. He was the Chancellor of Gujarat Vidyapith (university established by Mahatma Gandhi). Even during his term as the Prime Minister he used to visit and stay at Vidyapith during the month of October. He lived simply and used to write post cards himself even when he held the office of Prime Minister. Sardar Patel deputed him to conduct meetings of farmers in Kaira district which finally led to the establishment of the Amul Cooperative movement. During his rule, he withdrew intervention in Public Distribution System and rationing shops were literally lost due to cheap sugar and oil available in the market.

Personal Life and Family

Morarji Desai is survived by his eldest child, daughter, Virmati Ramanlal Desai and son Kanti Desai, six grandchildren, A grand son named Deepak Ramanlal Desai and three grand daughters, Mrs. Malti Mukund Desai, Mrs. Jyoti Ramesh Desai and Mrs. Purnima Manhar Desai, all 4 children of Mrs. Virmati Ramanlal Desai and their 6 great grand children, all of whom had settled out of India and two grand sons Bharat and Jagdeep Desai, sons of Mr. Kantilal Desai and their four great grand children, all settled in India. Grand daughter Jyoti Desai and her husband have relocated back to India at the end of 2008. Mr. Morarji Desai had total 5 chidren with his wife Gajaraben Desai. His 2 sons died very young and a daughter Indumati who was a medical doctor died while he was the Chief Minister of Bombay. The only one to hold any political ambition is Madhukeshwar Desai, one of his great grand sons, son of Jagdeep Desai, who has taken it upon himself to revive the legacy of his illustrious great grandfather. Madhukeshwar Desai is the National Vice-President of the Bharatiya Janata Yuva Morcha, the youth wing of the BJP.

Vishaal Desai, son of Bharat Desai, is a writer and filmmaker who graduated from The London Film School in 2009 and is currently running his own production company, 'A Thousand Faces Productions,' in Mumbai.

In 1978, Prime Minister Morarji Desai, a longtime practitioner of "urine therapy", spoke to Dan Rather on *60 Minutes* about the benefits of drinking urine. Desai stated that drinking urine was the perfect medical solution for the millions of Indians who cannot afford medical treatment., He was ridiculed by many in India and in Foreign countries for this habit.

27

Abul Kalam Muhiyuddin Ahmed Azad

Abul Kalam Muhiyuddin Ahmed Azad (11 November 1888 – 22 February 1958) was an Indian scholar and a senior political leader of the Indian independence movement. Following India's independence, he became the first Minister of Education in the Indian government. In 1992 he was posthumously awarded India's highest civilian award, the Bharat Ratna. There is also a theory which suggests that earlier when he was offered Bharat Ratna he promptly declined it saying that it should not be given to those who have been on the selection committee. Later he was awarded posthumously in 1992. He is commonly remembered as **Maulana Azad**; the word Maulana is an honorific meaning 'learned man', and he had adopted *Azad* (*Free*) as his pen name. His contribution to establishing the education foundation in India is recognised by celebrating his birthday as "National Education Day" across India.

As a young man, Azad composed poetry in Urdu language, as well as treatises on religion and philosophy. He rose to prominence through his work as a journalist, publishing works critical of the British Raj and espousing the causes of Indian nationalism. Azad became the leader of the Khilafat Movement, during which he came into close contact with the Indian leader Mahatma Gandhi. Azad became an enthusiastic supporter of Gandhi's ideas of non-violent civil disobedience, and worked to organise the non-co-operation movement in protest of the 1919 Rowlatt Acts. Azad committed himself to Gandhi's ideals, including promoting *Swadeshi* (indigenous) products and the cause of *Swaraj* (*Self-rule*) for India. In 1923, at an age of 35, he became the youngest person to serve as the President of the Indian National Congress.

Azad was one of the main organisers of the Dharasana Satyagraha in 1931, and emerged as one of the most important national leaders of the time, prominently leading the causes of Hindu-Muslim unity as well as espousing secularism and socialism. He served as Congress president from 1940 to 1945, during which the *Quit India* rebellion was launched. Azad was imprisoned, together with the entire Congress leadership, for three years. Azad became the most prominent Muslim opponent of the demand for a separate Muslim state of Pakistan and served in the interim national government.

Amidst communal turmoil following the partition of India, he worked for religious harmony. As India's Education Minister, Azad oversaw the establishment of a national education system with free primary education and modern institutions of higher education. He is also credited with the establishment of the Indian Institutes of Technology and the foundation of the University Grants Commission, an important institution to supervise and advance the higher education in the nation.

Early Life

Azad was born on 11 November 1888 in Makkah, Saudi Arabia. Azad's real name was Abul Kalam Ghulam Muhiyuddin who became known as Maulana Azad by everyone. His forefathers - madeup of scholars and soldiers - had immigrated to India from Herat, Afghanistan, after the Shi'a Safavids took over Persia and Babur established the

Sunni Mughal Empire in India. Azad's father was Maulana Muhammad Khairuddin, a scholar who authored a dozen of books and had thousands of disciples, while his mother was of a Bengali immigrant family already residing in Medina, the daughter of Sheikh Mohammad Zaher Watri, himself a reputed scholar from Medina who, like Abul Kalam Azad's father, had a reputation all over the Islamic world. Maulana Khairuddin lived with his family in the Bengal region until he left India during the First Indian War of Independence and settled in Mecca, where he met his wife, Zulaikha Begum (a member of the Bengali Muslim immigrant family residing in Medina) , and where Maulana Azad was born, but returned to Calcutta with his family in 1890. Azad began to master several languages, including Urdu, Hindi, Persian, Bengali, Arabic, English,. He was also trained in the Mazahibs of [Hanafi], [Maliki], Shafi'i and Hanbali fiqh, shariat, mathematics, philosophy, world history and science by reputed tutors hired by his family. An avid and determined student, the precocious Azad was running a library, a reading room, a debating society before he was twelve, wanted to write on the life of Ghazali at twelve, was contributing learned articles to ***Makhzan*** (the best known literary magazine of the day) at fourteen, was teaching a class of students, most of whom were twice his age, when he was merely fifteen and succeeded in completing the traditional course of study at the young age of sixteen, nine years ahead of his contemporaries, and brought out a magazine at the same age. In fact, in the field of journalism, he was publishing a poetical journal (***Nairang-e-Aalam***) and was already an editor of a weekly (***Al-Misbah***), in 1900, at the age of twelve and, in 1903, brought out a monthly journal, ***Lissan-us-Sidq***, which soon gained popularity. At the age of thirteen, he was married to a young Muslim girl, Zulaikha Begum. Azad compiled many treatises interpreting the Qur'an, the *Hadith*, and the principles of *Fiqh* and *Kalam*.

Revolutionary and Journalist

Azad developed political views considered radical for most

Muslims of the time and became a full-fledged Indian nationalist. He fiercely criticised the British for racial discrimination and ignoring the needs of common people across India. He also criticised Muslim politicians for focusing on communal issues before the national interest and rejected the All India Muslim League's communal separatism. Azad developed curiosity and interest in the pan-Islamic doctrines of Jamal al-Din al-Afghani and visited Afghanistan, Iraq, Egypt, Syria and Turkey. But his views changed considerably when he met revolutionary activists in Iraq and was influenced by their fervent anti-imperialism and nationalism. Against common Muslim opinion of the time, Azad opposed the partition of Bengal in 1905 and became increasingly active in revolutionary activities, to which he was introduced by the prominent Hindu revolutionaries Sri Aurobindo and Shyam Sundar Chakravarty. Azad initially evoked surprise from other revolutionaries, but Azad won their praise and confidence by working secretly to organise revolutionaries activities and meetings in Bengal, Bihar and Bombay (now called Mumbai).

Azad's education had been shaped for him to become a cleric, but his rebellious nature and affinity for politics turned him towards journalism. He established an Urdu weekly newspaper in 1912 called **Al-Hilal** and openly attacked British policies while exploring the challenges facing common people. Espousing the ideals of Indian nationalism, Azad's publications were aimed at encouraging young Muslims into fighting for independence and Hindu-Muslim unity. His work helped improve the relationship between Hindus and Muslims in Bengal, which had been soured by the controversy surrounding the partition of Bengal and the issue of separate communal electorates.

With the onset of World War I, the British stiffened censorship and restrictions on political activity. Azad's *Al-Hilal* was consequently banned in 1914 under the *Press Act*. Azad started a new journal, the ***Al-Balagh***, which increased its active support for nationalist causes and communal unity. In this period Azad also became active in his support for the

Khilafat agitation to protect the position of the Sultan of Ottoman Turkey, who was the caliph for Muslims worldwide. The Sultan had sided against the British in the war and the continuity of his rule came under serious threat, causing distress amongst Muslim conservatives. Azad saw an opportunity to energise Indian Muslims and achieve major political and social reform through the struggle. With his popularity increasing across India, the government outlawed Azad's second publication under the *Defence of India Regulations Act* and arrested him. The governments of the Bombay Presidency, United Provinces, Punjab and Delhi prohibited his entry into the provinces and Azad was moved to a jail in Ranchi, where he was incarcerated until 1 January 1920.

Non-co-operation

Upon his release, Azad returned to a political atmosphere charged with sentiments of outrage and rebellion against British rule. The Indian public had been angered by the passage of the Rowlatt Acts in 1919, which severely restricted civil liberties and individual rights. Consequently, thousands of political activists had been arrested and many publications banned. The killing of unarmed civilians at Jallianwala Bagh in Amritsar on 13 April 1919 had provoked intense outrage all over India, alienating most Indians, including long-time British supporters from the authorities. The Khilafat struggle had also peaked with the defeat of the Ottoman Empire in World War I and the raging Turkish War of Independence, which had made the caliphate's position precarious. India's main political party, the Indian National Congress came under the leadership of Mahatma Gandhi, who had aroused excitement all over India when he led the farmers of Champaran and Kheda in a successful revolt against British authorities in 1918. Gandhi organised the people of the region and pioneered the art of *Satyagraha*—combining mass civil disobedience with complete non-violence and self-reliance.

Taking charge of the Congress, Gandhi also reached out

to support the Khilafat struggle, helping to bridge Hindu-Muslim political divides. Azad and the Ali brothers warmly welcomed Congress support and began working together on a programme of *non-co-operation* by asking all Indians to boycott British-run schools, colleges, courts, public services, the civil service, police and military. Non-violence and Hindu-Muslim unity were universally emphasised, while the boycott of foreign goods, especially clothes were organised. Azad joined the Congress and was also elected president of the All India Khilafat Committee. Although Azad and other leaders were soon arrested, the movement drew out millions of people in peaceful processions, strikes and protests.

This period marked a transformation in Azad's own life. Along with fellow Khilafat leaders Dr. Mukhtar Ahmad Ansari, Hakim Ajmal Khan and others, Azad grew personally close to Gandhi and his philosophy. The three men founded the Jamia Millia Islamia in Delhi as an institution of higher education managed entirely by Indians without any British support or control. Both Azad and Gandhi shared a deep passion for religion and Azad developed a close friendship with him. He adopted the Prophet Muhammad's ideas by living simply, rejecting material possessions and pleasures. He began to spin his own clothes using *khadi* on the *charkha*, and began frequently living and participating in the ashrams organised by Gandhi. Becoming deeply committed to *ahinsa* (*non-violence*) himself, Azad grew close to fellow nationalists like Jawaharlal Nehru, Chittaranjan Das and Subhas Chandra Bose. He strongly criticised the continuing suspicion of the Congress amongst the Muslim intellectuals from the Aligarh Muslim University and the Muslim League.

The rebellion began a sudden decline when with rising incidences of violence; a nationalist mob killed 22 policemen in Chauri Chaura in 1922. Fearing degeneration into violence, Gandhi asked Indians to suspend the revolt and undertook a five-day fast to repent and encourage others to stop the rebellion. Although the movement stopped all over India, several Congress leaders and activists were disillusioned with Gandhi. The following year, the caliphate was overthrown by Mustafa Kemal Atatürk and the Ali brothers grew distant and critical of Gandhi and the Congress. Azad's close friend Chittaranjan Das co-founded the Swaraj Party, breaking from Gandhi's leadership. Despite the circumstances, Azad remained firmly committed to Gandhi's ideals and leadership. In 1923, he became the youngest man to be elected Congress president. Azad led efforts to organise the Flag Satyagraha in Nagpur. Azad served as president of the 1924 Unity Conference in Delhi, using his position to work to re-unite the Swarajists and the Khilafat leaders under the common banner of the Congress. In the years following the movement, Azad travelled across India, working extensively to promote Gandhi's vision, education and social reform.

Congress Leader

Azad became an inspiring personality in the field of politics. Azad became an important national leader, and served on the Congress Working Committee and in the offices of general secretary and president many times. The political environment in India re-energised in 1928 with nationalist outrage against the Simon Commission appointed to propose constitutional reforms. The commission included no Indian members and did not even consult Indian leaders and experts. In response, the Congress and other political parties appointed a commission under Motilal Nehru to propose constitutional reforms from Indian opinions. In 1928, Azad endorsed the Nehru Report, which was criticised by the Ali brothers and Muslim League politician Muhammad Ali Jinnah. Azad endorsed the ending of separate electorates based on religion, and called for an independent India to be committed to secularism. At the 1928 Congress session in Guwahati, Azad endorsed Gandhi's call for dominion status for India within a year. If not granted, the Congress would adopt the goal of complete political independence for India. Despite his affinity for Gandhi, Azad also drew close to the young radical leaders

Jawaharlal Nehru and Subhash Bose, who had criticised the delay in demanding full independence. Azad developed a close friendship with Nehru and began espousing socialism as the means to fight inequality, poverty and other national challenges. Azad decided the name of Muslim political party Majlis-e-Ahrar-ul-Islam. He was also a friend of Syed Ata Ullah Shah Bukhari founder of All India Majlis-e-Ahrar. When Gandhi embarked on the Dandi Salt March that inaugurated the Salt Satyagraha in 1930, Azad organised and led the nationalist raid, albeit non-violent on the Dharasana salt works to protest the salt tax and restriction of its production and sale. The biggest nationalist upheaval in a decade, Azad was imprisoned along with millions of people, and would frequently be jailed from 1930 to 1934 for long periods of time. Following the Gandhi-Irwin Pact in 1934, Azad was amongst millions of political prisoners released. When elections were called under the Government of India Act 1935, Azad was appointed to organise the Congress election campaign, raising funds, selecting candidates and organising volunteers and rallies across India. Azad had criticised the Act for including a high proportion of un-elected members in the central legislature, and did not himself contest a seat. He again declined to contest elections in 1937, and helped head the party's efforts to organise elections and preserve co-ordination and unity amongst the Congress governments elected in different provinces.

At the 1936 Congress session in Lucknow, Azad was drawn into a dispute with Sardar Vallabhbhai Patel, Dr. Rajendra Prasad and Chakravarthi Rajagopalachari regarding the espousal of socialism as the Congress goal. Azad had backed the election of Nehru as Congress president, and supported the resolution endorsing socialism. In doing so, he aligned with Congress socialists like Nehru, Subhash Bose and Jayaprakash Narayan. Azad also supported Nehru's re-election in 1937, at the consternation of many conservative Congressmen. Azad supported dialogue with Jinnah and the Muslim League between 1935 and 1937 over a Congress-

League coalition and broader political co-operation. Less inclined to brand the League as obstructive, Azad nevertheless joined the Congress's vehement rejection of Jinnah's demand that the League be seen exclusively as the representative of Indian Muslims.

Quit India

In 1938, Azad served as an intermediary between the supporters of and the Congress faction led by Congress president Subhash Bose, who criticised Gandhi for not launching another rebellion against the British and sought to move the Congress away from Gandhi's leadership. Azad stood by Gandhi with most other Congress leaders, but reluctantly endorsed the Congress's exit from the assemblies in 1939 following the inclusion of India in World War II. Nationalists were infuriated that the viceroy had entered India into the war without consulting national leaders. Although willing to support the British effort in return for independence, Azad sided with Gandhi when the British ignored the Congress overtures. Azad's criticism of Jinnah and the League intensified as Jinnah called Congress rule in the provinces as "Hindu Raj," calling the resignation of the Congress ministries as a "Day of Deliverance" for Muslims. Jinnah and the League's separatist agenda was gaining popular support amongst Muslims. Muslim religious and conservative leaders criticised Azad as being too close to the Congress and placing politics before faith. As the Muslim League adopted a resolution calling for a separate Muslim state in its session in Lahore in 1940, Azad was elected Congress president in its session in Ramgarh. Speaking vehemently against Jinnah's *Two-Nation Theory*—the notion that Hindus and Muslims were distinct nations—Azad lambasted religious separatism and exhorted all Muslims to preserve a united India, as all Hindus and Muslims were Indians who shared deep bonds of brotherhood and nationhood. In his presidential address, Azad said:

"... Full eleven centuries have passed by since then.

Islam has now as great a claim on the soil of India as Hinduism. If Hinduism has been the religion of the people here for several thousands of years Islam also has been their religion for a thousand years. Just as a Hindu can say with pride that he is an Indian and follows Hinduism, so also we can say with equal pride that we are Indians and follow Islam. I shall enlarge this orbit still further. The Indian Christian is equally entitled to say with pride that he is an Indian and is following a religion of India, namely Christianity."

In face of increasing popular disenchantment with the British across India, Gandhi and Patel advocated an all-out rebellion demanding immediate independence. The situation had grown precarious as the Japanese conquered Burma and approached India's borders, which left Indians insecure but resentful of the British inability to protect India. Azad was wary and sceptical of the idea, aware that India's Muslims were increasingly looking to Jinnah and had supported the war. Feeling that a struggle would not force a British exit, Azad and Nehru warned that such a campaign would divide India and make the war situation even more precarious. Intensive and emotional debates took place between Azad, Nehru, Gandhi and Patel in the Congress Working Committee's meetings in May and June 1942. In the end, Azad became convinced that decisive action in one form or another had to be taken, as the Congress had to provide leadership to India's people and would lose its standing if it did not.

Supporting the call for the British to "Quit India", Azad began exhorting thousands of people in rallies across the nation to prepare for a definitive, all-out struggle. As Congress president, Azad travelled across India and met with local and provincial Congress leaders and grass-roots activists, delivering speeches and planning the rebellion. Despite their previous differences, Azad worked closely with Patel and Dr. Rajendra Prasad to make the rebellion as effective as possible. On 7 August 1942 at the Gowalia Tank in Mumbai, Congress president Azad inaugurated the struggle with a vociferous speech exhorting Indians into action. Just two days later, the British arrested Azad and the entire Congress leadership. While Gandhi was incarcerated at the Aga Khan Palace in Pune, Azad and the Congress Working Committee were imprisoned at a fort in Ahmednagar, where they would remain under isolation and intense security for nearly four years. Outside news and communication had been largely prohibited and completely censored. Although frustrated at their incarceration and isolation, Azad and his companions attested to feeling a deep satisfaction at having done their duty to their country and people.

Azad occupied the time playing bridge and acting as the referee in tennis matches played by his colleagues. In the afternoons, Azad began working on his classic Urdu work, the ***Ghubhar-i-Khatir***. Sharing daily chores, Azad also taught the Persian and Urdu languages, as well as Indian and world history to several of his companions. The leaders would generally avoid talking of politics, unwilling to cause any arguments that could exacerbate the pain of their imprisonment. However, each year on 26 January, the leaders would gather to remember their cause and pray together. **Azad, Nehru and Patel** would briefly speak about the nation and the future. Azad and Nehru proposed an initiative to forge an agreement with the British in 1943. Arguing that the rebellion had been mis-timed, Azad attempted to convince his colleagues that the Congress should agree to negotiate with the British and call for the suspension of disobedience if the British agreed to transfer power. Although his proposal was overwhelmingly rejected, Azad and a few others agreed that Gandhi and the Congress had not done enough. When they learnt of Gandhi holding talks with Jinnah in Mumbai in 1944, Azad criticised Gandhi's move as counter-productive and ill-advised.

Partition of India

With the end of the war, the British agreed to transfer

power to Indian hands. All political prisoners were released in 1946 and Azad led the Congress in the elections for the new Constituent Assembly of India, which would draft India's constitution. He headed the delegation to negotiate with the British Cabinet Mission, in his sixth year as Congress president. While attacking Jinnah's demand for Pakistan and the mission's proposal of 16 June 1946 that envisaged the partition of India, Azad became a strong proponent of the mission's earlier proposal of 16 May. The proposal advocated a federation with a weak central government and great autonomy for the provinces. Additionally, the proposal called for the "grouping" of provinces on religious lines, which would informally band together the Muslim-majority provinces. While Gandhi and others were suspicious of this clause, Azad argued that the Jinnah's demand for Pakistan would be buried and the concerns of the Muslim community would be assuaged. Under Azad and Patel's backing, the Working Committee approved the resolution against Gandhi's advice. Jawaharlal Nehru replaced Azad as Congress president and led the Congress into the interim government. Azad was appointed to head the Department of Education. However, Jinnah's *Direct Action Day* agitation for Pakistan, launched on 16 August sparked communal violence across India. Thousands of people were killed as Azad travelled across Bengal and Bihar to calm the tensions and heal relations between Muslims and Hindus. Despite Azad's call for Hindu-Muslim unity, Jinnah's popularity amongst Muslims soared and the League entered a coalition with the Congress in December, but continued to boycott the constituent assembly. Later in his autobiography, Azad indicted Patel having become more pro-partition than the Muslim League, largely due to the League's not co-operating with the Congress in the provisional government on any issue.

Azad had grown increasingly hostile to Jinnah, who had described him as the "Muslim Lord Haw-Haw" and a "Congress Showboy." Despite being a learned scholar of Islam and a *Maulana*, Azad had been assailed by Muslim religious leaders for his commitment to nationalism and secularism, which were deemed un-Islamic. Muslim League politicians accused Azad of allowing Muslims to be culturally and politically dominated by the Hindu community. Azad continued to proclaim his faith in Hindu-Muslim unity:

> "I am proud of being an Indian. I am part of the indivisible unity that is Indian nationality. I am indispensable to this noble edifice and without me this splendid structure is incomplete. I am an essential element, which has gone to build India. I can never surrender this claim."

Amidst more incidences of violence in early 1947, the Congress-League coalition struggled to function. The provinces of Bengal and Punjab were to be partitioned on religious lines, and on 3 June 1947 the British announced a proposal to partition India on religious lines, with the princely states free to choose between either dominion. The proposal was hotly debated in the All India Congress Committee, with Muslim leaders Saifuddin Kitchlew and Khan Abdul Ghaffar Khan expressing fierce opposition. Azad privately discussed the proposal with Gandhi, Patel and Nehru, but despite his opposition was unable to deny the popularity of the League and the unworkability of any coalition with the League. Faced with the serious possibility of a civil war, Azad abstained from voting on the resolution, remaining silent and not speaking throughout the AICC session, which ultimately approved the plan.

Post-Independence

India's partition and independence on 15 August 1947 brought with it a scourge of violence that swept the Punjab, Bengal, Bihar, Delhi and many other parts of India. Millions of Hindus and Sikhs fled the newly created Pakistan for India, and millions of Muslims fled for West Pakistan and East Pakistan, created out of East Bengal. Violence claimed the lives of an estimated one million people. Azad took up responsibility for the safety of Muslims in India, touring affected areas in Bengal, Bihar, Assam and the Punjab, guiding the organisation of refugee camps, supplies and security. Azad gave speeches to large crowds encouraging peace and calm in the border areas and encouraging Muslims across the country to remain in India and not fear for their safety and security. Focusing on bringing the capital of Delhi back to peace, Azad organised security and relief efforts, but was drawn into a dispute with the Deputy prime minister and Home Minister Sardar Vallabhbhai Patel when he demanded the dismissal of Delhi's police commissioner, who was a Sikh accused by Muslims of overlooking attacks and neglecting their safety. Patel argued that the commissioner was not biased, and if his dismissal was forced it would provoke anger amongst Hindus and Sikhs and divide the city police. In Cabinet meetings and discussions with Gandhi, Patel and Azad clashed over security issues in Delhi and Punjab, as well as the allocation of resources for relief and rehabilitation. Patel opposed Azad and Nehru's proposal to reserve the houses vacated by Muslims who had departed for Pakistan for Muslims in India displaced by the violence. Patel argued that a secular government could not offer preferential treatment for any religious community, while Azad remained anxious to assure the rehabilitation of Muslims in India, secularism, religious freedom and equality for all Indians. He supported provisions for Muslim citizens to make avail of Muslim personal law in courts.

Azad remained a close confidante, supporter and advisor to prime minister Nehru, and played an important role in framing national policies. Azad masterminded the creation of national programmes of school and college construction and spreading the enrolment of children and young adults into schools, to promote universal primary education. Elected to the lower house of the Indian Parliament, the Lok Sabha in 1952 and again in 1957, Azad supported Nehru's socialist economic and industrial policies, as well as the advancing social rights and economic opportunities for women and underprivileged Indians. In 1956, he served as president of the UNESCO General Conference held in Delhi. Azad spent the final years of his life focusing on writing his book *India Wins Freedom*, an exhaustive account of India's freedom struggle and its leaders, which was published in 1957.

As India's first Minister of Education, he emphasised on educating the rural poor and girls. As Chairman of the Central Advisory Board of Education, he gave thrust to adult illiteracy, universal primary education, free and compulsory for all children up to the age of 14, girls *education, and diversification of secondary education and vocational training.* Addressing the conference on All India Education on 16 January 1948, Maulana Azad emphasised,

We must not for a moment forget, it is a birthright of every individual to receive at least the basic education without which he cannot fully discharge his duties as a citizen.

He oversaw the setting up of the Central Institute of Education, Delhi, which later became the Department of Education of the University of Delhi as "a research centre for solving new educational problems of the country". Under his leadership, the Ministry of Education established the first Indian Institute of Technology in 1951 and the University Grants Commission in 1953., He also laid emphasis on the development of the Indian Institute of Science, Bangalore and the Faculty of Technology of the Delhi University. He foresaw a great future in the IITs for India:

I have no doubt that the establishment of this Institute will form a landmark in the progress of higher technological education and research in the country.

28

Jehangir Ratanji Dadabhoy Tata

Jehangir Ratanji Dadabhoy Tata (29 July 1904 – 29 November 1993) was a French-born Indian aviator and business tycoon. He was the former Chairman of Tata Sons. He became India's first licensed pilot in 1929. In 1983, he was awarded the French Legion of Honour and, in 1992, India's highest civilian award, the Bharat Ratna.

Early Life

J. R. D. Tata was born in Paris, France, the second child of Parsi father Ratanji Dadabhoy Tata and his French wife, Suzanne "Sooni" Brière. His father was a first cousin of Jamsetji Tata, a pioneer industrialist in India. He had one elder sister Sylla, another younger sister Rodabeh two younger brother Darab and Jimmy Tata. As his mother was French, he spent much of his childhood in France and as a result, French was his first language. Tata also served in the French Foreign Legion for one year in the regiment **Le Saphis** during the Second World War. After he left the service the whole regiment perished on an expedition in Morocco.

He attended the Cathedral and John Connon School, Bombay. Tata was educated in London, Japan, France and India. When his father joined the Tata company he moved the whole family to London. During this time, J.R.D's mother died at an early age of 43 while his father was in India and his family was in France. After his mother's death Ratanji Dadabhoy Tata decided to move his family to India and sent J.R.D to England for higher studies in October 1923. He was enrolled in a "crammer" school, and was interested in studying Engineering at Cambridge. Just as the crammer course was ending and he was hoping to enter Cambridge, a law was passed in France to draft into the army, for two years, all French boys at the age of 20. As a citizen of France J.R.D had to enlist in the army for at least 1 year. In between the crammer and his time in the army, he spent brief spell at home in Bombay. After joining the French Army he was posted into the regiment called Le Saphis (The Sepoys). Soon the Colonel of the regiment found that there was a member of his Squadron who could not only read and write French and English, but also could type, so he assigned him as a secretary in his office. Tata was once again transferred to a more luxurious office of a colonel. After a 12 month period of conscription in the French Army he wanted to proceed to Cambridge for further education, but his father decided to bring him back to India and he joined Tata Company. In 1929, JRD renounced his French citizenship and became an Indian citizen, and started working at Tata. In 1930 JRD married Thelma Vicaji, the daughter of 'Prince' Vicaji, a colourful lawyer whom he hired to defend him on a charge of driving his Bugatti too fast along Bombay's main promenade, Marine Drive. Previously he had been engaged to Dinbai Mehta, the future mother of The Economist editor Shapur Kharegat.

Career

J. R. D. Tata was inspired early by pioneer Louis Blériot, and took to flying. On February 10, 1929, Tata obtained the first pilot licence issued in India.[6] He later came to be known as the father of Indian civil aviation. He founded India's first commercial airline, Tata Airlines in 1932, which became Air

India in 1946, now India's national airline.He and Nevill Vintcent worked together in building Tata Airlines. They were also friends.

He joined Tata & Sons as an unpaid apprentice in 1925. In 1938, at the age of 34, JRD was elected Chairman of Tata & Sons making him the head of the largest industrial group in India. He took over as Chairman of Tata Sons from his uncle Nowroji Saklatwala. For decades, he directed the huge Tata Group of companies, with major interests in Steel, Engineering, Power, Chemicals and Hospitality. He was famous for succeeding in business while maintaining high ethical standards - refusing to bribe politicians or use the black market.

Under his chairmanship, the assets of the Tata Group grew from US$100 million to over US$5 billion. He started with 14 enterprises under his leadership and half a century later on July 26, 1988, when he left, Tata & Sons was a conglomerate of 95 enterprises which they either started or in which they had controlling interest.

He was the trustee of the Sir Dorabji Tata Trust from its inception in 1932 for over half a century. Under his guidance, this Trust established Asia's first cancer hospital, the Tata Memorial Center for Cancer, Research and Treatment, in Bombay in 1941. It also founded the Tata Institute of Social Sciences (TISS, 1936), the Tata Institute of Fundamental Research (TIFR, 1945), and the National Center for Performing Arts.

In 1945, he founded Tata Motors. In 1948, JRD Tata launched Air India International as India's first international airline. In 1953, the Indian Government appointed JRD Tata as Chairman of Air India and a director on the Board of Indian Airlines - a position he retained for 25 years. For his crowning achievements in aviation, he was bestowed with the title of Honorary Air Commodore of India.

JRD Tata cared greatly for his workers. In 1956, he initiated a program of closer 'employee association with management' to give workers a stronger voice in the affairs of the company. He firmly believed in employee welfare and espoused the principles of an eight-hour working day, free medical aid, workers' provident scheme, and workmen's accident compensation schemes,which were later, adopted as statutory requirements in India. He was also a founding member of the first Governing Body of NCAER, the National Council of Applied Economic Research in New Delhi,India's first independent economic policy institute established in 1956. In 1968, he founded Tata Consultancy Services. In 1979, Tata Steel instituted a new practice: a worker being deemed to be "at work" from the moment he leaves home for work till he returns home from work. This made the company financially liable to the worker for any mishap on the way to and from work. In 1987, he founded Titan Industries. Jamshedpur was also selected as a UN Global Compact City because of the quality of life, conditions of sanitation, roads and welfare that were offered by Tata Steel.

Awards and Honours

JRD Tata received a number of awards. He was conferred the honorary rank of Group Captain by the Indian Air Force, was promoted to the Air Commodore rank (equivalent to Brigadier in army), and was further promoted on 1 April 1974 to the Air Vice Marshal rank. Several international awards for aviation were given to him - The Tony Jannus Award in March 1979, the Gold Air Medal of the Federation Aeronautique Internationale in 1995, the Edward Warner Award of the International Civil Aviation Organisation, Canada in 1986 and the Daniel Guggenheim Award in 1988. He received the Padma Vibhushan in 1955 . The French Legion of Honour was bestowed on him in 1983. In 1992, because of his selfless humanitarian endeavours, JRD Tata was awarded India's highest civilian honour, the Bharat Ratna. In the same year, JRD Tata was also bestowed with the United Nations Population Award for his crusading endeavours towards initiating and successfully implementing the family planning movement in India, much before it became an official government policy. In his memory Government of Maharashtra termed its first double decker bridge as Bharatratne JRD Tata over bridge at Kasarwadi phata,Pune.

Death

JRD Tata died in Geneva, Switzerland on November 29, 1993 at the age of 89 due to Kidney Infection. On his death, the Indian Parliament was adjourned in his memory:— an honour not usually given to persons who are not Members of Parliament. He is buried in the Père Lachaise Cemetery in Paris.

29

Satyajit Ray

Satyajit Ray (Shôtôjit Rae, listen (help·info); 2 May 1921 – 23 April 1992) was an Indian filmmaker, regarded as one of the greatest auteurs of world cinema. Ray was born in the city of Calcutta into a Bengali family prominent in the world of arts and literature. Starting his career as a commercial artist, Ray was drawn into independent filmmaking after meeting French filmmaker Jean Renoir and viewing Vittorio De Sica's Italian neorealist 1948 film *Bicycle Thieves* during a visit to London.

Ray directed 36 films, including feature films, documentaries and shorts. He was also a fiction writer, publisher, illustrator, calligrapher, graphic designer and film critic. He authored several short stories and novels, primarily aimed at children and adolescents. Feluda, the sleuth, and Professor Shonku, the scientist in his science fiction stories, are popular fictional characters created by him.

Ray's first film, *Pather Panchali* (1955), won eleven international prizes, including *Best Human Documentary* at the Cannes Film Festival. This film, *Aparajito* (1956), and

Apur Sansar (1959) form *The Apu Trilogy.* Ray did the scripting, casting, scoring, and editing, and designed his own credit titles and publicity material. Ray received many major awards in his career, including 32 Indian National Film Awards, a number of awards at international film festivals and award ceremonies, and an Academy Award in 1992. The Government of India honoured him with the Bharat Ratna in 1992.

Life and career

Early life and background

Satyajit Ray's ancestry can be traced back for at least ten generations.[1] Ray's grandfather, Upendrakishore Ray Chowdhury was a writer, illustrator, philosopher, publisher, amateur astronomer and a leader of the Brahmo Samaj, a religious and social movement in nineteenth century Bengal. He also set up a printing press by the name of U. Ray and Sons, which formed a crucial backdrop to Satyajit's life. Sukumar Ray, Upendrakishore's son and father of Satyajit, was a pioneering Bengali writer of nonsense rhyme and children's literature, an illustrator and a critic. Ray was born to Sukumar and Suprabha Ray in Calcutta.

Sukumar Ray died when Satyajit was barely three, and the family survived on Suprabha Ray's meager income. Ray studied at Ballygunge Government High School, Calcutta, and completed his BA in economics at Presidency College, Calcutta, though his interest was always in fine arts. In 1940, his mother insisted that he study at the Visva-Bharati University at Santiniketan, founded by Rabindranath Tagore. Ray was reluctant due to his love of Calcutta, and the low opinion of the intellectual life at Santiniketan His mother's persuasion and his respect for Tagore finally convinced him to try. In Santiniketan, Ray came to appreciate Oriental art. He later admitted that he learned much from the famous painters Nandalal Bose and Benode Behari Mukherjee. Later he produced a documentary film, *The Inner Eye,* about Mukherjee. His visits to Ajanta, Ellora and Elephanta stimulated his admiration for Indian art.

In 1943, Ray started work at D.J. Keymer, a British-run advertising agency, as a "junior visualiser," earning eighty rupees a month. Although he liked visual design (graphic design) and he was mostly treated well, there was tension between the British and Indian employees of the firm. The British were better paid, and Ray felt that "the clients were generally stupid." Later, Ray also worked for Signet Press, a new publishing house started by D. K. Gupta. Gupta asked Ray to create cover designs for books to be published by Signet Press and gave him complete artistic freedom. Ray designed covers for many books, including Jibanananda Das's *Banalata Sen*, and *Rupasi Bangla*, Bibhutibhushan Bandyopadhyay's Chander Pahar, Jim Corbett's *Maneaters of Kumaon,* and Jawaharlal Nehru's *Discovery of India.* He worked on a children's version of *Pather Panchali,* a classic Bengali novel by Bibhutibhushan Bandyopadhyay, renamed as *Aam Antir Bhepu* (*The mango-seed whistle*). Designing the cover and illustrating the book, Ray was deeply influenced by the work. He used it as the subject of his first film, and featured his illustrations as shots in his ground-breaking film.

Along with Chidananda Dasgupta and others, Ray founded the Calcutta Film Society in 1947. They screened many foreign films, many of which Ray watched and seriously studied. He befriended the American GIs stationed in Calcutta during World War II, who kept him informed about the latest American films showing in the city. He came to know a RAF employee, Norman Clare, who shared Ray's passion for films, chess and western classical music.

In 1949, Ray married Bijoya Das, his first cousin and long-time sweetheart. The couple had a son, Sandip, who is now a film director. In the same year, French director Jean Renoir came to Calcutta to shoot his film *The River*. Ray helped him to find locations in the countryside. Ray told Renoir about his idea of filming *Pather Panchali,* which had long been on his mind, and Renoir encouraged him in the project. In 1950, D.J. Keymer sent Ray to London to work at its headquarters office. During his three months in London, Ray watched 99 films. Among these was the neorealist film *Ladri di biciclette* (*Bicycle Thief*) (1948) by Vittorio De Sica, which had a profound impact on him. Ray later said that he came out of the theatre determined to become a film-maker.

The Apu years (1950–59)

Ray decided to use *Pather Panchali* (1928), the classic bildungsroman of Bengali literature, as the basis for his first film. The semi-autobiographical novel describes the maturation of Apu, a small boy in a Bengal village.

Ray gathered an inexperienced crew, although both his cameraman Subrata Mitra and art director Bansi Chandragupta went on to achieve great acclaim. The cast consisted of mostly amateur actors. He started shooting in late 1952 with his personal savings and hoped to raise more money once he had some passages shot, but did not succeed on his terms. As a result, Ray shot *Pather Panchali* over three years, an unusually long period, based on when he or his production manager Anil Chowdhury could raise additional funds.[11] He refused funding from sources who wanted a change in script or supervision over production. He also ignored advice from the government to incorporate a happy ending, but he did receive funding that allowed him to complete the film.[12] Ray showed an early film passage to Anglo-Irish director John Huston, who was in India scouting locations for *The Man Who Would Be King*. The passage was of the vision which Apu and his sister have of the train running through the countryside, the only sequence which Ray had yet filmed due to his small budget. Huston notified Monroe Wheeler at the New York Museum of Modern Art (MOMA) that a major talent was on the horizon.

With a loan from the West Bengal government, Ray finally completed the film. It was released in 1955 to great critical and popular success. It earned numerous prizes and had long runs in both India and abroad. In India, the reaction to the film was enthusiastic; *The Times of India* wrote that "It is absurd to compare it with any other Indian cinema [...] *Pather Panchali* is pure cinema." In the United Kingdom, Lindsay Anderson wrote a glowing review of the film. But, the reaction was not uniformly positive. After watching the movie, François Truffaut is reported to have said, "I don't want to see a movie of peasants eating with their hands." Bosley Crowther, then the most influential critic of *The New York Times*, wrote a scathing review of the film. Its American distributor Ed Harrison was worried Crowther's review would dissuade audiences, but the film had an exceptionally long run when released in the United States.

Ray's international career started in earnest after the success of his next film, *Aparajito* (*The Unvanquished*). This film shows the eternal struggle between the ambitions of a young man, Apu, and the mother who loves him. Critics such as Mrinal Sen and Ritwik Ghatak rank it higher than Ray's first film. *Aparajito* won the Golden Lion at the Venice Film Festival, bringing Ray considerable acclaim. Before completing *The Apu Trilogy*, Ray directed and released two other films: the comic *Parash Pathar* (*The Philosopher's Stone*), and *Jalsaghar* (*The Music Room*), a film about the decadence of the Zamindars, considered one of his most important works.

While making *Aparajito*, Ray had not planned a trilogy, but after he was asked about the idea in Venice, it appealed to him.[17] He finished the last of the trilogy, *Apur Sansar* (*The World of Apu*) in 1959. Critics Robin Wood and Aparna Sen found this to be the supreme achievement of the trilogy. Ray introduced two of his favourite actors, Soumitra Chatterjee and Sharmila Tagore, in this film. It opens with Apu living in a Calcutta house in near-poverty. He becomes involved in an unusual marriage with Aparna. The scenes of their life together form "one of the cinema's classic affirmative depictions of married life." They suffer tragedy. After *Apur Sansar* was harshly criticised by a Bengali critic, Ray wrote an article defending it. He rarely responded to critics during his filmmaking career, but also later defended his film *Charulata*, his personal favourite.

Ray's film successes had little influence on his personal life in the years to come. He continued to live with his wife and children in a rented house, with his mother, uncle and other members of his extended family.

From *Devi* to *Charulata* (1959–64)

During this period, Ray composed films on the British Raj period (such as *Devi*), a documentary on Tagore, a comic film (*Mahapurush*) and his first film from an original screenplay (*Kanchenjungha*). He also made a series of films that, taken together, are considered by critics among the most deeply felt portrayals of Indian women on screen.

Ray followed *Apur Sansar* with *Devi* (*The Goddess*), a film in which he examined the superstitions in Hindu society. Sharmila Tagore starred as Doyamoyee, a young wife who is deified by her father-in-law. Ray was worried that the censor board might block his film, or at least make him re-cut it, but *Devi* was spared. In 1961, on the insistence of Prime minister Jawaharlal Nehru, Ray was commissioned to make a documentary on Rabindranath Tagore, on the occasion of the poet's birth centennial, a tribute to the person who likely most influenced Ray. Due to limited footage of Tagore, Ray faced the challenge of making a film out of mainly static material. He said that it took as much work as three feature films.

In the same year, together with Subhas Mukhopadhyay and others, Ray was able to revive *Sandesh*, the children's magazine which his grandfather once published. Ray had been saving money for some years to make this possible. A duality in the name (*Sandesh* means both "news" in Bengali and also a sweet popular dessert) set the tone of the magazine (both educational and entertaining). Ray began to make illustrations for it, as well as to write stories and essays for children. Writing became his major source of income in the years to come.

In 1962, Ray directed *Kanchenjungha*. Based on his first

original screenplay, it was his first film in colour. The film tells of an upper-class family spending an afternoon in Darjeeling, a picturesque hill town in West Bengal. They try to arrange the engagement of their youngest daughter to a highly paid engineer educated in London. He had first conceived shooting the film in a large mansion, but later decided to film it in the famous hill town. He used the many shades of light and mist to reflect the tension in the drama. Ray noted that while his script allowed shooting to be possible under any lighting conditions, a commercial film contingent present at the same time in Darjeeling failed to shoot a single scene, as they only wanted to do so in sunshine.

In the sixties, Ray visited Japan and took particular pleasure in meeting the filmmaker Akira Kurosawa, for whom he had very high regard. While at home, he would take an occasional break from the hectic city life by going to places such as Darjeeling or Puri to complete a script in isolation.

In 1964 Ray made *Charulata* (*The Lonely Wife*); it was the culmination of this period of work, and regarded by many critics as his most accomplished film. Based on "Nastanirh", a short story of Tagore, the film tells of a lonely wife, Charu, in 19th-century Bengal, and her growing feelings for her brother-in-law Amal. Critics have referred to this as Ray's Mozartian masterpiece. He said the film contained the fewest flaws among his work, and it was his only work which, given a chance, he would make exactly the same way. Madhabi Mukherjee's performance as Charu, and the work of both Subrata Mitra and Bansi Chandragupta in the film, have been highly praised. Other films in this period include *Mahanagar* (*The Big City*), *Teen Kanya* (*Three Daughters*), *Abhijan* (*The Expedition*) and *Kapurush o Mahapurush* (*The Coward and the Holy Man*).

New directions (1965–82)

In the post-*Charulata* period, Ray took on projects of increasing variety, ranging from fantasy to science fiction to detective films to historical drama. Ray also made considerable formal experimentation during this period. He expressed contemporary issues of Indian life, responding to a perceived lack of these issues in his films. The first major film in this period is *Nayak* (*The Hero*), the story of a screen hero travelling in a train and meeting a young, sympathetic female journalist. Starring Uttam Kumar and Sharmila Tagore, in the twenty-four hours of the journey, the film explores the inner conflict of the apparently highly successful matinée idol. In spite of the film's receiving a "Critics prize" at the Berlin Festival, it had a generally muted reception.

In 1967, Ray wrote a script for a film to be called *The Alien*, based on his short story "Bankubabur Bandhu" ("Banku Babu's Friend") which he wrote in 1962 for *Sandesh*, the Ray family magazine. Columbia Pictures was the producer for what was a planned US-India co-production, and Peter Sellers and Marlon Brando were cast as the leading actors. Ray found that his script had been copyrighted and the fee appropriated by Mike Wilson. Wilson had initially approached Ray through their mutual friend, Arthur C. Clarke, to represent him in Hollywood. Wilson copyrighted the script credited to *Mike Wilson & Satyajit Ray*, although he contributed only one word. Ray later said that he never received a penny for the script.[28] After Brando dropped out of the project, the project tried to replace him with James Coburn, but Ray became disillusioned and returned to Calcutta.[28] Columbia expressed interest in reviving the project several times in the 1970s and 1980s, but nothing came of it. When *E.T.* was released in 1982, Clarke and Ray saw similarities in the film to his earlier *Alien* script. The Indian director Satyajit Ray claimed that this film plagiarized his script. Ray said that Steven Spielberg's movie "would not have been possible without my script of 'The Alien' being available throughout America in mimeographed copies." Spielberg denied any plagiarism by saying, "I was a kid in high school when this script was circulating in Hollywood." (Spielberg actually graduated high school in 1965 and released his first film in 1968. Besides *The Alien*, two other unrealised projects which Ray had intended to direct were adaptations of the ancient Indian epic, the *Mahâbhârata*, and E. M. Forster's 1924 novel *A Passage to India.*

In 1969, Ray released what would be commercially the most successful of his films. Based on a children's story written by his grandfather, *Goopy Gyne Bagha Byne* (*The Adventures of Goopy and Bagha*), it is a musical fantasy. Goopy the singer and Bagha the drummer, endowed with three gifts by the King of Ghosts, set out on a fantastic journey. They try to stop an impending war between two neighbouring kingdoms. Among his most expensive enterprises, the film project was difficult to finance. Ray abandoned his desire to shoot it in colour, as he turned down an offer that would have forced him to cast a certain Hindi film actor as the lead.

Ray made a film from a novel by the young poet and writer, Sunil Gangopadhyay. Featuring a musical motif structure acclaimed as more complex than *Charulata, Aranyer Din Ratri* (*Days and Nights in the Forest*) traces four urban young men going to the forests for a vacation. They try to leave their daily lives behind. All but one of them become involved in encounters with women, which becomes a deep study of the Indian middle class. According to Robin Wood, "a single sequence [of the film] ... would offer material for a short essay".

After *Aranyer*, Ray addressed contemporary Bengali life. He completed what became known as the *Calcutta trilogy*: *Pratidwandi* (1970), *Seemabaddha* (1971), and *Jana Aranya* (1975), three films that were conceived separately but had thematic connections. *Pratidwandi* (*The Adversary*) is about an idealist young graduate; if disillusioned at the end of film, he is still uncorrupted. *Jana Aranya* (*The Middleman*) showed a young man giving in to the culture of corruption to make a living. *Seemabaddha* (*Company Limited*) portrayed an already successful man giving up his morality for further gains. In the first film, *Pratidwandi*, Ray introduces a new, elliptical narrative style, such as scenes in negative, dream sequences, and abrupt flashbacks. In the 1970s, Ray adapted two of his popular stories as detective films. Though mainly addressed to children and young adults, both *Sonar Kella* (*The Golden Fortress*) and *Joy Baba Felunath* (*The Elephant God*) found some critical following.

Ray considered making a film on the Bangladesh Liberation War but later abandoned the idea. He said that, as a filmmaker, he was more interested in the travails of the refugees and not the politics. In 1977, Ray completed *Shatranj Ke Khiladi* (*The Chess Players*), a Hindi film based on a story by Munshi Premchand. It was set in Lucknow in the state of Oudh, a year before the Indian rebellion of 1857. A commentary on issues related to the colonisation of India by the British, this was Ray's first feature film in a language other than Bengali. It is his most expensive and star-studded film, featuring Sanjeev Kumar, Saeed Jaffrey, Amjad Khan, Shabana Azmi, Victor Bannerjee and Richard Attenborough.

In 1980, Ray made a sequel to *Goopy Gyne Bagha Byne*, a somewhat political *Hirak Rajar Deshe* (*Kingdom of Diamonds*). The kingdom of the evil Diamond King, or *Hirok Raj,* is an allusion to India during Indira Gandhi's emergency period. Along with his acclaimed short film *Pikoo* (*Pikoo's Diary*) and hour-long Hindi film, *Sadgati,* this was the culmination of his work in this period.

The last phase (1983–92)

Satyajit Ray became the first Indian to receive an Honorary Academy Award in 1992.

In 1983, while working on *Ghare Baire* (*Home and the World*), Ray suffered a heart attack; it would severely limit his productivity in the remaining 9 years of his life. *Ghare Baire* was completed in 1984 with the help of Ray's son (who operated the camera from then on) because of his health condition. He had wanted to film this Tagore novel on the dangers of fervent nationalism for a long time, and wrote a first draft of a script for it in the 1940s. In spite of rough patches due to Ray's illness, the film did receive some critical acclaim. It had the first kiss fully portrayed in Ray's films. In 1987, he made a documentary on his father, Sukumar Ray.

Ray's last three films, made after his recovery and with medical strictures in place, were shot mostly indoors, and have a distinctive style. They have more dialogue than his earlier films and are often regarded as inferior to his earlier body of work. The first, *Ganashatru* (*An Enemy of the People*) is an adaptation of the famous Ibsen play, and considered the weakest of the three. Ray recovered some of his form in his 1990 film *Shakha Proshakha* (*Branches of the Tree*). In it, an old man, who has lived a life of honesty, comes to learn of the corruption of three of his sons. The final scene shows the father finding solace only in the companionship of his fourth son, who is uncorrupted but mentally ill. Ray's last film, *Agantuk* (*The Stranger*), is lighter in mood but not in theme. When a long-lost uncle arrives to visit his niece in Calcutta, he arouses suspicion as to his motive. This provokes far-ranging questions in the film about civilisation.

In 1992, Ray's health deteriorated due to heart complications. He was admitted to a hospital, but never recovered. The Academy of Motion Picture Arts and Sciences awarded him an Honorary Academy Award. Ray became the first Indian to receive the honor. Twenty-four days before his death, Ray accepted the award in a gravely ill condition, saying that it is the "Best achievement of [his] movie-making career." He died on 23 April 1992 at the age of 70.

Film craft

Satyajit Ray considered script-writing to be an integral part of direction. Initially he refused to make a film in any language other than Bengali. In his two non-Bengali feature films, he wrote the script in English; translators interpreted it in Hindi or Urdu under Ray's supervision. Ray's eye for detail was matched by that of his art director Bansi Chandragupta. His influence on the early films was so important that Ray would always write scripts in English before creating a Bengali version, so that the non-Bengali Chandragupta would be able to read it. The craft of Subrata Mitra garnered praise for the cinematography of Ray's films.

A number of critics thought that his departure from Ray's crew lowered the quality of cinematography in the following films. Though Ray openly praised Mitra, his single-mindedness in taking over operation of the camera after *Charulata* caused Mitra to stop working for him after 1966. Mitra developed "bounce lighting", a technique to reflect light from cloth to create a diffused, realistic light even on a set. Ray acknowledged his debts to Jean-Luc Godard and François Truffaut of the French New Wave for introducing new technical and cinematic innovations.

Ray's regular film editor was Dulal Datta, but the director usually dictated the editing while Datta did the actual work. Because of financial reasons and Ray's meticulous planning, his films were mostly cut "on the camera" (apart from *Pather Panchali*). At the beginning of his career, Ray worked with Indian classical musicians, including Ravi Shankar, Vilayat Khan and Ali Akbar Khan. He found that their first loyalty was to musical traditions, and not to his film. He had a greater understanding of western classical forms, which he wanted to use for his films set in an urban milieu. Starting with *Teen Kanya*, Ray began to compose his own scores.

He used actors of diverse backgrounds, from famous film stars to people who had never seen a film (as in *Aparajito*). Robin Wood and others have lauded him as the best director of children, pointing out memorable performances in the roles of Apu and Durga (*Pather Panchali*), Ratan (*Postmaster*) and Mukul (*Sonar Kella*). Depending on the talent or experience of the actor, Ray varied the intensity of his direction, from virtually nothing with actors such as Utpal Dutt, to using the actor as "a puppet" (Subir Banerjee as young Apu or Sharmila Tagore as Aparna). Actors who had worked for Ray praised his customary trust but said he could also treat incompetence with "total contempt".

Literary works

Ray created two popular fictional characters in Bengali children's literature—Feluda, a detective, and Professor

Shonku, a scientist. The Feluda stories are narrated by Topshe, his teenage cousin, something of a Watson to Feluda's Holmes. The science fictions of Shonku are presented as a diary discovered after the scientist had mysteriously disappeared. Ray also wrote a collection of nonsense verse named *Today Bandha Ghorar Dim,* which includes a translation of Lewis Carroll's "Jabberwocky". He wrote a collection of humorous stories of Mullah Nasiruddin in Bengali.

His short stories were published as collections of 12 stories, in which the overall title played with the word twelve (for example *Aker pitthe dui,* or literally "Two on top of one"). Ray's interest in puzzles and puns is reflected in his stories. Ray's short stories give full rein to his interest in the macabre, in suspense and other aspects that he avoided in film, making for an interesting psychological study. Most of his writings have been translated into English. Most of his screenplays have been published in Bengali in the literary journal *Eksan.* Ray wrote an autobiography about his childhood years, *Jakhan Choto Chilam* (1982).

He also wrote essays on film, published as the collections: *Our Films, Their Films* (1976), *Bishoy Chalachchitra* (1976), and *Ekei Bole Shooting* (1979). During the mid-1990s, Ray's film essays and an anthology of short stories were also published in English in the West. *Our Films, Their Films* is an anthology of film criticism by Ray. The book contains articles and personal journal excerpts. The book is presented in two sections: Ray first discusses Indian film, before turning his attention toward Hollywood, specific filmmakers (Charlie Chaplin and Akira Kurosawa), and movements such as Italian neorealism. His book *Bishoy Chalachchitra* was published in translation in 2006 as *Speaking of Films.* It contains a compact description of his philosophy of different aspects of the cinema.

Ray as Calligrapher

Satyajit Ray designed four typefaces for roman script named Ray Roman, Ray Bizarre, Daphnis, and Holiday Script, apart from numerous Bengali ones for the *Sandesh* magazine.

Ray Roman and Ray Bizarre won an international competition in 1971. In certain circles of Calcutta, Ray continued to be known as an eminent graphic designer, well into his film career. Ray illustrated all his books and designed covers for them, as well as creating all publicity material for his films, i.e., Ray's artistic playing with the Bangla graphemes was also revealed in the cine posters and cine promo-brochures' covers. He also designed covers of several books by other authors. In his calligraphic technique there are deep impacts of: (a) Artistic pattern of European musical staff notation in the graphemic syntagms; (b) alpana ("ritual painting" mainly practised by Bengali women at the time of religious festival; the term denotes 'to coat with'. Generally categorised as "Folk"-Art cf. in Ray's graphemic representations.

Thus, so-called division between classical and folk art is blurred in Ray's representation of Bangla graphemes. The three-tier X-height of Bangla graphemes was presented in a manner of musical map and the contours, curves in between horizontal and vertical meeting-point, follow the patterns of alpana. It is also noticed that the metamorphosis of graphemes (This might be designated as "Archewriting") as a living object/subject in Ray's positive manipulation of Bangla graphemes.

Critical and popular response

Ray's work has been described as full of humanism and universality, and of a deceptive simplicity with deep underlying complexity. The Japanese director Akira Kurosawa said, "Not to have seen the cinema of Ray means existing in the world without seeing the sun or the moon." But his detractors find his films glacially slow, moving like a "majestic snail." Some find his humanism simple-minded, and his work anti-modern; they criticize him for lacking the new modes of expression or experimentation found in works of Ray's contemporaries, such as Jean-Luc Godard. As Stanley Kauffman wrote, some critics believe that Ray assumes that viewers "can be interested in a film that simply dwells in its characters, rather than one that imposes dramatic patterns on their lives." Ray said he could do nothing about the slow pace. Kurosawa defended him by saying that Ray's films were not slow, "His work can be described as flowing composedly, like a big river".

Critics have often compared Ray to artists in the cinema and other media, such as Chekhov, Renoir, De Sica, Hawks or Mozart. The writer V. S. Naipaul compared a scene in *Shatranj Ki Khiladi* (The Chess Players) to a Shakespearean play; he wrote, "only three hundred words are spoken but goodness! – terrific things happen." Even critics who did not like the aesthetics of Ray's films generally acknowledged his ability to encompass a whole culture with all its nuances. Ray's obituary in *The Independent* included the question, "Who else can compete?"

Political ideologues took issue with Ray's work. In a public debate during the 1960s, Ray and the Marxist filmmaker Mrinal Sen engaged in an argument. Sen criticised him for casting a matinée idol such as Uttam Kumar, whom he considered a compromise. Ray said that Sen only attacked "easy targets", i.e. the Bengali middle-classes. Advocates of socialism said that Ray was not "committed" to the cause of the nation's downtrodden classes; some critics accused him of glorifying poverty in *Pather Panchali* and *Ashani Sanket* (Distant Thunder) through lyricism and aesthetics. They said he provided no solution to conflicts in the stories, and was unable to overcome his bourgeois background. During the naxalite movements in the 1970s, agitators once came close to causing physical harm to his son, Sandip. Early in 1980, Ray was criticised by an Indian M.P. and former actress Nargis Dutt, who accused Ray of "exporting poverty." She wanted him to make films to represent "Modern India."

Legacy

Satyajit Ray is a cultural icon in India and in Bengali communities worldwide. Following his death, the city of Calcutta came to a virtual standstill, as hundreds of thousands of people gathered around his house to pay their last respects. Satyajit Ray's influence has been widespread and deep in Bengali cinema; a number of Bengali directors, including Aparna Sen, Rituparno Ghosh and Gautam Ghose in India, Tareq Masud and Tanvir Mokammel in Bangladesh, and Aneel Ahmad in England, have been influenced by his film craft. Across the spectrum, filmmakers such as Budhdhadeb Dasgupta, Mrinal Sen and Adoor Gopalakrishnan have acknowledged his seminal contribution to Indian cinema. Beyond India, filmmakers such as Martin Scorsese, James Ivory, Abbas Kiarostami, Elia Kazan, François Truffaut,[72] Carlos Saura, Isao Takahata and Danny Boyle have been influenced by his cinematic style, with many others such as Akira Kurosawa praising his work. Gregory Nava's 1995 film *My Family* had a final scene that repeated that of *Apur Sansar*. Ira Sachs's 2005 work *Forty Shades of Blue* was a loose remake of *Charulata*. Other references to Ray films are found, for example, in recent works such as *Sacred Evil*, the *Elements trilogy* of Deepa Mehta and even in films of Jean-Luc Godard.[77] According to Michael Sragow of *The Atlantic Monthly*, the "youthful coming-of-age dramas that have flooded art houses since the mid-fifties owe a tremendous debt to the Apu trilogy". The trilogy also introduced the bounce lighting technique. *Kanchenjungha* (1962) introduced a narrative structure that resembles later hyperlink cinema. *Pratidwandi* (1972) helped pioneer photo-negative flashback and X-ray digression techniques. Together with Madhabi Mukherjee, Ray was the first Indian film figure to be featured on a foreign stamp (Dominica).

Many literary works include references to Ray or his work, including Saul Bellow's *Herzog* and J. M. Coetzee's *Youth*. Salman Rushdie's *Haroun and the Sea of Stories* contains fish characters named *Goopy* and *Bagha*, a tribute to Ray's fantasy film. In 1993, UC Santa Cruz established the Satyajit Ray Film and Study collection, and in 1995, the Government of India set up Satyajit Ray Film and Television Institute for studies related to film. In 2007, the BBC declared that two *Feluda* stories would be made into radio programs. During the London Film Festival, a regular "Satyajit Ray Award" is given to a first-time feature director whose film best captures "the artistry, compassion and humanity of Ray's vision". Wes Anderson has claimed Ray as an influence on his work; his 2007 film, *The Darjeeling Limited*, set in India, is dedicated to Ray.

Awards, honours and recognitions

Ray received many awards, including 32 National Film Awards by the Government of India, and awards at international film festivals. At the 11th Moscow International Film Festival in 1979, he was awarded with the Honorable Prize for the contribution to cinema. At the Berlin Film Festival, he was one of only three filmmakers to win the Silver Bear for Best Director more than once and holds the record for the most number of Golden Bear nominations, with seven. At the Venice Film Festival, where he had previously won a Golden Lion for *Aparajito* (1956), he was awarded the Golden Lion Honorary Award in 1982. That same year, he received an honorary "Hommage à Satyajit Ray" award at the 1982 Cannes Film Festival.

Ray is the second film personality after Chaplin to have been awarded honorary doctorates by Oxford University. He was awarded the Dadasaheb Phalke Award in 1985 and the Legion of Honor by the President of France in 1987. The Government of India awarded him the highest civilian honour, Bharat Ratna shortly before his death. The Academy of Motion Picture Arts and Sciences awarded Ray an Honorary Oscar in 1992 for Lifetime Achievement. It was one of his favourite actresses, Audrey Hepburn, who represented the Academy on that day in Calcutta. Ray, unable to attend the ceremony due to his illness, gave his acceptance speech to the Academy via live video feed from the hospital bed. In 1992 he was posthumously awarded the *Akira Kurosawa Award for Lifetime Achievement in Directing* at the San Francisco International Film Festival; it was accepted on his behalf by actress Sharmila Tagore.

In 1992, the *Sight & Sound* Critics' Top Ten Poll ranked Ray at No. 7 in its list of "Top 10 Directors" of all time, making him the highest-ranking Asian filmmaker in the poll. In 2002, the *Sight & Sound* critics' and directors' poll ranked Ray at No. 22 in its list of all-time greatest directors, thus making him the fourth highest-ranking Asian filmmaker in the poll. In 1996, *Entertainment Weekly* magazine ranked Ray at No. 25 in its "50 Greatest Directors" list.[91] In 2007, *Total Film* magazine included Ray in its "100 Greatest Film Directors Ever" list.

30

Gulzarilal Nanda

Gulzarilal Nanda (4 July 1898 – 15 January 1998) was an Indian politician and Economist who specialized in labour issues. He was the Prime Minister of India for two short periods following the deaths of Jawaharlal Nehru in 1964 and Lal Bahadur Shastri in 1966. Both his terms ended after the ruling Indian National Congress's parliamentary party elected a new prime minister. He was awarded the Bharat Ratna, India's highest civilian award, in 1997.+

Early life

Nanda was born on 4 July 1898 in Sialkot in the Punjab Province of British India into a Punjabi Hindu family. (After the partition of British India into India and Pakistan in 1947, Sialkot became a part of the Punjab Province of Pakistan.) Nanda received his education in Lahore, Amritsar, Agra, and Allahabad.

Nanda worked as a research scholar on labour problems at Allahabad University (1920–1921), and became a Professor of Economics at National College in Bombay (Mumbai) in 1921. The same year, he joined the Indian Non-Cooperation

Movement against the British Raj. In 1922, he became secretary of the Ahmedabad Textile Labour Association where he worked until 1946. He was imprisoned for Satyagraha in 1932, and again from 1942 to 1944. He honored with "Proud Past Alumni" in the list of 42 members, from "Allahabad University Alumni Association", NCR, Ghaziabad (Greater Noida) Chapter 2007-2008 registered under society act 1860 with registration no. 407/2000.

Member of Bombay Legislative Assembly

In the British Raj, Nanda was elected to the Bombay Legislative Assembly in 1937, and served as parliamentary secretary (for Labor and Excise) to the Government of Bombay from 1937 to 1939. As Labour Minister of the Bombay Government during 1946–50, he successfully piloted the Labor Disputes Bill in the state assembly. He served as a Trustee of the Kasṭurba Memorial Trust. (Kasturba was the wife of Mahatma Gandhi.) He served as secretary of the Hindustan Mazdoor Sevak Sangh (Indian Labor Welfare Organization), and Chairman of the Bombay Housing Board. He was a member of the National Planning Committee. He was largely instrumental in organising the Indian National Trade Union Congress, and later became its president.

In 1947, Nanda went to Geneva, Switzerland as a government delegate to the International Labor Conference. He worked on The Freedom of Association Committee of the Conference, and visited Sweden, France, Switzerland, Belgium, and the UK to study labour and housing conditions in those countries.

In March 1950, Nanda joined the Indian Planning Commission as its vice-chairman. In September 1951, he was appointed Planning Minister in the Indian Government. He was also given charge of the portfolios of Irrigation and Power. He was elected to the Lok Sabha from Bombay in the general elections of 1952, and was reappointed Minister for Planning, Irrigation, and Power. He led the Indian Delegation to the Plan Consultative Committee held in Singapore in 1955, and the International Labor Conference held in Geneva in 1959.

Nanda was elected to the Lok Sabha in the 1957 elections, and was appointed Union Minister for Labour, Employment and Planning, and later, as Deputy Chairman of the Planning Commission. He visited the Federal Republic of Germany, Yugoslavia, and Austria in 1959.

Nanda was re-elected to the Lok Sabha in the 1962 elections from the Sabarkantha constituency in Gujarat. He initiated the Congress Forum for Socialist Action in 1962. He was Union Minister for Labour and Employment during 1962–1963, and Minister for Home Affairs during 1963 – 1966.

Interim Prime Minister

Nanda was the Prime Minister of India twice for thirteen days each: the first time after the death of Prime Minister Jawaharlal Nehru in 1964, and the second time after the death of Prime Minister Lal Bahadur Shastri in 1966. Both his terms were uneventful, yet they were sensitive of period because of the potential danger to the country following Nehru's death soon after a war with China in 1962 and Shastri's death after a war with Pakistan in 1965.

31

Aruna Asaf Ali

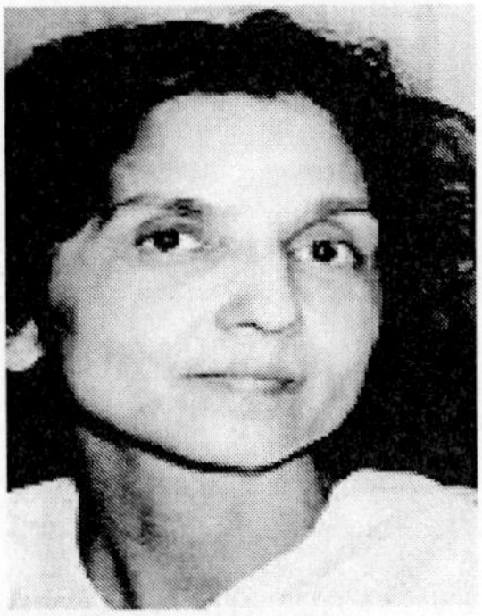

Aruna Asaf Ali (16 July 1909 – 29 July 1996), born **Aruna Ganguly**, was an Indian independence activist. She is widely remembered for hoisting the Indian National Congress flag at the Gowalia Tank maidan in Bombay during the Quit India Movement, 1942. She was 87 years old at the time of her death.

Early life

(AADIL)Aruna Asaf Ali was born as Aruna Ganguly on 16 July 1909 at Kalka, Punjab, British India, but now in the state of Haryana into a Bengali Brahmo family. She was educated at Sacred Heart Convent in Lahore and then in Nainital. She graduated and worked as a teacher. She taught at the Gokhale Memorial School in Calcutta. She met Asaf Ali, a leader in the Congress party at Allahabad and married him in 1928, despite parental opposition on grounds of religion (she was a Brahmo while he was a Muslim) and age (a difference of more than 20 years).

Freedom struggle: early days

She became an active member of Congress Party after marrying Asaf Ali and participated in public processions during the Salt Satyagraha. She was arrested on the charge that she was a vagrant and hence not released in 1931 under the Gandhi-Irwin Pact which stipulated release of all political prisoners. Other women co-prisoners refused to leave the premises unless she was also released and gave in only after Mohandas K. Gandhi intervened. A public agitation secured her release.

In 1932, she was held prisoner at the Tihar Jail where she protested the indifferent treatment of political prisoners by launching a hunger strike. Her efforts resulted in an improvement of conditions in the Tihar Jail but she was moved to Ambala and was subjected to solitary confinement. She was politically not very active after her release.

Family

Her father Upendranath Ganguly hailed from Barisal district of Eastern Bengal but settled in the United Province. He was a restaurant owner and a very adventurous man. Mother Ambalika Devi was the daughter of Trailokyanath Sanyal, a renowned Brahmo leader who wrote many beautiful Brahmo hymns. Upendranath Ganguly's younger brother Dhirendranath Ganguly (D G) was one of the earliest film directors. Another brother Nagendranath, a soil biologist was married to Rabindranath Tagore's only surviving daughter Mira Devi though they got separated after sometime. Her sister, Purnima Banerjee was a member of the Constituent Assembly of India.

Face of Quit India movement

On 8 August 1942, the All India Congress Committee passed the Quit India resolution at the Bombay session. The government responded by arresting the major leaders and all members of the Congress Working Committee and thus tried to pre-empt the movement from success. A young Aruna Asaf Ali presided over the remainder of the session on 9 August and hoisted the Congress flag at the Gowalia Tank maidan. This marked the commencement of the movement. The police fired upon the assembly at the session. Aruna was dubbed the *Heroine of the 1942 movement* for her bravery in the face of danger and was called *Grand Old Lady of the Independence movement* in her later years. Despite absence of direct leadership, spontaneous protests and demonstrations were held all over the country, as an expression of desire of India's youth to achieve independence.

Countdown to Independence

An arrest warrant was issued in her name but she went underground to evade the arrest and started underground movement in year 1942 . Her property was seized and sold. In the meanwhile, she also edited *Inquilab*, a monthly magazine of the Congress Party, along with Ram Manohar Lohia. In a 1944 issue, she exhorted youth to action by asking them to forget futile discussions about violence and non-violence and join the revolution. Leaders such as Jayaprakash Narayan and Aruna Asaf Ali were described as "the Political children of Gandhi but recent students of Karl Marx." The government announced a reward of Rs. 5,000/- for her capture. She fell ill and was for a period hiding in Dr Joshi's Hospital in Karol Bagh in Delhi. Mahatma Gandhi sent her a hand-written note to her to come out of hiding and surrender herself – as her mission was accomplished and as she could utilize the reward amount for the Harijan cause. However, she came out of hiding only after the warrant against her was withdrawn in 1946. She treasured the note from the Mahatma and it adorned her drawing room. However, she also faced criticism from Gandhi for her support of the Royal Indian Navy Mutiny, a movement she saw as the single greatest unifying factor of Hindus and Muslims at a time that was the peak of the movement for Pakistan.

Post-Independence

She was a member of the Congress Socialist Party, a caucus within the Congress Party for activists with socialist leanings. Disillusioned with the progress of the Congress Party on socialism she joined a new party, Socialist Party in

1948. She however left that party along with Metadata Granary and they visited Moscow along with Rajani Palme Dutt. Both of them joined the Communist Party of India in the early 1950s. On domestic front, she was bereaved when Asaf Ali died in 1953.

In 1954, she helped form the National Federation of Indian Women, the women's wing of CPI but left the party in 1956 following Nikita Khrushchev's disowning of Stalin. In 1958, she was elected the first Mayor of Delhi. She was closely associated with social activists and secularists of her era like Krishna Menon, Vimla Kapoor, Guru Radha Kishan, Premsagar Gupta, Rajani Palme joti, Sarla Sharma and Subhadra Joshi for social welfare and development in Delhi. She was the first elected Mayor of Delhi.

She and Narayanan started Link publishing house and published a daily newspaper, *Patriot* and a weekly, *Link* the same year. The publications became prestigious due to patronage of leaders such as Jawaharlal Nehru, Krishna Menon and Biju Patnaik. Later she moved out of the publishing house due to internal politics, stunned by greed taking over the creed of her comrades. In 1964, she rejoined the Congress Party but stopped taking part in active politics. Despite reservations about the emergency, she remained close to Indira Gandhi and Rajiv Gandhi.

Legacy

Aruna Asaf Ali was awarded International Lenin Peace Prize for the year 1964 and the Jawaharlal Nehru Award for International Understanding in 1991. She was awarded India's second highest civilian honour, the Padma Vibhushan in her lifetime in 1992, and finally the highest civilian award, the Bharat Ratna, posthumously in 1997. In 1998, a stamp commemorating her was issued. *Aruna Asaf Ali marg* in New Delhi was named in her honour. All India Minorities Front distributes the *Dr Aruna Asaf Ali Sadbhawana Award* annually.

Anecdote

Aruna Asaf Ali was well known for her Spartan lifestyle–she used public transport. In her eighties, once she was travelling in a crowded bus in Delhi and no seat was vacant. A fashionable young lady also boarded the bus and a gentleman trying to impress her, vacated his seat. This lady, in turn, offered the seat to Aruna Asaf Ali who accepted it. At this, that man protested, saying to the lady, "I vacated that seat for your sake, sister." Aruna Asaf Ali retorted with her quick wit, "Never mind, mother always comes before sister."

32

Avul Pakir Jainulabdeen Abdul Kalam

Avul Pakir Jainulabdeen Abdul Kalam born 15 October 1931) usually referred to as **Dr. A. P. J. Abdul Kalam**, is an Indian scientist and administrator who served as the 11th President of India from 2002 to 2007. Kalam was born and raised in Rameswaram, Tamil Nadu, studied physics at the St. Joseph's College, Tiruchirappalli, and aerospace engineering at the Madras Institute of Technology (MIT), Chennai.

Before his term as President, he worked as an Aerospace engineer with Defence Research and Development Organisation (DRDO) and Indian Space Research Organisation (ISRO). Kalam is popularly known as the *Missile Man of India* for his work on the development of ballistic missile and launch vehicle technology.[2] He played a pivotal organizational, technical and political role in India's *Pokhran-II* nuclear tests in 1998, the first since the original nuclear test by India in 1974. Some scientific experts have however called Kalam a man with no authority over nuclear physics but who just carried on the works of Homi J. Bhabha and Vikram Sarabhai.

Kalam was elected the President of India in 2002, defeating Lakshmi Sahgal and was supported by both the Indian National Congress and the Bharatiya Janata Party, the major political parties of India. He is currently a visiting professor at Indian Institute of Management Shillong, Indian Institute of Management Ahmedabad and Indian Institute of Management Indore, honorary fellow of Indian Institute of Science, Bangalore, Chancellor of the Indian Institute of Space Science and Technology Thiruvananthapuram, a professor of Aerospace Engineering at Anna University (Chennai), JSS University (Mysore) and an adjunct/visiting faculty at many other academic and research institutions across India.

Kalam advocated plans to develop India into a developed nation by 2020 in his book *India 2020*. He has received several prestigious awards, including the Bharat Ratna, India's highest civilian honour. Kalam is known for his motivational speeches and interaction with the student community in India. He launched his mission for the youth of the nation in 2011 called the *What Can I Give Movement* with a central theme to defeat corruption in India.

Early life and education

A. P. J. Abdul Kalam was born on 15 October 1931 in a Tamil Muslim family to Jainulabdeen, a boat owner and Ashiamma, a housewife, at Rameswaram, located in the Indian state of Tamil Nadu.He came from a poor background and started working at an early age to supplement his family's income. After completing school, Kalam distributed newspapers to financially contribute to his father's income. In his school years, he had average grades, but was described as a bright and hardworking student who had a strong desire to learn and spend hours on his studies, especially mathematics.

"I inherited honesty and self-discipline from my father; from my mother, I inherited faith in goodness and deep kindness as did my three brothers and sisters."

—A quote from Kalam's autobiography

After completing his school education at the Rameshwaram Elementary School, Kalam went on to attend Saint Joseph's College, Tiruchirappalli, then affiliated with the University of Madras, from where he graduated in physics in 1954.[12] Towards the end of the course, he was not enthusiastic about the subject and would later regret the four years he studied it. He then moved to Madras in 1955 to study aerospace engineering. While Kalam was working on a senior class project, the Dean was dissatisfied with the lack of progress and threatened revoking his scholarship unless the project was finished within the next three days. He worked tirelessly on his project and met the deadline, impressing the Dean who later said, "I [Dean] was putting you [Kalam] under stress and asking you to meet a difficult deadline". For him becoming a fighter pilot was a "dearest dream" but he failed to realise it as he bagged the ninth position when only eight slots were available in the IAF.

Career as scientist

This was my first stage, in which I learnt leadership from three great teachers—Dr. Vikram Sarabhai, Prof. Satish Dhawan and Dr. Brahm Prakash. This was the time of learning and acquisition of knowledge for me.

A. P. J. Abdul Kalam. After graduating from Madras Institute of Technology (MIT – Chennai) in 1960, Kalam joined Aeronautical Development Establishment of Defense Research and Development Organization (DRDO) as a scientist. Kalam started his career by designing a small helicopter for the Indian Army, but remained unconvinced with the choice of his job at DRDO. Kalam was also part of the INCOSPAR committee working under Vikram Sarabhai, the renowned space scientist.[9] In 1969, Kalam was transferred to the Indian Space Research Organization (ISRO) where he was the project director of India's first indigenous Satellite Launch Vehicle (SLV-III) which successfully deployed the *Rohini* satellite in near earth's orbit in July 1980. Joining ISRO was one of Kalam's biggest achievements in life and he is said to have found himself when he started to work on the SLV project. Kalam first started work on an expandable rocket project independently at DRDO in 1965. In 1969, Kalam received the government's approval and expanded the program to include more engineers.

Kalam addresses engineering students at IIT Guwahati

In 1963–64, he visited NASA's Langley Research Center in Hampton Virginia, Goddard Space Flight Center in Greenbelt, Maryland and Wallops Flight Facility situated at Eastern Shore of Virginia. During the period between the 1970s and 1990s, Kalam made an effort to develop the Polar SLV and SLV-III projects, both of which proved to be success.

Kalam was invited by Raja Ramanna to witness the country's first nuclear test Smiling Buddha as the representative of TBRL, even though he had not participated in the development, test site preparation and weapon designing. In the 1970s, a landmark was achieved by ISRO when the locally built *Rohini-1* was launched into space, using the SLV rocket. In the 1970s, Kalam also directed two projects, namely, *Project Devil* and *Project Valiant* , which sought to develop ballistic missiles from the technology of the successful SLV programme. Despite the disapproval of Union Cabinet, Prime Minister Indira Gandhi allotted secret funds for these aerospace projects through her discretionary powers under Kalam's directorship. Kalam played an integral role convincing the Union Cabinet to conceal the true nature of these classified aerospace projects. His research and educational leadership brought him great laurels and prestige in 1980s, which prompted the government to initiate an advanced missile program under his directorship. Kalam and Dr. V. S. Arunachalam, metallurgist and scientific adviser to the Defense Minister, worked on the suggestion by the then Defense Minister, R. Venkataraman on a proposal for simultaneous development of a quiver of missiles instead of taking planned missiles one by one. R Venkatraman was instrumental in getting the cabinet approval for allocating

3.88 billion rupees for the mission, named Integrated Guided Missile Development Program (I.G.M.D.P) and appointed Kalam as the chief executive. Kalam played a major part in developing many missiles under the mission including Agni, an intermediate range ballistic missile and Prithvi, the tactical surface-to-surface missile, although the projects have been criticised for mismanagement and cost and time overruns. He was the Chief Scientific Adviser to the Prime Minister and the Secretary of Defence Research and Development Organisation from July 1992 to December 1999. The *Pokhran-II* nuclear tests were conducted during this period where he played an intensive political and technological role. Kalam served as the Chief Project Coordinator, along with R. Chidambaram during the testing phase. Photos and snapshots of him taken by the media elevated Kalam as the country's top nuclear scientist.

In 1998, along with cardiologist Dr.Soma Raju, Kalam developed a low cost Coronary stent. It was named as "Kalam-Raju Stent" honouring them. In 2012, the duo, designed a rugged tablet PC for health care in rural areas, which was named as "Kalam-Raju Tablet".

Presidency

Kalam served as the 11th President of India, succeeding K. R. Narayanan. He won the 2002 presidential election with an electoral vote of 922,884, surpassing 107,366 votes won by Lakshmi Sahgal. He served from 25 July 2002 to 25 July 2007.

On 10 June 2002, the National Democratic Alliance (NDA) which was in power at the time, expressed to the leader of opposition, Indian National Congress president Sonia Gandhi that they would propose Kalam for the post of President. The Samajwadi Party and the Nationalist Congress Party backed his candidacy. After the Samajwadi Party announced its support for him, Narayanan chose not to seek a second term in office, leaving the field clear for Kalam.

I am really overwhelmed. Everywhere both in Internet and in other media, I have been asked for a message. I was thinking what message I can give to the people of the country at this juncture.

—Kalam responding to the announcement of his candidature by Prime Minister Atal Bihari Vajpayee

On 18 June, Kalam filed his nomination papers in the Parliament of India, accompanied by Vajpayee and his senior Cabinet colleagues.

The polling for the presidential election began on 15 July 2002 in the Parliament and the state assemblies with media claiming that the election was a one-sided affair and Kalam's victory was a foregone conclusion. The counting was held on 18 July. Kalam won the presidential election in a highly one-sided contest. He became the 11th president of the Republic of India. He moved into the Rashtrapati Bhavan after he was sworn in on 25 July. Kalam was the third President of India to have been honoured with a Bharat Ratna, India's highest civilian honour, before becoming the President. Dr. Sarvapali Radhakrishnan (1954) and Dr. Zakir Hussain (1963) were the earlier recipients of Bharat Ratna who later became the President of India. He was also the first scientist and the first bachelor to occupy Rashtrapati Bhawan.

During his term as President, he was affectionately known as the *People's President.* In his words, signing the Office of Profit Bill was the toughest decision he had taken during his tenure.

Kalam is criticised for inaction as a President in deciding the fate of 20 out of the 21 mercy petitions. Article 72 of the Constitution of India empowers the President of India to grant pardon, suspend and remit death sentences and commute the death sentence of convicts on death row. Kalam acted on only one mercy plea in his 5-year tenure as a President, rejecting the plea of rapist Dhananjoy Chatterjee, who was hanged thereafter. The most important of the 20 pleas is thought to be that of Afzal Guru, a Kashmiri terrorist who was convicted of conspiracy in the December 2001 attack on the Indian Parliament and was sentenced to death by the Supreme Court of India in 2004.[42] While the sentence was scheduled to be carried out on 20 October 2006, the pending action on the mercy plea resulted in him continuing in the death row.

At the end of his term, on 20 June 2007, Kalam expressed his willingness to consider a second term in office provided there was certainty about his victory in the 2007 presidential election.[43] However, two days later, he decided not to contest the Presidential election again stating that he wanted to avoid involving Rashtrapati Bhavan from any political processes. He did not have the support of the Left parties, Shiv Sena and UPA constituents to receive a renewed mandate.

Nearing the term expiry of the 12th President Pratibha Patil, whose tenure ended on 24 July 2012, media reports in April claimed that Kalam was likely to be nominated for his second term. After the reports, social networking sites were abuzz with activities extending their support for his candidature. BJP potentially backed his nomination, saying that the party will lend their support if Trinamool Congress, Samajwadi Party and Indian National Congress proposes his name for the 2012 presidential election. Just a month ahead of the election, Mulayam Singh Yadav and Mamata Banerjee also expressed their support to Kalam and revealed that they both would suggest his name. Days after expressing support, Mulayam Singh Yadav backed out, leaving Mamata Banerjee as a solitary supporter. On 18 June 2012, Kalam refused to contest 2012 presidential poll after much speculations.

Many, many citizens have also expressed the same wish. It only reflects their love and affection for me and the aspiration of the people. I am really overwhelmed by this support. This being their wish, I respect it. I want to thank them for the trust they have in me."

—Kalam's message to public upon denying to contest Presidential poll 2012.

Future India: 2020

In his book *India 2020*, Kalam strongly advocates an action plan to develop India into a knowledge superpower and a developed nation by the year 2020. He regards his work on India's nuclear weapons program as a way to assert India's place as a future superpower.

It was reported that, there was a considerable demand in South Korea for translated versions of books authored by him.

Kalam continues to take an active interest in other developments in the field of science and technology. He has proposed a research program for developing bio-implants. He is a supporter of Open Source over proprietary solutions and believes that the use of free software on a large scale will bring the benefits of information technology to more people.

Kalam set a target of interacting with 100,000 students during the two years after his resignation from the post of scientific adviser in 1999. In his own words, "I feel comfortable in the company of young people, particularly high school students. Henceforth, I intend to share with them experiences, helping them to ignite their imagination and preparing them to work for a developed India for which the road map is already available." He continued to interact with students during his term as a President and also during his post-presidency period as a visiting professor at Indian Institute of Management Ahmedabad and Indian Institute of Management Indore, Chancellor of Indian Institute of Space Science and Technology Thiruvananthapuram, a professor of Aerospace Engineering at Anna University (Chennai), JSS University (Mysore), and an adjunct/visiting faculty at many other academic and research institutions across India. Kalam is strong supporter of Space based solar power. In 2012 China proposed joint development between India and China towards developing a solar power satellite, during a visit by Kalam.

Popular culture

In May 2012, Kalam launched his mission for the youth of the nation called the *What Can I Give Movement* with a central theme to defeat corruption. He also has interests in writing Tamil poetry and in playing veenai, a South Indian string instrument.

He was nominated for the MTV Youth Icon of the Year award in 2003 and in 2006. In the 2011 Hindi film *I Am Kalam*, Kalam is portrayed as an extremely positive influence to a poor but bright Rajasthani boy named Chhotu, who renames himself Kalam in honour of his idol.

Awards and honours

A. P. J. Abdul Kalam's 79th birthday was recognised as *World Student's Day* by United Nations. He has also received honorary doctorates from 40 universities. The Government of India has honoured him with the Padma Bhushan in 1981 and the Padma Vibhushan in 1990 for his work with ISRO and DRDO and his role as a scientific advisor to the Government. In 1997, Kalam received India's highest civilian honour, the Bharat Ratna, for his immense and valuable contribution to the scientific research and modernisation of defence technology in India. In 2005, Switzerland declared 26 May as science day to commemorate Kalam's visit in the country.

33

Madurai Shanmukhavadivu Subbulakshmi

Madurai Shanmukhavadivu Subbulakshmi 16 September 1916 – 11 December 2004), also known as **M.S.**, was a renowned Carnatic vocalist.

She was the first musician ever to be awarded the Bharat Ratna, India's highest civilian honor.[1] She is the first Indian musician to receive the Ramon Magsaysay award, often considered Asia's Nobel Prize, in 1974 with the citation reading "Exacting purists acknowledge Srimati M. S. Subbulakshmi as the leading exponent of classical and semi-classical songs in the Karnataka tradition of South India."

Biography

Early years

Subbulakshmi (Kunjamma to her family) was born in Madurai, Madras Presidency, India to veena player Shanmukavadiver Ammal and Subramania Iyer. Her grandmother Akkammal was a violinist.

She started learning Carnatic music at an early age and trained in Carnatic music under the tutelage of Semmangudi

Srinivasa Iyer and subsequently in Hindustani music under Pandit Narayanrao Vyas.

Her mother, from the devadasi community, was a music exponent and a regular stage performer, and Subbulakshmi grew up in an environment very conducive to musical learning. Her musical interests were also shaped by regular interactions with Karaikudi Sambasiva Iyer, Mazhavarayanendal Subbarama Bhavathar and Ariyakudi Ramanuja Iyengar.

Subbulakshmi gave her first public performance, at the age of eleven, in the year 1927, in the 100 pillar hall inside the Rockfort Temple, Tiruchirappalli; with Mysore Chowdiah on the violin and Dakshinamurthy Pillai on the mriganga.

Move to Madras

In 1936 Subbulakshmi moved to Madras (now Chennai). She also made her film debut in *Sevasadan* in 1938.

Musical style and performance

Singing career

M.S. Subbulakshmi began her Carnatic classical music training under her mother Shanmugavadivu; and later in Hindustani classical training under Pandit Narayan Rao Vyas. Subbulakshmi first recording was released when she was 10 years old.

Subbulakshmi gave her first performance at the prestigious Madras Music Academy in 1929,when she was 13 years old . The performance consisted of singing bhajans (Hindu hymns). The academy was known for its discriminating selection process, and they broke tradition by inviting a young girl as a key performer. Her performance was described as spellbinding and earned her many admirers and the moniker of musical genius from critics. Soon after her debut performances, Subbulakshmi became one the leading Carnatic vocalists.

By the age of seventeen, Subbulakshmi was giving concerts

on her own, including major performances at the Madras Music Academy.

She traveled to London, New York, Canada, the Far East, and other places as India's cultural ambassador. Her concerts at

- Edinburgh International Festival of Music and Drama in 1963
- Carnegie Hall, New York; the UN General Assembly on UN day in 1966
- Royal Albert Hall, London in 1982
- Festival of India in Moscow in 1987

were significant landmarks in her career. In 1969 she was accompanied by Indian Railways Advisor SN Venkata Rao to Rameshwaram, where she famously sang several songs in front of each idol in the Rameshwaram temple.

After the death of her husband Kalki Sadasivam in 1997, she stopped all her public performances.

Films

M.S. also acted in a few Tamil films in her youth. Her first movie Sevasadanam was released on 2 May 1938. F.G. Natesa Iyer was the lead actor, opposite Subbulakshmi, in this film, directed by K. Subramanyam. It was a critical and commercial success.[12] Ananda Vikatan favourably reviewed the film on 8 May 1938:

"We should always expect somethings from Subramaniam's direction - for instance depiction of social ills.. If we have to say only two words about this talkie based on Premchand's story it is - Go see (it)."

Sevasadanam is one of the early Tamil films to be set in a contemporary social setting and to advocate reformist social policies. The film is an adapted version of Premchand's novel Bazaar-e-Husn. The veteran Marxist leader N. Sankaraiah, has described Sevasadanam as an "unusual film" for choosing the subject of marriages between young girls and old men (which had social sanction). According to him, the film successfully broughout the "sufferings of the girl" (acted by M.S.) and the "mental agony of the aged husband".(acted by F.G.Natesa Iyer).Tamil film critic and historian Aranthai Narayanan observes in his book*Thamizh Cinemavin Kathai* (The Story of Tamil Cinema) that "Seva Sadhanam proved a turning point in the history of Tamil cinema. In the climax, the aged husband, now a totally changed man, was shown as casting aside with utter contempt his `sacred thread', which symbolises his Brahmin superiority. It came as a stunning blow to the then Brahmin orthodoxy."

MS Subbulakshmi also played the male role of Narada in "Savitri" (1941) to raise money for launching Kalki, her husband's nationalist Tamil weekly. Her title role of the Rajasthani saint-poetess Meera in the eponymous 1945 film gave her national prominence. This movie was re-made in Hindi in 1947.

34

Chidambaram Subramaniam

Chidambaram Subramaniam (commonly known as **CS**) (January 30, 1910 – November 7, 2000), was an Indian statesman (Indian Independence activist, State minister, Central minister and Governor of state). He was the man who ushered in an era of self-sufficiency in food production in India.

Early Life and Education

Subramaniam was born on January 30, 1910, to Chidambaram and his wife, in a village called Senguttaipalayam, Pollachi taluk, Coimbatore district. Subramaniam completed his early education in Pollachi before moving to Chennai where he did a B.Sc in Physics at the Presidency College, Chennai. Later he took a degree in law at the Law college, Chennai. During college days he along with contemporary stalwarts like Periyasami Thooran, K.M.Ramasami, O.V.Alagesan, Justice Palanisami started "Vanamalr Sangam" & published underground magazine called "PITHAN" edited by P.Thooran & Published by K.M.Ramasami at Gobichettipalayam.

Political Career

He was an active member in Civil disobedience movement in his college days. He was imprisoned during the Quit India Movement in 1942. A protégé of Rajaji, Subramaniam was trained in the rudiments of politics and administration. He was a Minister (Education, Law and Finance) in the then Madras State from 1952 to 1962. He was the Leader of the House in the Madras Legislative Assembly for 10 years from 1952. He was elected to the Lok Sabha in 1962 and was the Minister for Steel and Mines. Subsequently, he handled important portfolios like agriculture (in 1965 when he spearheaded the Green Revolution), and later the portfolios of Finance and Defence. He was the finance minister during the emergency. He also worked as the Deputy Chairman of the Planning Commission from 2 May 1971 to 22 July 1972.

When the historic split in the Congress took place in 1969, he cast his lot with Indira Gandhi and became the interim president of the faction she headed. He stood by her when she clamped the Emergency in 1975, but parted ways later and joined the Congress (Urs) faction led by Devraj Urs

Subramaniam was appointed Governor of Maharashtra in 1990. He transformed the Raj Bhavan into a beehive of activity by holding frequent meetings with leading academics, industrialists, representatives of non-governmental organisations and prominent citizens on issues crucial to the community. He had to resign after a newspaper reporter overheard and published an informal remark of his criticising the style of functioning of the then Indian Prime Minister, Mr P.V. Narasimha Rao.

Achievements

Subramaniam participated in the freedom struggle actively and went to prison. He was later elected to the Constituent Assembly and had a hand in the framing of the Constitution of India.

Subramaniam is best known as the architect of India's modern agricultural development policy, after the success of his programme which led to a record production of wheat in 1972 — an achievement termed as the Indian Green Revolution. As Minister for Food and Agriculture, he played a decisive role in the introduction of high-yielding varieties of seeds and more intensive application of fertilizers which paved the way for increased output of cereals in the late 60s and attainment of self-sufficiency in food-grains in the country. About his contribution, Dr. Norman E. Borlaug, the Nobel Laureate, writes: "The vision and influence of Mr. Subramaniam in bringing about agricultural change and in the very necessary political decisions needed to make the new approach effective, should never be under-emphasized. The groundwork for this advance (in the production of wheat) was solidly laid during that period (1964–67) when Mr. Subramaniam was the guiding political force instituting change.

Among his protégés who are notable in their own right are M.S. Swaminathan, who played a major role in translating the dream of a 'green revolution' into reality; former Agriculture Secretary B. Sivaraman (who, along with Subramaniam and Swaminathan, formed the three 'S's instrumental in heralding the Green Revolution), and Verghese Kurien Chairman of the National Dairy Development Board.

He was the founder of National Agro Foundation, Chennai and Bharathidasan Institute of Management, Tiruchirappalli.

Honours

He has received the following awards

- Bharat Ratna (the nation's highest civilian honour) in 1998.
- Y.B. Chavan National Integration Award.
- U Thant peace award and Norman Borlaug award in 1996.
- Anuvrat award (1988).

A commemorative coin of him, was released in August 2010.

Publications

- *War on Poverty*
- *The New Strategy in Indian Agriculture*
- *Some Countries which I visited Round The World*
- *The India of My Dreams*

35

Jayaprakash Narayan

Jayaprakash Narayan (listen (help·info); 11 October 1902 – 8 October 1979), popularly referred to as **JP** or **Lok Nayak** (Hindi for "people's hero"), was an Indian independence activist, social reformer and political leader, remembered especially for leading the mid-1970s opposition against Prime Minister Indira Gandhi, for whose overthrow he called a "total revolution". His biography, *Jayaprakash,* was written by his nationalist friend and an eminent writer of Hindi literature, Ramavriksha Benipuri. In 1999, he was posthumously awarded the Bharat Ratna, India's highest civilian award, in recognition of his social work. Other awards include the Magsaysay award for Public Service in 1965. The Patna airport is also named after him.

Early life

Jayprakash Narayan was born on 11 October 1902 [1] in the village of *Sitabdiara*, U.P Ballia, India.[2] He came from a Kayastha family.[3] He was Harsu Dayal Srivastava and Phul Rani Devi's fourth child.His father Harsudayal was a junior official in the Canal Department of the State government and was often touring the region. When Narayan was 9 years old he left his village to enroll in 7th class of the collegiate school at Patna. While in school, Jayaprakash read magazines like Saraswati, Prabha and Pratap, books like Bharat- Bharati, and poems by Maithilsharan Gupta and Bharatendu Harishchandra which described the courage and valour of the Rajput kings. Jayaprakash also read the Bhagwad Gita. His essay, "The present state of Hindi in Bihar" won a best essay award. He excelled in school and by 1918 completed school and undertook the 'State Public Matriculation Examination' and won a District merit scholarship to Patna college.

In October 1920, Narayan was married to Braj Kishore Prasad's daughter Prabhavati Devi, a freedom fighter in her own right.[4] At the time of marriage, Jayaprakash was 18 years and Prabhavati was 14 years of age, which was a normal age for marriage in that period. After their wedding, since Narayan was working in Patna and it was difficult for his wife to stay with him, on the invitation of Gandhi, Prabhavati became an inmate at the Ashram of Gandhi. Jayaprakash, along with some friends, went to listen to Maulana Abul Kalam Azad speak about the Non-cooperation movement launched by Gandhi against the passing of the Rowlatt Act of 1919. The Maulana was a brilliant orator and his call to give up English education was "like leaves before a storm: Jayaprakash was swept away and momentarily lifted up to thc skies. That brief experience of soaring up with the winds of a great idea left imprints on his inner being". Jayaprakash took the Maulana's words to heart and left Patna College with just 20 days remaining for his examinations. He joined the Bihar Vidyapeeth, a college run by the Congress.

Higher Education in America

After exhausting the courses at the Vidyapeeth, Jayaprakash decided to go to America to pursue his studies. At age 20, Jayaprakash sailed aboard the cargo ship Janus while Prabhavati remained at Sabarmati. Jayaprakash reached California on October 8, 1922 and gained admission to Berkeley in January 1923. To pay for his education, Jayaprakash picked grapes, set them out to dry, packed fruits at a canning factory, washed dishes, worked as a mechanic at a garage and at a slaughter house, sold lotions and accepted teaching jobs. All these jobs gave Jayaprakash an insight regarding the difficulties the working class faced.Jayaprakash was forced to transfer to Iowa State when fees at Berkeley were doubled. He was forced to transfer to many universities thereafter. He pursued his favourite subject, sociology and received much help from Professor Edward Ross, the father of Sociology.

In Wisconsin, Jayaprakash was introduced to Karl Marx's *Das Kapital*. News of the success of the Russian revolution of 1917 made Jayaprakash conclude that Marxism was the way to alleviate the suffering masses. He delved into books by Indian intellectual and Communist theoretician M.N. Roy. His paper on Sociology, "Social Variation", was declared as the best of the year.

Politics

Sandip Das, a biographer, says that

> "... in 1920, he joined the non-cooperation struggle and gave up his studies. He joined the Bihar Vidyapeeth established by the Congress to pursue his education. The determination to continue the boycott of British educational institutions led him to study in the United States."

Returning from the US in late 1929 as a supporter of Marxist theories, Narayan joined the Indian National Congress on the invitation of Jawaharlal Nehru in 1929; Mahatma Gandhi became his mentor in the Congress. He shared the same house at *Kadam Kuan* in Patna with his close friend and nationalist Ganga Sharan Sinha (Shrivastava). with whom he shared the most cordial and lasting friendship.

During the Indian independence movement he was arrested, jailed, and tortured several times by the British.He won particular fame during the Quit India movement.

After being jailed in 1932 for civil disobedience against British rule, Narayan was imprisoned in Nasik Jail, where he met Ram Manohar Lohia, Minoo Masani, Achyut Patwardhan, Ashok Mehta, Yusuf Desai and other national leaders. After his release, the Congress Socialist Party, or (CSP), a left-wing group within the Congress, was formed with Acharya Narendra Deva as President and Narayan as General secretary.

When Mahatma Gandhi launched the Quit India Movement in August, 1942, Yogendra Shukla scaled the wall of Hazaribagh Central Jail along with Jayaprakash Narayan, Suraj Narayan Singh, Gulab Chand Gupta, Ramnandan Mishra and Shaligram Singh with a view to starting an underground movement for freedom. As Jayaprakash Narayan was ill then, Yogendra Shukla walked a distance to Gaya, a distance of about 124 kilometres, with Jayaprakash Narayan on his shoulders.

Bihar Movement and Total Revolution

Narayan returned to prominence in State politics in the late 1960s. 1974 ushered in a year of high inflation, unemployment and lack of supplies and essential commodities. Jayaprakash was asked to lead a peaceful agitation by the Navanirman Andolan of Gujarat. On April 8, 1974, at the age of 72, he led a silent procession at Patna. The procession was lathi charged. On June 5, 1974, Jayaprakash addressed a mammoth crowd at Gandhi Maidan in Patna. He declared, "This is a revolution, friends! We are not here merely to see the Vidhan Sabha dissolved. That is only one milestone on our journey. But we have a long way to go... After 27 years of freedom, people of this country are wracked by hunger, rising prices, corruption... oppressed by every kind of injustice... it is a Total Revolution we want, nothing less!" In

1974, he led the students' movement in the state of Bihar which gradually developed into a popular people's movement known as the Bihar movement. It was during this movement that JP gave a call for peaceful Total Revolution. Together with V. M. Tarkunde, he found the Citizens for Democracy in 1974 and the People's Union for Civil Liberties in 1976, both NGOs, to uphold and defend civil liberties.

Emergency

When Indira Gandhi was found guilty of violating electoral laws by the Allahabad High Court, Narayan called for Indira to resign, and advocated a program of social transformation which he termed *Sampoorna kraanti* (Total Revolution). Instead she proclaimed a national Emergency on the midnight of June 25, 1975, immediately after Narayan had called for the PM's resignation and had asked the military and the police to disregard unconstitutional and immoral orders; JP, opposition leaders, and dissenting members of her own party (the 'Young Turks') were arrested on that day.

Jayaprakash Narayan attracted a gathering of 100,000 people at the Ramlila grounds and thunderously recited *Rashtrakavi* Ramdhari Singh 'Dinkar''s wonderfully evocative poetry: *Singhasan Khaali Karo Ke Janata Aaati Hai.*

Narayan was kept as *detenu* at Chandigarh even after he had asked for a month's parole for mobilising relief in areas of Bihar gravely affected by flood. His health suddenly deteriorated on October 24, and he was released on November 12; diagnosis at Jaslok Hospital, Bombay, revealed kidney failure; he would be on dialysis for the rest of his life.

The "Free JP" campaign was launched in the UK by Surur Hoda and chaired by Nobel Peace Prize winner Noel-Baker for the release of Jayaprakash Narayan.

After Indira revoked the emergency on January 18, 1977 and announced elections, it was under JP's guidance that the Janata Party (a vehicle for the broad spectrum of the anti-

Indira Gandhi opposition) was formed. The Janata Party was voted into power, and became the first non-Congress party to form a government at the Centre. On the call of Narayan many youngsters joined the JP movement.

Death

Narayan died in Patna, Bihar, on 8 October 1979, three days before his 77th birthday, due to effects of diabetes and heart ailments. In March 1979, while he was in hospital, his death had been erroneously announced by the Indian prime minister, causing a brief wave of national mourning, including the suspension of parliament and regular radio broadcasting, and the closure of schools and shops. When he was told about the gaffe a few weeks later, he smiled.

Family

Jayaprakash was married to Prabhavati Devi, daughter of lawyer and nationalist Brij Kishore Prasad in October 1920. Prabhavati was very independent and on Gandhi's invitation, went to stay at his ashram while Jayaprakash continued his studies.

Awards

- Bharat Ratna, 1999 (Posthmus)for Public Affairs[
- Rashtrabhushan Award of FIE Foundation, Ichalkaranji
- Ramon Magsaysay Award,1965 for Public Service.

Artistic depictions of JP

- Prakash Jha directed a 112-minute film "Loknayak ",based on the life of Jaya Prakash Narayan (JP). Chetan Pandit played the role of JP in that film.
- Achyut Potdar played role of JP in ABP News show Pradhanmantri (TV Series) and Aaj Tak Aandolan.

36

Ravi Shankar

Ravi Shankar, 7 April 1920 – 11 December 2012), his name often preceded by the title Pandit, was an Indian musician who was one of the best-known exponents of the sitar in the second half of the 20th century as well as a composer of Hindustani classical music.

Shankar was born in Varanasi and spent his youth touring Europe and India with the dance group of his brother Uday Shankar. He gave up dancing in 1938 to study sitar playing under court musician Allauddin Khan. After finishing his studies in 1944, Shankar worked as a composer, creating the music for the *Apu Trilogy* by Satyajit Ray, and was music director of All India Radio, New Delhi, from 1949 to 1956.

In 1956, he began to tour Europe and the Americas playing Indian classical music and increased its popularity there in the 1960s through teaching, performance, and his association with violinist Yehudi Menuhin and Beatles guitarist George Harrison. Shankar engaged Western music by writing concerti for sitar and orchestra, and toured the world in the 1970s and 1980s. From 1986 to 1992 he served as a nominated member of Rajya Sabha, the upper chamber of the Parliament of India. In 1999, Shankar was awarded India's highest civilian honour, the Bharat Ratna. He continued to perform up until the end of his life.

Early life

Shankar was born Robindro Shaunkor Chowdhury on 7 April 1920 in Varanasi, to a Bengali Brahmin family as the youngest of seven brothers. His father, Shyam Shankar, a Middle Temple barrister and scholar who served as *dewan* of Jhalawar, used the Sanskrit spelling of the family name and removed its last part. Shyam was married to Shankar's mother Hemangini Devi, and later worked as a lawyer in London, England. There he married a second time while Devi raised Shankar in Varanasi, and did not meet his son until he was eight years old. Shankar shortened the Sanskrit version of his first name, Ravindra, to Ravi, for "sun".

At the age of ten, after spending his first decade in Varanasi, Shankar went to Paris with the dance group of his brother, choreographer Uday Shankar. By the age of 13 he had become a member of the group, accompanied its members on tour and learned to dance and play various Indian instruments. Uday's dance group toured Europe and the United States in the early to mid-1930s and Shankar learned French, discovered Western classical music, jazz, cinema and became acquainted with Western customs. Shankar heard the lead musician for the Maihar court, Allauddin Khan, in December 1934 at a music conference in Kolkata and Uday convinced the Maharaja of Maihar in 1935 to allow Khan to become his group's soloist for a tour of Europe. Shankar was sporadically trained by Khan on tour, and Khan offered Shankar training to become a serious musician under the condition that he abandon touring and come to Maihar.

Career

Training and Work in India

Shankar's parents had died by the time he returned from the European tour, and touring the West had become difficult due to political conflicts that would lead to World War II. Shankar gave up his dancing career in 1938 to go to Maihar and study Indian classical music as Khan's pupil, living with his family in the traditional *gurukul* system. Khan was a rigorous teacher and Shankar had training on *sitar* and *surbahar*, learned *ragas* and the musical styles *dhrupad*, *dhamar*, and *khyal*, and was taught the techniques of the instruments *rudra veena*, *rubab*, and *sursingar*. He often studied with Khan's children Ali Akbar Khan and Annapurna Devi. Shankar began to perform publicly on *sitar* in December 1939 and his debut performance was a *jugalbandi* (duet) with Ali Akbar Khan, who played the string instrument *sarod*.

Shankar completed his training in 1944. Following his training, he moved to Mumbai and joined the Indian People's Theatre Association, for whom he composed music for ballets in 1945 and 1946. Shankar recomposed the music for the popular song "Sare Jahan Se Achcha" at the age of 25. He began to record music for HMV India and worked as a music director for All India Radio (AIR), New Delhi, from February 1949 to January 1956. Shankar founded the Indian National Orchestra at AIR and composed for it; in his compositions he combined Western and classical Indian instrumentation. Beginning in the mid-1950s he composed the music for the *Apu Trilogy* by Satyajit Ray, which became internationally acclaimed. He was music director for several Hindi movies including *Godaan* and *Anuradha*.

1956–69: International career

V. K. Narayana Menon, director of AIR Delhi, introduced the Western violinist Yehudi Menuhin to Shankar during Menuhin's first visit to India in 1952. Shankar had performed as part of a cultural delegation in the Soviet Union in 1954 and Menuhin invited Shankar in 1955 to perform in New York City for a demonstration of Indian classical music, sponsored by the Ford Foundation. Shankar declined to attend due to problems in his marriage, but recommended Ali Akbar Khan to play instead. Khan reluctantly accepted and performed with *tabla* (percussion) player Chatur Lal in the Museum of Modern Art, and he later became the first Indian classical musician to perform on American television and record a full *raga* performance, for Angel Records.

Shankar heard about the positive response Khan received and resigned from AIR in 1956 to tour the United Kingdom, Germany, and the United States. He played for smaller audiences and educated them about Indian music, incorporating *ragas* from the South Indian Carnatic music in his performances, and recorded his first LP album *Three Ragas* in London, released in 1956. In 1958, Shankar participated in the celebrations of the tenth anniversary of the United Nations and UNESCO music festival in Paris. From 1961, he toured Europe, the United States, and Australia, and became the first Indian to compose music for non-Indian films. Chatur Lal accompanied Shankar on *tabla* until 1962, when Alla Rakha assumed the role. Shankar founded the Kinnara School of Music in Mumbai in 1962.

Shankar befriended Richard Bock, founder of World Pacific Records, on his first American tour and recorded most of his albums in the 1950s and 1960s for Bock's label. The Byrds recorded at the same studio and heard Shankar's music, which led them to incorporate some of its elements in theirs, introducing the genre to their friend George Harrison of the Beatles. Harrison became interested in Indian classical music, bought a *sitar* and used it to record the song "Norwegian Wood (This Bird Has Flown)". This led to Indian music being used by other musicians and created the raga rock trend.

Harrison met Shankar in London in June 1966 and visited India later that year for six weeks to study *sitar* under Shankar in Srinagar. During the visit, a documentary film about

Shankar named *Raga* was shot by Howard Worth, and released in 1971. Shankar's association with Harrison greatly increased Shankar's popularity and Ken Hunt of Allmusic would state that Shankar had become "the most famous Indian musician on the planet" by 1966. In 1967, he performed at the Monterey Pop Festival and won a Grammy Award for Best Chamber Music Performance for *West Meets East*, a collaboration with Yehudi Menuhin. The same year, the Beatles won the Grammy Award for Album of the Year for *Sgt. Pepper's Lonely Hearts Club Band*, which included "Within You Without You" by Harrison, a song that was influenced by Indian classical music. Shankar opened a Western branch of the Kinnara School of Music in Los Angeles, California, in May 1967, and published an autobiography, *My Music, My Life*, in 1968. In 1968, he scored for the movie *Charly*. He performed at the Woodstock Festival in August 1969, and found he disliked the venue. In the 1970s Shankar distanced himself from the hippie movement.

1970–2012: International Career

In October 1970 Shankar became chair of the department of Indian music of the California Institute of the Arts after previously teaching at the City College of New York, the University of California, Los Angeles, and being guest lecturer at other colleges and universities, including the Ali Akbar College of Music. In late 1970, the London Symphony Orchestra invited Shankar to compose a concerto with *sitar*. *Concerto for Sitar and Orchestra* was performed with André Previn as conductor and Shankar playing the *sitar*. Hans Neuhoff of *Musik in Geschichte und Gegenwart* has criticised the usage of the orchestra in this concert as "amateurish". George Harrison organized the charity Concert for Bangladesh in August 1971, in which Shankar participated. After the musicians had tuned up on stage for over a minute, the crowd broke into applause, to which the amused Shankar responded: "If you like our tuning so much, I hope you will enjoy the playing more." Although interest in Indian music had decreased in the early 1970s, the concert album became one of the best-selling recordings to feature the genre and won Shankar a second Grammy Award.

During the 1970s, Shankar and Harrison worked together again, recording *Shankar Family & Friends* in 1973 and touring North America the following year to a mixed response after Shankar had toured Europe with the Harrison-sponsored Music Festival from India. The demanding schedule weakened Shankar, and he suffered a heart attack in Chicago in November 1974, causing him to miss a portion of the tour. In his absence, Shankar's sister-in-law, singer Lakshmi Shankar, conducted the touring orchestra. The touring band visited the White House on invitation of John Gardner Ford, son of U.S. President Gerald Ford. Shankar toured and taught for the remainder of the 1970s and the 1980s and released his second concerto, *Raga Mala*, conducted by Zubin Mehta, in 1981. Shankar was nominated for an Academy Award for Best Original Music Score for his work on the 1982 movie *Gandhi*, but lost to John Williams' *E.T.*

He served as a member of the Rajya Sabha, the upper chamber of the Parliament of India, from 12 May 1986 to 11 May 1992, after being nominated by Indian Prime Minister Rajiv Gandhi. Shankar composed the dance drama *Ghanashyam* in 1989. His liberal views on musical cooperation led him to contemporary composer Philip Glass, with whom he released an album, *Passages*, in 1990.

37

Amartya Kumar Sen

Amartya Kumar Sen (born 3 November 1933), is an Indian economist who since 1972 has taught and worked in the United Kingdom and the United States. He has made contributions to welfare economics, social choice theory, economic and social justice, economic theories of famines, and indexes of the measure of well-being of citizens of developing countries. He was awarded the Nobel Memorial Prize in Economic Sciences in 1998 for his work in welfare economics.

He is currently the Thomas W. Lamont University Professor and Professor of Economics and Philosophy at Harvard University. He is also a senior fellow at the Harvard Society of Fellows, distinguished fellow of All Souls College, Oxford and a Fellow of Trinity College, Cambridge, where he previously served as Master from 1998 to 2004. Sen's books have been translated into more than thirty languages over a period of forty years.

Early life and education

Sen was born in Santiniketan, West Bengal, India, to Ashutosh Sen and his wife Amita. Rabindranath Tagore is said to have given Amartya Sen his name. Sen's family was originally from Wari, Dhaka, in present-day Bangladesh, and both of his parents were born in Manikganj, Dhaka. His father Ashutosh Sen was a professor of chemistry at Dhaka University who moved with his family to West Bengal during the Partition of India and worked at various educational institutions, eventually becoming Chairman of the West Bengal Public Service Commission. Sen's mother Amita Sen was the daughter of Kshiti Mohan Sen, a scholar and close associate of Rabindranath Tagore who became the second Vice Chancellor of Visva-Bharati University. She was also first cousin (through her father) of Sukumar Sen, ICS the First-Chief Election Commissioner of India, Ashoke Kumar Sen, M.P. and sometime Union Law Minister, and Amiya Sen, a distinguished Barrister.

Sen began his high-school education at St Gregory's School in Dhaka in 1941. After his family moved to West Bengal following the partition of the country in 1947, he studied at Visva-Bharati University school and then at Presidency College, Kolkata, where he earned a First Class First in his B.A. (Honours) in Economics (awarded by the University of Calcutta). The same year, 1953, he moved to Trinity College, Cambridge, where he earned a First Class (Starred First) MA (Honours) in 1956. He was elected President of the Cambridge Majlis. While still an undergraduate student of Trinity, he met the economist Prasanta Chandra Mahalanobis, the principal architect of India's (later much reviled) economic policy based on the soviet model of nationalized heavy industry. Mahalanobis, who was much impressed with Sen, returned to Calcutta and immediately recommended the brilliant Cambridge undergraduate to Triguna Sen, the then Education Minister of West Bengal, who had been instrumental in turning the National Council into the new Jadavpur University.

After Sen completed his Tripos examination and enrolled for a PhD in Economics at Trinity College, Cambridge, he returned to India on a two-year leave. Triguna Sen immediately appointed him Professor and founding Head of Department of Economics at Jadavpur University, Calcutta, something quite extraordinary because Sen had hardly even begun his PhD studies at Trinity and was 23 years of age. This still remains the youngest age at which anybody has been appointed to a professorship or a head of departmentship in India. During his tenure at Jadavpur University, Sen had economic methodologist A.K. Dasgupta, who was then teaching at Benares Hindu University, as his supervisor. After two full years of full-time teaching in Jadavpur, Sen returned to Cambridge in 1959 to complete his PhD.

Subsequently, Sen won a Prize Fellowship at Trinity College, which gave him four years of freedom to do anything he liked. He took the radical decision of studying philosophy. That proved to be of immense help to his later research. Sen related the importance of studying philosophy thus: "The broadening of my studies into philosophy was important for me not just because some of my main areas of interest in economics relate quite closely to philosophical disciplines (for example, social choice theory makes intense use of mathematical logic and also draws on moral philosophy, and so does the study of inequality and deprivation), but also because I found philosophical studies very rewarding on their own."[6] However, his deep interest in philosophy can be dated back to his college days in Presidency, when he both read books on philosophy and debated philosophical themes.

To Sen, Cambridge was like a battlefield. There were major debates between supporters of Keynesian economics on the one hand, and the "neo-classical" economists skeptical of Keynes, on the other. Sen was lucky to have close relations with economists on both sides of the divide. Meanwhile, thanks to its good "practice" of democratic and tolerant social choice, Sen's own college, Trinity College, was an oasis very much removed from the discord. However, because of a lack of enthusiasm for social choice theory whether in Trinity or

Cambridge, Sen had to choose a quite different subject for his Ph.D. thesis, after completing his B.A. He submitted his thesis on "The Choice of Techniques" in 1959 under the supervision of the "brilliant but vigorously intolerant" post-Keynesian, Joan Robinson. According to Quentin Skinner, Sen was a member of the secret society Cambridge Apostles during his time at Cambridge.

Professorships

Between 1960 and 1961, Sen was a visiting Professor at Massachusetts Institute of Technology. He was also a visiting Professor at UC-Berkeley, Stanford, and Cornell. He has taught economics also at the University of Calcutta and at the Delhi School of Economics (where he completed his *magnum opus* Collective Choice and Social Welfare in 1970), where he was a Professor from 1961 to 1972, a period which is considered to be a Golden Period in the history of DSE. In 1972, he joined the London School of Economics as a Professor of Economics where he taught until 1977. From 1977 to 1986 he taught at the University of Oxford, where he was first a Professor of Economics at Nuffield College, Oxford and then the Drummond Professor of Political Economy and a Fellow of All Souls College, Oxford. In 1986, he joined Harvard as the Thomas W. Lamont University Professor of Economics. In 1998 he was appointed as Master of Trinity College, Cambridge. In January 2004, Sen returned to Harvard. He is also a contributor to the Eva Colorni Trust at the former London Guildhall University. In June 2005 he received an Honorary Doctor of Economics, politics and international institutions degree from University of Pavia.

Membership and associations

He has served as president of the Econometric Society (1984), the International Economic Association (1986–1989), the Indian Economic Association (1989) and the American Economic Association (1994). He has also served as President of the Development Studies Association (1980–1982) and is an Honorary Vice-President of the Royal Economic Society, which he has been since 1988.

He presently serves as Honorary Director of Center for Human and Economic Development Studies at Peking University in China and is also a board council member of the Prime Minister of India's Global Advisory Council of Overseas Indians.

Research

Sen's papers in the late 1960s and early 1970s helped develop the theory of social choice, which first came to prominence in the work by the American economist Kenneth Arrow, who, while working at the RAND Corporation, had most famously shown that all voting rules, be they majority rule or two thirds-majority or status quo, must inevitably conflict with some basic democratic norm. Sen's contribution to the literature was to show under what conditions Arrow's impossibility theorem would indeed come to pass as well as to extend and enrich the theory of social choice, informed by his interests in history of economic thought and philosophy.

In 1981, Sen published *Poverty and Famines: An Essay on Entitlement and Deprivation* (1981), a book in which he argued that famine occurs not only from a lack of food, but from inequalities built into mechanisms for distributing food. Sen also argued that the Bengal famine was caused by an urban economic boom that raised food prices, thereby causing millions of rural workers to starve to death when their wages did not keep up.

Sen's interest in famine stemmed from personal experience. As a nine-year-old boy, he witnessed the Bengal famine of 1943, in which three million people perished. This staggering loss of life was unnecessary, Sen later concluded. He presents data that there was an adequate food supply in Bengal at the time, but particular groups of people including rural landless labourers and urban service providers like haircutters did not have the monetary means to acquire food as its price rose rapidly due to factors that include British military acquisition, panic buying, hoarding, and price gouging, all connected to the war in the region. In *Poverty and Famines*, Sen revealed that in many cases of famine, food supplies were not significantly reduced. In Bengal, for example, food production, while down on the previous year, was higher than in previous non-famine years. Thus, Sen points to a number of social and economic factors, such as declining wages, unemployment, rising food prices, and poor food-distribution systems. These issues led to starvation among certain groups in society. His capabilities approach focuses on positive freedom, a person's actual ability to be or do something, rather than on negative freedom approaches, which are common in economics and simply focuses on non-interference. In the Bengal famine, rural laborers' negative freedom to buy food was not affected. However, they still starved because they were not positively free to do anything, they did not have the functioning of nourishment, nor the capability to escape morbidity.

In addition to his important work on the causes of famines, Sen's work in the field of development economics has had considerable influence in the formulation of the *Human Development Report*, published by the United Nations Development Programme. This annual publication that ranks countries on a variety of economic and social indicators owes much to the contributions by Sen among other social choice theorists in the area of economic measurement of poverty and inequality.

Sen's revolutionary contribution to development economics and social indicators is the concept of 'capability' developed in his article "Equality of What". He argues that governments should be measured against the concrete capabilities of their citizens. This is because top-down development will always trump human rights as long as the definition of terms remains in doubt (is a 'right' something that must be provided or something that simply cannot be taken away?). For instance, in the United States citizens have a hypothetical "right" to vote. To Sen, this concept is fairly empty. In order for citizens to have a capacity to vote, they first must have "functionings." These "functionings" can range from the very broad, such as the availability of education, to the very specific, such as transportation to the polls. Only when such barriers are removed can the citizen truly be said to act out of personal choice. It is up to the individual society to make the list of minimum capabilities guaranteed by that society. For an example of the "capabilities approach" in practice, see Martha Nussbaum's *Women and Human Development*.

He wrote a controversial article in *The New York Review of Books* entitled "More Than 100 Million Women Are Missing" (see Missing women of Asia), analyzing the mortality impact of unequal rights between the genders in the developing world, particularly Asia. Other studies, such as one by Emily Oster, have argued that this is an overestimation, though Oster has recanted some of her conclusions.

38

Gopinath Bordoloi

Gopinath Bordoloi (1890–1950) was the first Prime Minister of undivided Assam before independence and later Chief Minister of the Indian state of Assam, and also a leading Indian independence activist. He was a follower of the Gandhian principle of non-violence as a political tool. Due to his unselfish dedication towards Assam and its people, the then Governor of Assam Jayram Das Doulatram conferred him with the title "Lokapriya" (loved by all).

Early Life and Education

Gopinath Bordoloi was born on 6 June 1890 at Raha. His father was Buddheswar Bordoloi and mother Praneswari Bordoloi. He lost his mother when he was only 12 years old. He got admitted in Cotton College after passing matriculation in 1907. He passed I.A. in 1st Div. In 1909 and took admission in the renowned Scottish Church College, Calcutta and graduated in 1911. He then passed M.A. from Calcutta University in 1914. He studied Law for three years but came back to Guwahati without sitting in the final examination. Then on request of Tarun Ram Phukan, he took up the temporary job as Headmaster of Sonaram High School. During that period, he sat and passed in the Law examination and started practising in 1917 in Guwahati.

Political Life

Assam Association was the only political organisation of Assam in that period. Assam Congress was formed in 1922 as a branch of the Indian National Congress. Gopinath Bordoloi's political life started when he joined the Indian National Congress as a volunteer in that year. He actively participated in the fight for independence. He was arrested in 1922 due to active participation in the Non-co-operation movement and was put in jail for 1-year. When the movement was called off following Chauri Chaura incident, he went back to practising law. From 1930 to 1933 he kept himself away from political activity and got involved in various social works after becoming member of Guwahati Municipal Board and Local Board. In addition, he was constantly demanding a separate University and High Court for Assam.

In 1935 Government of India Act was articulated with a view to form British India. Congress decided to participate in the Regional Assembly election in 1936. They won 38 seats and became the party with majority in Assembly, but due to a dubious law meant to reduce the power of Ministers and the Cabinet, they decided to remain as opposition party instead of forming the government. Gopinath Bordoloi was elected as the leader of the opposition party. With the support of other parties apart from Congress Md. Sadulla formed the Cabinet of Ministers. Congress party was gaining people's support as the government remained unaware of the basic problems of Assam. Md. Sadulla Cabinet Ministers resigned in September,1938. Then the Governor invited Gopinath Bordoloi to form the government and accordingly they took oath in 21 September.

The reasons of Gopinath Bordoloi becoming Prime Minister of undivided Assam were his political prowess, superb personality, truthfulness and behaviour which attracted not only his colleagues but also people of various communities. Congress got recognition as a powerful political party in Assam by virtue of his ability and intelligence. His contributions as Chief Ministers were mainly to stop Land Tax, stop giving lands to migrant Muslims to secure the right of indigenous people etc.

The new government didn't last long as World War II began in 1939. Gopinath Bordoloi's Cabinet resigned in 1940 following appeal by Mohandas K. Gandhi. He was arrested again in December 1940. However, he was released before completing one year in jail due to ill health. When Quit India movement was launched in August 1942, Congress party was declared outlawed and all leaders were arrested.

In the meantime Md. Sadulla formed the government with the promise to help British in World War II and indulged again in communial activities. Gopinath Bordoloi was released from jail in 1944 and he straightaway started opposing the government with the help of other leaders. Md. Sadulla offered him to discuss the matters. An agreement was reached which included immediate release of all political prisoners, removing the ban on procession or meeting, correcting the process of rehabilitation of migrant Muslims etc.

In July 1945, British announced their decision to form a new constitution for India after holding the central and regional election. Congress too participated in the election in 1946 and they became the major party in Assembly with 61 seats out of 108. They formed the Government and Gopinath Bordoloi was made Prime Minister unanimously.

Cabinet commission and Bordoloi's role

British Government formed a Cabinet Commission in 1946 to discuss the demands for Indian Independence. The members held meetings with Congress and Muslim League in Shimla and Delhi. Their plan included grouping of states into 3 categories for selecting the candidates to form the constitutional body with Assam and Bengal in third group. Gopinath Bordoloi sensed the ominous sign for Assam in the plan as the inclusion would mean the local representative will become minority in comparison to Bengal. That would be devastating for rights of people of Assam.

The Assam Pradesh Congress committee decided to go against the grouping plan. Gopinath Bordoloi told the Indian National Congress working committee, Cabinet committee and Viceroy that the representative of Assam will form the Constitution of Assam themselves and will decide whether to join the group or not among themselves. Subsequently, the Cabinet commission announced that the grouping will be mandatory for every state and they may later withdraw from the group if they want. This further complicated the situation. Bordoloi met the National Congress leaders to discuss it with no result. He then with Assam Congress Committee decided to start mass agitation in Assam. After that only the National Congress working committee advised them to pass a unanimous decision in Assembly. Later, the members of the Assembly suggested a working formula in which ten representative from Assam would form their own constitution without joining any group and would merge with national committee to form the Indian constitution.

Jawaharlal Nehru and Muslim League were ignorant enough to this grim situation and joined hands to implement the grouping plan. Gopinath Bordoloi requested Mohandas Gandhi for suggestion and the later advised him to continue opposing the grouping vehemently.

In 1947, Lord Mountbeten took over as new Viceroy. He held separate meeting with Muslim League, Congress and Mahatma Gandhi. They decided to go for Partition as a permanent solution instead of grouping. India and Pakistan became separate independent countries.

Thus Gopinath Bordoloi played a major role in securing the future of Assam which would have been included in East Pakistan otherwise. Whether any other leader could have shown the light other than him during that crisis period is in doubt.

Contribution as Chief Minister

After India's Independence, he worked closely with Sardar Vallabhbhai Patel to secure the sovereignty of Assam against China on the one hand and East Pakistan on the other. He also helped to organise the rehabilitation of millions of Hindu refugees who had fled East Pakistan due to widespread violence and intimidation in the aftermath of Partition. His work formed the basis for ensuring communal harmony, democracy and stability which effectively kept Assam secure and progressive right up to the 1971 war over East Pakistan's independence. He was instrumental in establishing Guwahati University, High Court of Assam, Assam Medical College, Assam Veterinary College etc. Gopinath Bordoloi was also a gifted writer. He wrote several books like ***Annasaktiyog***, ***Shreeramachandra***, ***Hajrat Mohammad***, and ***Budhhadeb*** while in jail. For all his life he was a stern believer in Gandhian principles. He led a simple life in spite of being a Chief Minister. He died on 5 August 1950.

He was awarded the Bharat Ratna posthumously in 1999.

39

Lata Mangeshkar

Lata Mangeshkar (born 28 September 1929) is an Indian singer, and occasional music-composer. She is one of the best-known and most respected playback singers in India. Mangeshkar's career started in 1942 and has spanned over seven decades. She has recorded songs for over a thousand Hindi films and has sung songs in over thirty-six regional Indian languages and foreign languages, though primarily in Marathi and Hindi. She is the elder sister of singers Asha Bhosle, Hridaynath Mangeshkar, Usha Mangeshkar and Meena Mangeshkar. She is the second vocalist to have ever been awarded the Bharat Ratna, India's highest civilian honour.

Mangeshkar was featured in the *Guinness Book of World Records* from 1974 to 1991 for having made the most recordings in the world. The claim was that she had recorded approximately 25,000 solo, duet, and chorus-backed songs in 20 Indian languages between 1948 to 1974. The category was removed in 1991 and re-introduced in 2011. In 2011 *Guinness* officially acknowledged Mangeshkar's sister Asha Bhosle as the most recorded artist in music history.

Early Life

Lata Mangeshkar was born in a Marathi-speaking Gomantak Maratha family, in the princely state of Sangli, part of the Maharashtra. Her father, Pandit Deenanath Mangeshkar was a classical singer and theater actor. Her mother Shevanti (Shudhamati) who was from Thalner, Maharashtra, was Deenanath's second wife. The family's last name used to be Hardikar; Deenanath changed it to Mangeshkar in order to identify his family with his native town, Mangeshi in Goa. Lata was named "Hema" at her birth. Her parents later renamed her Lata after a female character, Latika, in one of her father's plays, *BhaawBandhan*. Lata is the eldest child of her parents. Meena, Asha, Usha and Hridaynath are her siblings in sequence.

Mangeshkar took her first lessons from her father. At the age of five, she started to work as an actress in her father's musical plays (*Sangeet Natak* in Marathi). On the first day in the school, she started teaching songs to other children. When the teacher stopped her, she was so angry that she stopped going to the school. Other sources cite that she left school because they would not allow her to bring Asha with her, as she would often bring her younger sister with her.

Singing Career

In 1942, when Mangeshkar was 13, her father died of heart disease. Master Vinayak (Vinayak Damodar Karnataki), the owner of Navyug Chitrapat movie company and a close friend of the Mangeshkar family, took care of them. He helped Lata get started in a career as a singer and actress.

Mangeshkar sang the song "Naachu Yaa Gade", Khelu Saari Mani Haus Bhaari" which was composed by Sadashivrao Nevrekar for Vasant Joglekar's Marathi movie *Kiti Hasaal* (1942), but the song was dropped from the final cut. Vinayak gave her a small role in Navyug Chitrapat's Marathi movie *Pahili Mangalaa-gaur* (1942), in which she sang "Natali Chaitraachi Navalaai" which was composed by Dada

Chandekar. Her first Hindi song was "Mata Ek Sapoot Ki Duniya Badal De Tu" for the Marathi film, *Gajaabhaau* (1943). Mangeshkar moved to Mumbai in 1945 when Master Vinayak's company moved its headquarters there. She started taking lessons in Hindustani classical music from Ustad Amanat Ali Khan . She sang "Paa Lagoon Kar Jori" for Vasant Joglekar's Hindi-language movie *Aap Ki Seva Mein* (1946), which was composed by Datta Davjekar. The dance in the film was performed by Rohini Bhate who later became a famous classical dancer. Mangeshkar and her sister Asha played minor roles in Vinayak's first Hindi-language movie, *Badi Maa* (1945). In that movie, Lata also sang a bhajan, "Maata Tere Charnon Mein." She was introduced to music director Vasant Desai during the recording of Vinayak's second Hindi-language movie, *Subhadra* (1946).

Following the partition of India in 1947, Ustad Amanat Ali Khan migrated to newly formed Pakistan, so Mangeshkar started to learn classical music under Amanat Khan Devaswale. Pandit Tulsidas Sharma, a pupil of Ustad Bade Ghulam Ali Khan, also trained her.

After Vinayak's death in 1948, music director Ghulam Haider mentored her as a singer. Haider introduced Mangeshkar to producer Sashadhar Mukherjee, who was working then on the movie *Shaheed* (1948), but Mukherjee dismissed Mangeshkar's voice as "too thin." An annoyed Haider responded that in the coming years the producers and the directors would "fall at Lata's feet" and "beg her" to sing in their movies. Haider gave Lata her first major break with the song "Dil Mera Toda," from the movie *Majboor* (1948).

Initially, Mangeshkar is said to have imitated the acclaimed singer Noor Jehan, but later she developed her own style of singing. Lyrics of songs in Hindi movies are primarily composed by Urdu poets and contain a higher proportion of Urdu words, including the dialogue. Actor Dilip Kumar once made a mildly disapproving remark about Mangeshkar's Maharashtrian accent while singing Hindi/Urdu songs; so for a period of time, Lata took lessons in Urdu from an Urdu teacher named Shafi.

One of her first major hits was "Aayega Aanewaala," a song in the movie *Mahal* (1949), which was composed by music director Khemchand Prakash and lip-synced on screen by actress Madhubala.

1950s

In the 1950s, Mangeshkar sang songs composed by various music directors of the period, including Anil Biswas (in films such as Tarana and Heer), Shankar Jaikishan, Naushad Ali, S. D. Burman, Pandit Husan Lal Bhagat Ram (in films like Bari Behan, Meena Bazaar, Afsana, Aadhi Raat, Ansoo, Chhoti Bhabi, Adal-e-Jehangir) C. Ramchandra, Hemant Kumar, Salil Chowdhury, Khayyam, Ravi, Sajjad Hussain, Roshan, Kalyanji-Anandji, Vasant Desai, Sudhir Phadke, Hansraj Behl, Madan Mohan, and Usha Khanna. She made her debut in Tamil playback singing with Vanaradham in 1956 (Uran Khotala dubbed in Tamil) with Tamil song Enthan Kannalan picturised on Nimmi in the dubbed version composed by Naushad.

Mangeshkar sang many raga-based songs for Naushad in movies such as *Baiju Bawra* (1952), *Mughal-E-Azam* (1960), and *Kohinoor* (1960). *Ae Chorre Ki Jaat Badi Bewafa*, a duet with G. M. Durrani, was her first song for composer, Naushad. The duo, Shankar-Jaikishan, chose Mangeshkar for *Aag*, *Aah* (1953), *Shree 420* (1955), and *Chori Chori* (1956). Before 1957, composer S. D. Burman chose Mangeshkar as the leading female singer for his musical scores in *Sazaa* (1951), *House No. 44* (1955), and *Devdas* (1955). However a rift developed between Lata and Burman in 1957, and Lata did not sing Burman's compositions again until 1962.

Mangeshkar won a Filmfare Award for Best Female Playback Singer for Salil Chowdhury's composition "Aaja Re Pardesi," from *Madhumati* (1958). In the early fifties, Lata Mangeshkar's association with C. Ramchandra produced songs in movies such as Anarkali, Albela, Asha, Pehli Jhhalak, Shin Shinkai Bublaa Boo, Azad and Amardeep. For Madan Mohan, she performed for films like Adalat, Railway Platform, Dekh Kabira Roya and Chacha Zindabad.

1960s

Mangeshkar's song "Pyar Kiya To Darna Kya" from *Mughal-e-Azam* (1960), composed by Naushad and picturized on Madhubala, still remains famous . The Hawaiian-themed number "Ajeeb Dastaan Hai Yeh" from *Dil Apna Aur Preet Parai* (1960) was composed by Shankar Jaikishan and picturized on Meena Kumari.

In 1961, Mangeshkar recorded two popular bhajans, "Allah Tero Naam" and "Prabhu Tero Naam", for Burman's assistant, Jaidev. In 1962, she was awarded her second Filmfare Award for the song "Kahin Deep Jale Kahin Dil" from *Bees Saal Baad*, composed by Hemant Kumar.

On 27 January 1963, against the backdrop of the Sino-Indian War, Mangeshkar sang the patriotic song "Aye Mere Watan Ke Logo" (literally, "Oh, People of My Country") in the presence of Jawaharlal Nehru, the then Prime Minister of India. The song, composed by C. Ramchandra and written by Kavi Pradeep, is said to have brought the Prime Minister to tears.

In 1963, Mangeshkar returned to collaboration with S. D. Burman. She also sang for R. D. Burman's very first film *Chhote Nawaab* and later for his films such as *Bhoot Bangla* (1965), *Pati Patni* (1966), *Baharon ke Sapne* (1967) and *Abhilasha* (1969). She also recorded several popular songs for S. D. Burman, including "Aaj Phir Jeene Ki Tamanna Hai", "Gata Rahe Mera Dil" (duet with Kishore Kumar) and "Piya Tose" from *Guide* (1965), and "Hothon Pe Aisi Baat" from *Jewel Thief* (1967).

During the 1960s, Lata Mangeshkar continued her association with Madan Mohan which included the songs "Aap Ki Nazron Ne Samjha" from *Anpadh* (1962), "Lag Ja

Gale" and "Naina Barse Rim Jhim" from *Woh Kaun Thi?* (1964), "Woh Chup Rahen To" from *Jahan Ara* (1964), "Tu Jahan Jahan Chalega" from *Mera Saaya* (1966) and "Teri Aankho Ke Siva" from *Chirag* (1969).

The 1960s also witnessed the beginning of Mangeshkar's association with Laxmikant-Pyarelal, the music directors for whom she sang the most popular songs in her career. Starting in 1963, Laxmikant-Pyarelal association with Lata Mangeshkar grew stronger over the years. Lata Mangeshkar sang over 700 songs for the composer duo over a period of 35 long years, most of which became huge hits. She sang for *Parasmani* (1963), *Mr. X in Bombay* (1964), *Aaye Din Bahar Ke* (1966), *Milan* (1967), *Anita* (1967) *Shagird (1968),* Mere Hamdam Mere Dost *(1968),* Intaquam *(1969),* Do Raaste *(1969) and* Jeene Ki Raah *for which she got her 3rd Filmfare Award.*

She also sang several playback songs for Marathi films, composed by Marathi music directors including Hridaynath Mangeshkar, Vasant Prabhu, Srinivas Khale, Sudhir Phadke and herself (under the name *Anandghan*). During the 1960s and 1970s, she also sang several Bengali songs, composed by music directors like Salil Chowdhury and Hemant Kumar. She also made her Kannada debut in 1967 for the film *Krantiveera Sangolli Rayanna* by recording two songs for the music director Lakshman Berlekar. The song "Bellane Belagayithu" was received well and appreciated.

In this period Lata Mangeshkar has recorded duets with Mukesh, Manna Dey, Mahendra Kapoor, Mohammed Rafi, and Kishore Kumar. For a brief period during the 1960s, she was not on good terms with Mohammed Rafi over the issue of royalty payments to singers. Mangeshkar wanted Rafi to back her in demanding a half-share from the five percent song royalty that the film's producer conceded to select composers. But Rafi took a diametrically opposite view, and believed that a playback singer's claim on the filmmaker ended with the payment of the agreed fee for the song. This led to tensions between the two. After an argument during the recording of the song *Tasveer Teri Dil Mein* (Maya, 1961), the two refused to sing with each other. The music director Jaikishan later negotiated a reconciliation between the two.

1970s

In 1972, Meena Kumari's last film, *Pakeezah*, was released. It featured popular songs including "Chalte Chalte" and "Inhi Logon Ne" sung by Lata Mangeshkar, and composed by Ghulam Mohammed. She recorded many popular songs for S. D. Burman's last films, including "Rangeela Re" from *Prem Pujari* (1970), "Khilte Hain Gul Yahaan" from *Sharmeelee* (1971), and "Piya Bina" from *Abhimaan* (1973). She recorded many popular songs for Madan Mohan's last films, including *Dastak* (1970), *Heer Raanjha* (1970), *Dil Ki Rahen* (1973), *Hindustan Ki Kasam* (1973), *Hanste Zakhm* (1973), *Mausam* (1975) and *Laila Majnu* (1976).

Lata Mangeshkar's most notable songs in 1970s were composed by Laxmikant-Pyarelal (Laxmi-Pyare) and Rahul Dev Burman. She recorded several songs composed by Laxmi-Pyare in 1960s and 1970s, many of them written by the lyricist Anand Bakshi. She also recorded many hit songs with Rahul Dev Burman in the films *Amar Prem* (1972), *Caravan* (1971), *Kati Patang* (1971), and *Aandhi* (1975). The two are noted for their songs with the lyricists Majrooh Sultanpuri, Anand Bakshi and Gulzar.

In 1973, she won the National Film Award for Best Female Playback Singer for the song "Beeti Na Bitai" from the film *Parichay*, composed by R. D. Burman, and written by Gulzar. In 1974, she sang her only Malayalam song "Kadali Chenkadali" for the film *Nellu*, composed by Salil Chowdhury, and written by Vayalar Ramavarma. In 1975, she again won the national award, this time for the song "Roothe Roothe Piya" from the film *Kora Kagaz*, composed by Kalyanji Anandji.

From 1970s onwards, Lata Mangeshkar has also staged many concerts in India and abroad, including several charity concerts. Her first concert overseas was at the Royal Albert

Hall, London, in 1974. She also released an album of Mirabai's bhajans, *Chala Vaahi Des*, composed by her brother Hridaynath Mangeshkar. Some of the bhajans in the album include "Saanware Rang Raachi" and "Ud Jaa Re Kaaga". In the early 1970s, she released other non-film albums, such as her collection of Ghalib ghazals, an album of Marathi folk songs (koḷi-geete), an album of Ganesh aartis (all composed by her brother Hridaynath) and an album of *abhangs* of Sant Tukaram composed by Shrinivas Khale.

In 1978, Raj Kapoor direct Satyam Shivam Sundaram Lata Mangeshkar lends her voice to the main theme song "Satyam Shivam Sundaram", which was among the chart-toppers of the year. The story of was inspired by Lata Mangeshkar reveals Raj Kapoor's daughter Ritu Nanda in her latest book.

I visualised the story of a man falling for a woman with an ordinary countenance but a golden voice and wanted to cast Lata Mangeshkar in the role. The book quotes Raj Kapoor as saying.

In late 1970s and early 1980s, she worked with the children of composers she had earlier worked with. Some of these composers included Rahul Dev Burman (son of Sachin Dev Burman), Rajesh Roshan (son of Roshan), Anu Malik (son of Sardar Malik), and Anand-Milind (sons of Chitragupt). She also sang many songs in Assamese language and had a very good relationship with Dada Saheb Phalke award winner singing legend Late Bhupen Hazarika. She sang many songs under his guidance and in *Rudaali* the song "Dil hoom hoom kare" made a highestrecord of sales that year.

1980s onwards

From 1980s onwards, Lata Mangeshkar worked with music directors including Shiv-Hari in *Silsila* (1981), *Faasle* (1985), *Vijay* (1988) and *Chandni* (1989). Ram Laxman in *Ustadi Ustad Se* (1981), *Bezubaan* (1982), *Woh Jo Hasina* (1983), *Ye Kesa Farz* (1985) and *Maine Pyar Kiya* (1989) which was a musical hit. In 1988, Mangeshkar made a come back to Tamil films with two back to back renditions "Aaraaro Aaraaro" and "Valai Osai" for composer Ilayaraja's compositions for the films *Aanand* and *Sathya* respectively.

In June 1985, the United Way of Greater Toronto invited the Lata Mangeshkar to perform at Maple Leaf Gardens. She filled 12,000 seats, raising $150,000 for the charity.

During the 1990s, she recorded with music directors including Anand-Milind, Nadeem-Shravan, Jatin Lalit, Dilip Sen-Sameer Sen, Uttam Singh, Anu Malik, Aadesh Shrivastava and A. R. Rahman. She recorded some non-film songs, including ghazals with Jagjit Singh. She has also sung with S. P. Balasubrahmanyam, Udit Narayan, Hariharan, Kumar Sanu, Suresh Wadkar, Mohammed Aziz, Abhijeet Bhattacharya, Roop Kumar Rathod, Vinod Rathod, Gurdas Maan and Sonu Nigam.

In 1990, Mangeshkar launched her own production house for Hindi movies which produced the Gulzar-directed movie *Lekin...*. She won her third National Film Award for Best Female Playback Singer for her rendition of the song "Yaara Sili Sili" from the film, which was composed by her brother Hridaynath.

Mangeshkar has sung for almost all the Yash Chopra films and films from his production house Yash Raj Films at that time, including *Chandni* (1989), *Lamhe* (1991), *Darr* (1993), *Yeh Dillagi* (1994), *Dilwale Dulhania Le Jayenge* (1995), *Dil To Pagal Hai* (1997) and later on *Mohabbatein* (2000), *Mujhse Dosti Karoge!* (2002) and *Veer-Zaara* (2004).

During 1990, Mangeshkar records with Ram Laxman in *Patthar Ke Phool* (1991), *100 Days* (1991), *Mehboob Mere Mehboob* (1992), *Saatwan Aasman* (1992), *I Love You (1992 film)* (1992), *Dil Ki Baazi* (1993), *Antim Nyay* (1993), *The Melody of Love* (1993), *The Law* (1994), *Hum Aapke Hain Koun..!* (1994), *Megha* (1996), *Lav Kush* (1997), *Manchala* (1999), and *Dulhan Banoo Main Teri* (1999).

A. R. Rahman recorded a few songs with Mangeshkar during this period, including “Jiya Jale” (*Dil Se..*), “Khamoshiyan Gungunane Lagin” (*One 2 Ka 4*), “Ek Tu Hi Bharosa” (*Pukar*), “Pyaara Sa Gaon” (*Zubeidaa*),”So Gaye Hain” (*Zubeidaa*) “Lukka chuppi” (*Rang De Basanti*) and “O Paalanhaare” (*Lagaan*). She made an appearance in the film *Pukar* singing this song.

In 1994, Lata Mangeshkar released *Shraddanjali-My Tribute To The Immortals*. The special feature of the album is that Lata offer her tributes to immortal singers of the time by rendering a few of their songs in her own voice. There are songs of K.L. Saigal, Rafi, Hemant Kumar, Mukesh, Punkaj Mallick and Kishore Kumar, Geeta dutt, Zohrabai, Amirbai, Parul Ghosh and Kanan Devi.

Mangeshkar sang both, Rahul Dev Burman’s first and last song. In 1994, she sang last song *Kuch Na Kaho* for Rahul Dev Burman in 1942: A Love Story.

In 1999, Lata Eau de Parfum, a perfume brand named after her, was launched.

In 1999, Mangeshkar was nominated as a member of Rajya Sabha. However, she did not attend the Rajya Sabha sessions regularly, inviting criticism from several members of the House, including the Deputy Chairperson Najma Heptullah, Pranab Mukherjee and Shabana Azmi. She stated the reason for her absence as ill-health; it was also reported that she had not taken a salary, allowance or a house in Delhi for being a Member of Parliament.

In 2001, Lata Mangeshkar was awarded Bharat Ratna, India’s highest civilian honor. In the same year, she established the Master Deenanath Mangeshkar Hospital in Pune, managed by the Lata Mangeshkar Medical Foundation (founded by the Mangeshkar family in October 1989). In 2005, she designed a jewellery collection called Swaranjali, which was crafted by Adora, an Indian diamond export company. Five pieces from the collection raised £105,000 at a Christie's auction, and a part of the money was donated for the 2005 Kashmir earthquake relief. Also in 2001, she recorded her first Hindi song with the composer Ilaiyaraaja, for the film *Lajja*; she had earlier recorded Tamil and Telugu songs composed by Ilaiyaraaja.

Lata Mangeshkar's song "Wada Na Tod" is in the film *Eternal Sunshine of the Spotless Mind* (2004) and on the film's soundtrack.

On 21 June 2007, she released an album *Saadgi*, featuring eight ghazal-like songs written by Javed Akhtar and composed by Mayuresh Pai. On 12 April 2011, she released another album *Sarhadein: Music Beyond Boundaries* the album has a rare duet *Tera Milna Bara Acha Lage* by Lata Mangeshkar and Mehdi Hasan (written by Pakistan's Farhat Shahzad). The album features Usha Mangeshkar, Suresh Wadkar, Hariharan, Sonu Nigam, Rekha Bhardwaj and another Pakistani singer, Ghulam Ali.

After 14 years, Lata Mangeshkar recorded a song for composer Nadeem-Shravan *Kese Piya Sai Mein Kaho* for Bewafaa (2005). After *Kitne Ajeeb Rishte Hain Yahan Par* for *Page 3* (2005) and *Daata Sun Le* for *Jail* (2009), *Shamir Tandon* once again recorded a song with Lata Mangeshkar *Tere Hasne Sai Mujheko* for the film *Satrangee Parachute* (2011).

On 28 November 2012, Lata Mangeshkar launched her own music label LM Music with an album of bhajans. She sang along with younger sister Usha on the album.

Non-singing career

Music direction

Lata Mangeshkar composed music for the first time in 1955 for Marathi movie *Ram Ram Pavhane*. Later in 1960s, she composed music for following Marathi movies under the pseudonym of *Anand Ghan*.

- 1960 - *Ram Ram Pavhana*

- 1963 - *Maratha Tituka Melvava*
- 1963 - *Mohityanchi Manjula*
- 1965 - *Sadhi Manase*
- 1969 - *Tambadi Mati*

She won Maharashtra State Government's Best Music Director Award for the film *Sadhi Manase*. The song "Airanichya Deva Tula" from the same film received best song award.

Production

Lata Mangeshkar has produced four films:

- 1953 - *Vaadal* (Marathi)
- 1953 - *Jhaanjhar* (Hindi), co-produced with C. Ramchandra
- 1955 - *Kanchan* (Hindi)
- 1990 - *Lekin...* (Hindi)

Awards and recognitions

Lata Mangeshkar has won several awards and honors, including Bharat Ratna (India's Highest Civilian Award), Padma Bhushan (1969), Padma Vibhushan (1999), Dada Saheb Phalke Award (1989), Maharashtra Bhushan Award (1997), NTR National Award (1999), Bharat Ratna (2001), ANR National Award (2009), three National Film Awards, and 12 Bengal Film Journalists' Association Awards. She has also won four Filmfare Best Female Playback Awards. In 1969, she made the unusual gesture of giving up the Filmfare Best Female Playback Award, in order to promote fresh talent. She was later awarded Filmfare Lifetime Achievement Award in 1993.

In 1984, the State Government of Madhya Pradesh instituted the *Lata Mangeshkar Award* in honour of Lata Mangeshkar. The State Government of Maharashtra also instituted a Lata Mangeshkar Award in 1992.

In 1974, The Guinness Book of Records listed Lata

Mangeshkar as the most recorded artist in the history, stating that she had reportedly recorded "not less than 25,000 solo, duet and chorus backed songs in 20 Indian languages" between 1948 and 1974. Her record was contested by Mohammed Rafi, who was claimed to have sung around 28,000 songs. After Rafi's death, in its 1984 edition, the Guinness Book of World Records stated Lata Mangeshkar's name for the "Most Recordings", but also stated Rafi's claim. The later editions of Guinness Book stated that Lata Mangeshkar had sung no fewer than 30,000 songs between 1948 and 1987.

Although the entry has not been printed in Guinness editions since 1991, several sources claim that she has recorded thousands of songs, with estimates ranging up to figures as large as 50,000. However, even the earliest Guinness claim of 25,000 songs (between 1948–1974) was claimed to be exaggerated by several other sources, with one of them stating that the number of songs sung by Lata Mangeshkar in Hindi films till 1991 was found to be 5250. Mangeshkar herself stated that she does not keep a record of the number of songs recorded by her, and that she did not know from where Guinness Book editors got their information. In 2011 Asha Bhosle was officially acknowledged by *Guinness* as the most recorded artist in music history, surpassing Mangeshkar.

40

Bismillah Khan

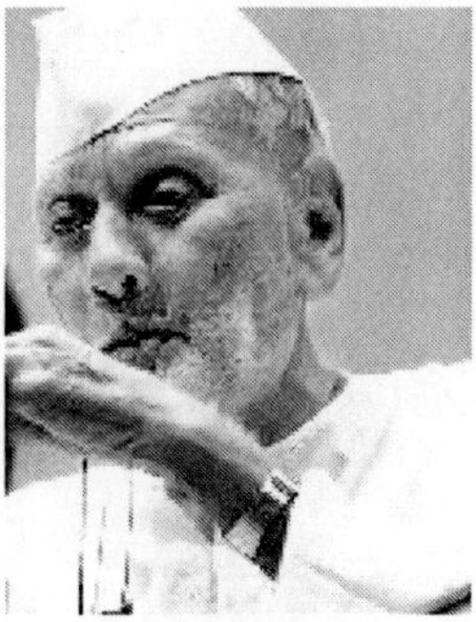

Bismillah Khan 21 March 1913 – 21 August 2006), often referred to by the honorific title Ustad, was an Indian musician credited with popularising the shehnai, a subcontinental wind instrument of the oboe class. While the shehnai had long held importance as a folk instrument played primarily during traditional ceremonies, Khan is credited with elevating its status and bringing it to the concert stage.

He was awarded India's highest civilian honour, the Bharat Ratna, in 2001, becoming the Third classical musician after M. S. Subbulakshmi and Ravi Shankar to be accorded this distinction

Early life

Bismillah Khan was born on 21 March 1913 in Dumraon, Bihar in northern India. He was the second son of Paigambar Khan and Mitthan. His parents had initially named him Qamaruddin to rhyme with their first-born son Shamshuddin. However, his grandfather, Rasool Bux Khan, the shehnai master of the court of Bhojpur, exclaimed "Bismillah!" ("In the name of Allah!") at the sight of him and thereafter he came to be known by this name.

His ancestors were court musicians and used to play in Naqqar khana in the princely states of Bhojpur, now in Bihar. His father was a shehnai player in the court of Maharaja Keshav Prasad Singh of Dumraon Estate, Bihar.

At the age of six, he moved to Varanasi.[2] He received his training under his uncle, the late Ali Baksh 'Vilayatu', a shehnai player attached to Varanasi's Vishwanath Temple.

Bihar Government has proposed setting up of a museum, a town hall-cum-library and installation of a life-size statue at his birthplce in Dumraon.

Religious Beliefs

Though a pious Shi'ite Muslim, he was also, like many Indian musicians, regardless of religion, a devotee of Saraswati, the Hindu Goddess of wisdom and arts, and often played at Hindu temples, including the famous Vishwanath Temple in Varanasi, on the banks of the river Ganga. He also performed for spiritual master Prem Rawat.

Career

Bismillah Khan was perhaps single-handedly responsible for making the shehnai a famous classical instrument. He brought the shehnai to the center stage of Indian music with his concert in the Calcutta All India Music Conference in 1937. He was credited with having almost monopoly over the instrument as he and the shehnai are almost synonyms.

Khan is one of the finest musicians in post-independent Indian classical music and one of the best examples of Hindu-Muslim unity in India. He played the shehnai to audiences across the world. He was known to be so devoted to his art form that he referred to shehnai as his begum (wife in Urdu) after his wife died. On his death, as an honour, his shehnai was buried with him. He was known for his vision of spreading peace and love through music.

"Even if the world ends, the music will still survive.

"Music has no caste."

Performances at Red Fort

Khan had the rare honor of performing at Delhi's Red Fort on the eve of India's Independence in 1947. He also performed raga Kafi from the Red Fort on the eve of India's first Republic Day ceremony, on 26 January 1950. His recital had become a cultural part of India's Independence Day celebrations, telecast on Doordarshan every year on 15 August. After the prime minister's speech from Lal Qila (the Red Fort,) in Old Delhi, Doordarshan would broadcast a live performance by the shehnai maestro. This tradition dated from the days of Pandit Nehru.

Popular Culture

Khan had a brief association with movies. He played the shehnai for Rajkumar's role of *Appanna* in the Kannada movie *Sanaadi Appanna*. He acted in *Jalsaghar*, a movie by Satyajit Ray and provided sound of shehnai in *Goonj Uthi Shehnai* (1959). Noted director Goutam Ghose directed *Sange Meel Se Mulaqat*, a documentary about the life of Khan. In the 1967 film *The Graduate*, there is a poster advertising "Bismillah Khan and the seven musicians" on a busy street of Berkeley, California.

Students

Khan seldom accepted students. He thought that if he would be able to share his knowledge it wouldn't be useful as it would only give his students a little knowledge. Some of his followers include S. Ballesh, as well as Khan's own sons, Nazim Hussain and Nayyar Hussain.

Personal Life

On 17 August 2006, Khan was taken ill and admitted to the Heritage Hospital, Varanasi for treatment. He died after four days on 21 August 2006 due to a cardiac arrest. He is survived by five daughters, three sons and a large number of grandchildren and great-grandchildren, and his adopted daughter Dr Soma Ghosh (famous Hindustani shastriya sangeet exponent)

The Government of India declared a day of national mourning on his death. His body along with a Shehnai was buried at Fatemain burial ground of old Varanasi under a neem tree with 21-gun salute from Indian Army.

Legacy

Sangeet Natak Akademi, New Delhi, instituted the 'Ustad Bismillah Khan Yuva Puraskar' in 2007, in his honour. It is given to young artists in the field of music, theatre and dance.

Awards and recognitions

Awards

- Bharat Ratna (2001)
- Fellow of Sangeet Natak Akademi (1994).
- Talar Mausiquee from Republic of Iran (1992).
- Padma Vibhushan (1980)
- Padma Bhushan (1968)
- Padma Shri (1961)
- Sangeet Natak Akademi Award (1956)
- Tansen Award by Govt. of Madhya Pradesh.
- Three medals in All India Music Conference, Calcutta (1937)
- "Best Performer" in All India Music Conference, Allahabad (1930)

Recognitions

Bismillah Khan had honorary doctorates from

- Banaras Hindu University, Varanasi
- Visva Bharati University, Santiniketan

Others include

- Was invited by the then Prime Minister of India Pandit

Jawaharlal Nehru to play shehnai on the first Independence Day (15 August 1947) in Delhi's Red Fort.

- Participated in World Exposition in Montreal
- Participated in Cannes Art Festival
- Participated in Osaka Trade Fair
- His 80th birthday was celebrated by World Music Institute in New York

Discography

Albums

- *Sanaadi Appanna* - Played shehnai for Rajkumar's role in the movie.
- *Goonj Uthi Shehnai* (1959) - Provided shehnai
- *Maestro's Choice* (February 1994)
- *Megh Malhar, Vol. 4* (the other piece in the album is by Kishori Amonkar) (September 1994)
- *Live at the Queen Elizabeth Hall* (September 2000)
- *Live in London, Vol. 2* (September 2000)

Contributing artist

- *The Rough Guide to the Music of India and Pakistan* (1996, World Music Network)

41

Bhimsen Gururaj Joshi

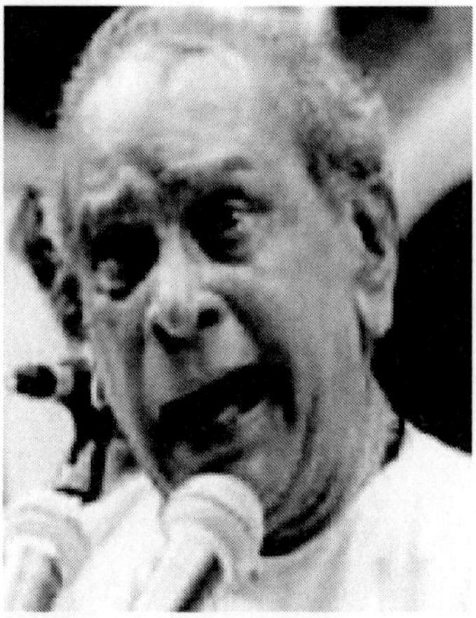

Bhimsen Gururaj Joshi February 4, 1922 – January 24, 2011) He was an Indian vocalist in the Hindustani classical tradition. He is known for the *khayal* form of singing, as well as for his popular renditions of devotional music (*bhajans* and *abhangs*).

In 1998, he was awarded the Sangeet Natak Akademi Fellowship the highest honour conferred by Sangeet Natak Akademi, India's National Academy for Music, Dance and Drama. Subsequently received the Bharat Ratna, India's highest civilian honour, in 2008.

Early Life

Bhimsen Gururaj Joshi was born in a town called Gadag in the erstwhile Dharwad (today Gadag) district of Karnataka in a Kannada Madhwa Brahmin family on 4 February 1922 to Gururaj Joshi (a pure Kannadiga teacher and Sanskrit scholar who had authored a Kannada-English dictionary, and Godavaraibai, a home-maker. Bhimsen was the eldest among 16 siblings. He lost his mother at a young age and was raised by his step mother.

As a child, Bhimsen was fascinated with music and musical instruments like Harmonium and Tanpura[7] and would often follow processions accompanied by music bands. This exercise often tired him and he would curl up somewhere and sleep, forcing the parents to go to the police after efforts to trace him fail. Fed up, his father Gururajacharya Joshi come up with the solution, writing "Joshi mastarara maga" (son of teacher Joshi) on Bhimsen's shirts. This worked and those who found the boy sleeping would safely deposit him back to his house.

Musical Training

His first music teacher was Agasara Channappa of Kurtakoti, who had trained with the veteran singer Inayat Khan. After learning ragas Bhairav and Bhimpalasi, Bhimsen Joshi left him for Pandit Shyamacharya Joshi, who hailed from Bagalkot and was a priest and classical singer. Pandit Shyamacharya taught him to sing as well as play the harmonium. Shree Shamacharya Joshi was a descendant of Great Haridasa Shree Mahipati Dasaru. As revealed by Shree Shamacharya Joshi himself when he was live, it was a turning point in Bhimsen Joshi's life that Shree Shyamacharya Joshi went to Bombay for recording his songs by HMV where Shree Bhimsen Joshi also accompanied him and due to ill health Shree Shayamacharya Joshi returned to Bagalkot after recording few songs and asked Shree Bhimsen Joshi to render rest of the songs which Shree Bhimsen Joshi did and this proved to be a major breakthrough for Shree Bhimsen Joshi in the initial stage of his career.

Search for a Guru

Joshi heard a recording of Abdul Karim Khan's Thumri "Piya Bin Nahi Aavat Chain" in Raga Jhinjhoti when he was a child, which inspired him to become a musician. During this time, he also heard Pandit Sawai Gandharva at a performance in Kundgol. In 1933, the 11-year-old Joshi left Dharwad for Bijapur to find a master and learn music. With the help of money lent by his co-passengers in the train, Bhimsen reached Dharwad first and later went to Pune. Later he moved to Gwalior and got into Madhava Music School, a school run by Maharajas of Gwalior, with the help of famous *sarod* player Hafiz Ali Khan. He traveled for three years around North India, including in Delhi, Kolkata, Gwalior, Lucknow and Rampur, trying to find a good guru. Eventually, his father succeeded in tracking him down in Jalandar and brought young Bhimsen back home.

Sawai Gandharva

In 1936, Sawai Gandharva, a native of Dharwad, agreed to be his guru. Joshi stayed at his house in the *guru-shishya* (teacher-student) tradition. Joshi continued his training with Sawai Gandharva till 1940.

Career

Joshi first performed live in 1941 at the age 19. His debut album, containing a few devotional songs in Marathi and Hindi, was released by HMV the next year in 1942. Later Joshi moved to Mumbai in 1943 and worked as a radio artist. His performance at a concert in 1946 to celebrate his guru Sawai Gandharva's 60th birthday won him accolades both from the audience and his guru.

Hindustani classical music

Joshi's performances have been acknowledged by music critics such as S. N. Chandrashekhar of the Deccan Herald to be marked by spontaneity, accurate notes, dizzyingly-paced *taans* which make use of his exceptional voice training, and a mastery over rhythm. The Hindu, in an article written after he was awarded the Bharat Ratna, said: *Bhimsen Joshi was ever the wanderer, engendering brilliant phrases and tans more intuitively than through deliberation.* Joshi occasionally employed the use of *sargam* and *tihaais*, and often sang traditional compositions of the Kirana gharana. His music often injected surprising and sudden turns of phrase, for example through the unexpected use of boltaans. Over the years, his repertoire tended to favor a relatively small number of complex and serious ragas; however, he remained one of the most prolific exponents of Hindustani classical music. Some of Joshi's more popular ragas include Shuddha Kalyan, Miyan Ki Todi, Puriya Dhanashri, Multani, Bhimpalasi, Darbari, and Ramkali. He was a purist who has not dabbled in experimental forms of music, except for a series of Jugalbandi recordings with the Carnatic signer M. Balamuralikrishna.

Joshi's singing has been influenced by many musicians, including Smt. Kesarbai Kerkar, Begum Akhtar and Ustad Amir Khan. Joshi assimilated into his own singing various elements that he liked in different musical styles and Gharanas.

Devotional Music

In devotional music, Joshi was most acclaimed for his Hindi, Kannada and Marathi Bhajan singing. He has recorded bhakti songs in Marathi, *Santavani* and Kannada, *Dasavani*.[12]

Patriotic Music

Bhimsen Joshi was widely recognized in India due to his performance in the Mile Sur Mera Tumhara music video (1988), which begins with him. The video was created for the purpose of national integration in India, and highlights the diversity of Indian culture. Bhimsen Joshi was also a part of Jana Gana Mana produced by A. R. Rahman on the occasion of 50th year of Indian Republic.

Playback Singing

Joshi sang for several films, including *Basant Bahar* (1956) with Manna Dey, *Birbal My Brother* (1973) with Pandit Jasraj. He also sang for the films *Tansen* (1958) and *Ankahee* (1985) where latter fetched him National Film Award for Best Male Playback Singer. His song 'Bhagyadalakshmi baaramma', a

Purandara Dasa composition, was used by Anant Nag and Shankar Nag in the Kannada film *Nodi Swami Naavu Irodhu Heege.* He also sang as a playback singer for the Marathi film Gulacha Ganapati, produced and directed by P. L. Deshpande

Sawai Gandharva Music Festival

Joshi along with his friend Vasantrao Deshpande organized the Sawai Gandharva Music Festival as an homage to his guru, Sawai Gandharva, along with the Arya Sangeet Prasarak Mandal in 1953, marking Gandharva's first death anniversary. The festival has been held ever since, typically on the second weekend of December in Pune, Maharashtra and has become not only a cultural event for the city, but an annual pilgrimage for Hindustani Classical Music lovers all over the world. Joshi conducted the festival annually since 1953, until his retirement in 2002.

Legacy

Bhimsen Joshi was known for his powerful voice, amazing breath control, fine musical sensibility and unwavering grasp of the fundamentals, representing a subtle fusion of intelligence and passion that imparted life and excitement to his music. A classicist by training, and temperament, Bhimsen Joshi was renowned for having evolved an approach that sought to achieve a balance between what may be termed as "traditional values and mass-culture tastes" and as such he went on to have supposedly the largest commercially recorded repertoire in Hindustani vocal music. Pt. Joshi's iconic status in the music world has earned him a whole generation of suni shagirds who by merely listening to him have picked up his style and not through any formal tutelage. His greatest endeavour in perpetuating his legacy could be the Sawai Gandharva Festival held at Pune. annually since the year 1953 which seeks to promote a certain music culture.

Narayan Deshpande, Shrikant Deshpande, and others are some of his more well-known disciples.

Personal Life

Bhimsen married twice. His first wife was Sunanda Katti, the daughter of his maternal uncle, whom he married in 1944. He had four children from Sunanda; Raghavendra, Usha, Sumangala, and Anand. In 1951, he married Vatsala Mudholkar, his co-actor in the Kannada play Bhagya-Shree in 1951. Although bigamous marriages among Hindus were prohibited by law in the Bombay Presidency, he did not divorce or separate from Sunanda. With Vatsala, he had three children; Jayant, Shubhada, and Shrinivas. Initially, both his wives and families lived together, but when this did not work out, his first wife moved out with the family to live in a rented house in Limayewadi in Sadashiv Peth, Pune, where Bhimsen continued to visit them.

Bhimsen had a passion for cars. He was a swimmer, an enthusiast of yoga and a football player. He had acknowledged his weakness for alcohol but became a teetotaller after it started affecting his career.

Illness and Death

Joshi was admitted to Sahyadri Super Speciality Hospital on December 31, 2010 with gastrointestinal bleeding and bilateral pneumonia. Due to difficulty in breathing, he was put on ventilator support. He suffered convulsions and was put on dialysis too during his stay in hospital. Though he recovered briefly for three days when he was taken off the ventilator, his condition deteriorated thereafter. He died on 24 January 2011. He was cremated at Vaikunth Crematorium in Pune with full state honors.

Awards and recognitions

- 1972 - Padma Shree[
- 1976 - Sangeet Natak Akademi Award
- 1985 - Padma Bhushan
- 1985 - National Film Award for Best Male Playback Singer

- 1986 - "First platinum disc"[
- 1999 - Padma Vibhushan
- 2000 - "Aditya Vikram Birla Kalashikhar Puraskar"[22]
- 2002 - Maharashtra Bhushan[
- 2003 - "Swathi Sangeetha Puraskaram" by Government of Kerala
- 2009 - Bharat Ratna
- 2008 - "Swami Haridas Award"
- 2009 - "Lifetime achievement award" by Delhi government[
- 2010 - "S V Narayanaswamy Rao National Award" by Rama Seva Mandali, Bangalore

42

Chintamani Nagesa Ramachandra Rao

Chintamani Nagesa Ramachandra Rao FRS, also known as **C.N.R. Rao** (born 30 June 1934), is an Indian chemist who has worked mainly in solid-state and structural chemistry. He currently serves as the Head of the Scientific Advisory Council to the Prime Minister of India. Rao has honorary doctorates from 60 universities from around the world. He has authored around 1,500 research papers and 45 scientific books. He is the recipient of most of the major scientific awards, and is member of all major scientific organisations.

On 16 November 2013, the Government of India announced his selection for Bharat Ratna, the highest civilian award in India, making him the third scientist after C.V. Raman and A. P. J. Abdul Kalam to receive the award. He, along with the legendary cricketer Sachin Tendulkar, was conferred the award on 4 February 2014 by President Pranab Mukherjee in a special ceremony in the Durbar Hall of the Rashtrapati Bhavan.

Early life and education

C.N.R. Rao was born in Bangalore in a Kannada family to Hanumantha Nagesa Rao and Nagamma Nagesa Rao. He was an only child, and his learned parents made an academic environment. He was well versed in Hindu literature from his mother and in English from his father at an early age. He did not attend elementary school but was home-tutored by his mother, who was particularly skilled in arithmetic and Hindu literature. He entered middle school in 1940, at age six. Although he was the youngest in his class, he used to tutor his classmates in mathematics and English. He passed lower secondary examination (class VII) in first class in 1944. He was ten years old, and his father rewarded him with four annas (twenty-five paisa). He attended Acharya Patashala high school in Basavanagudi, which made a lasting influence on his interest in chemistry. His father enrolled him to a Kannada-medium course to encourage his mother tongue, but at home used English for all conversation. He completed secondary school leaving certificate in first class in 1947. He studied BSc at Central College, Bangalore. Here he developed his communication skills in English and also learnt Sanskrit. He obtained his bachelor's degree from Mysore University in 1951, in first class, and only at the age of seventeen. He initially thought of joining Indian Institute of Science (IISc) for a diploma or a postgraduate degree in chemical engineering, but a teacher persuaded him to attend Banaras Hindu University. He obtained a master's in chemistry from BHU two years later. In 1953 he was granted a scholarship for PhD in IIT Kharagpur. But four foreign universities, MIT, Penn State, Columbia and Purdue also offered him financial support. He chose Purdue. His first research paper was published in the *Agra University Journal of Research* in 1954. He completed PhD in 1958, only after two years and nine months, at age twenty-four.

Profession

Rao returned to Bangalore in 1959 to join IISC as a lecturer. He got a monthly salary of Rs 500. He started his own research with six PhD students. After three years he got permanent appointment in the Department of Chemistry at the Indian Institute of Technology Kanpur. The Director P.K. Kelkar directly appointed him as Head of the department. He worked there from 1963 to 1976. In 1964, C.V. Raman informed him that he was elected as a fellow of the Indian Academy of Sciences. In 1976 he returned to IISc to set up a solid state and structural chemistry unit. He became Director of the IISc from 1984 to 1994. He has also been a visiting professor at Purdue University, the University of Oxford, the University of Cambridge and University of California, Santa Barbara. He was the Jawaharlal Nehru Professor at the University of Cambridge and Professorial Fellow at the King's College, Cambridge during 1983–1984.

Rao is currently the National Research Professor, Linus Pauling Research Professor and Honorary President of Jawaharlal Nehru Centre for Advanced Scientific Research, Bangalore which he founded in 1989. He was appointed Chair of the Scientific Advisory Council to the Indian Prime Minister in January 2005, a position which he had occupied earlier during 1985–89. He is also the director of the International Centre for Materials Science (ICMS).

Rao is one of the world's foremost solid state and materials chemists. He has contributed to the development of the field over five decades. His work on transition metal oxides has led to basic understanding of novel phenomena and the relationship between materials properties and the structural chemistry of these materials.

Rao was one of the earliest to synthesize two-dimensional oxide materials such as La_2CuO_4. His work has led to a systematic study of compositionally controlled metal-insulator transitions. Such studies have had a profound impact in application fields such as colossal magneto resistance and high temperature superconductivity. Oxide semiconductors have unusual promise. He has made immense contributions to nanomaterials over the last two decades, besides his work on hybrid materials.

He is the author of around 1500 research papers. He has authored and edited 45 books. Rao serves on the board of the Science Initiative Group.

Awards and recognition

Scientific awards

- DSc from Mysore University in 1961
- Marlow Medal by the Faraday Society of England in 1967
- Shanti Swarup Bhatnagar Prize for Science and Technology in Chemical Science in 1968
- Royal Society of Chemistry (London) Medal in 1981
- Member of many of the world's scientific associations, including the National Academy of Sciences, American Academy of Arts and Sciences, the Royal Society (London, 1982), French Academy, Japanese Academy, Serbian Academy of Sciences and Arts and the Pontifical Academy.
- Honorary doctorates from several universities including Bordeaux, Caen, Colorado, Khartoum, Liverpool, Northwestern, Novosibirsk, Oxford, Purdue, Stellenbosch, Universite Joseph Fourier, Wales, Wroclaw, Notre Dame, Uppsala, Aligarh Muslim, Anna, AP, Banaras, Bengal Engineering, Bangalore, Burdwan, Bundelkhand, Delhi, Hyderabad, IGNOU, IIT Bombay, Kharagpur, Delhi, Patna, JNTU, Kalyani, Karnataka, Kolkata, Kuvempu, Lucknow, Mangalore, Manipur, Mysore, Osmania, Punjab, Roorkee, Sikkim Manipal, SRM, Tumkur, Sri Venkateswara, Vidyasagar, and Visveswaraya Technological University.
- Hevrovsky Gold Medal of the Czechoslovak Academy of Sciences in 1989
- Centenary Medal of the Royal Society of Chemistry, London in 2000
- Hughes Medal by the Royal Society in 2000
- Doctor of Science from University of Calcutta in 2004
- Somiya Award of the International Union of Materials Research in 2004
- India Science Award in 2004
- Dan David Prize from Tel Aviv University in 2005[J] shared

with George Whitesides and Robert Langer.

- Foreign fellow of Bangladesh Academy of Sciences]
- *Nikkei Asia Prize* for Science, Technology and Innovation, by Nihon Keizai Shimbun, Inc., Japan in 2008[21]
- Royal Medal by the Royal Society in 2009
- August-Wilhelm-von-Hofmann Medal by the German Chemical Society in 2010.
- Ernesto Illy Trieste Science Prize for materials research in 2011
- 2012 Award for International Scientific Cooperation from the Chinese Academy of Sciences in 2013
- Elected honorary foreign member of Chinese Academy of Sciences in 2013
- Distinguished Academician Award from IIT Patna in 2013

Indian governmental honours

- Padma Shri in 1974
- Padma Vibhushan in 1985
- Karnataka Ratna by the Karnataka State Government in 2001
- Bharat Ratna in 2014

Foreign honours

- Great Cross of the National Order of Scientific Merit from the President of Brazil in 2002
- Chevalier de la Légion d'honneur (Knight of the Legion of Honour, France) in 2005
- Order of Friendship by the President of Russia in 2009

Personal Life

Rao is married to Indumati Rao in 1960. They have two children, Sanjay and Suchitra. His son Sanjay Rao is engaged in popularising science in Bangalore's schools. His daughter Suchitra is married to K.M. Ganesh, the director of the Indian Institute of Science Education and Research (IISER) at Pune, Maharashtra. Rao is quite technophobic. He removed computers from his tables and never check his email by himself. He also said that he uses mobile phone only for talking to his wife.

43

Sachin Ramesh Tendulkar

Sachin Ramesh Tendulkar born 24 April 1973) is a former Indian cricketer widely acknowledged as one of the greatest batsmen of all time, popularly holding the title "God of Cricket" among his fans.[2] Some commentators, such as former West Indian batsman Brian Lara, have labelled Tendulkar the greatest cricketer of all time. He took up cricket at the age of eleven, made his Test debut against Pakistan at the age of sixteen, and went on to represent Mumbai domestically and India internationally for close to twenty-four years. He is the only player to have scored one hundred international centuries, the first batsman to score a double century in a One Day International, the only player to complete more than 30,000 runs in international cricket. and the 16th player and first Indian to aggregate 50,000 runs or more in all forms of domestic and international recognised cricket.

In 2002, *Wisden Cricketers' Almanack* ranked him the second greatest Test batsman of all time, behind Don Bradman, and the second greatest ODI batsman of all time, behind Viv Richards.[12] Later in his career, Tendulkar was a part of the Indian team that won the 2011 World Cup, his first win in six World Cup appearances for India. He had previously been named "Player of the Tournament" at the 2003 edition of the tournament, held in South Africa. In 2013, he was the only Indian cricketer included in an all-time Test World XI named to mark the 150th anniversary of *Wisden Cricketers' Almanack*.

Tendulkar received the Arjuna Award in 1994 for his outstanding sporting achievement, the Rajiv Gandhi Khel Ratna award in 1997, India's highest sporting honour, and the Padma Shri and Padma Vibhushan awards in 1999 and 2008, respectively, India's fourth and second highest civilian awards. After a few hours of his final match on 16 November 2013, the Prime Minister's Office announced the decision to award him the Bharat Ratna, India's highest civilian award. He is the youngest recipient to date and the first ever sportsperson to receive the award. He also won the 2010 Sir Garfield Sobers Trophy for cricketer of the year at the ICC awards.[21] In 2012, Tendulkar was nominated to the Rajya Sabha, the upper house of the Parliament of India.[22] He was also the first sportsperson and the first person without an aviation background to be awarded the honorary rank of group captain by the Indian Air Force. In 2012, he was named an Honorary Member of the Order of Australia.

In December 2012, Tendulkar announced his retirement from ODIs. He retired from Twenty20 cricket in October 2013[27] and subsequently announced his retirement from all forms of cricket, retiring on 16 November 2013 after playing his 200th and final Test match, against the West Indies in Mumbai's Wankhede Stadium. Tendulkar played 664 international cricket matches in total, scoring 34,357 runs.

44

Pt Madan Mohan Malaviya

Humble Beginnings

Pt Madan Mohan Malaviya or Mahamana Malaviya, as he was popularly known, was born on 25th December 1861 at Prayag, in a family of six brothers and two sisters. His grandfather Pt Premdhar and father Pt Baijnath were Sanskrit scholars. His father, Pt Baijnath, was also an excellent Kathavacak (narrator of the stories from Bhagawat). After initial training in Sanskrit, Malaviyaji joined the Saraswati School for study in English. He passed his B.A. from Muir Central College in 1884. He was married in 1878 to Kumari Devi of Mirzapur.

Early Dream

Malaviyaji wanted to be a good Kathavacak like his father. But his dreams were drowned "in the tears of his mother" and the poverty in the house. Circumstances forced him in 1884 to join the Government School as a teacher for a salary of Rs.40 per month.

Legal Practice

After his graduation and the job of a teacher in 1884, Malaviyaji could pursue his education only from 1889 and passed LLB course in 1891. He first practiced in the District court in 1891 and then in the High Court from 1893. According to Sir Tej Bahadur Sapru "Soon he became a brilliant Civil Lawyer". Sir Mirza Ismail said "I have heard a great lawyer say that if Mr.Malaviya had so willed it, he would have been an ornament to the legal profession". He decided to give up his roaring practice during his 50th birthday and retired in 1913 to serve the country. Gopala Krishna Gokhale said "Malaviyaji's sacrifice is a real one. Born in a poor family, he started earning thousands monthly. He tasted luxury and wealth but giving heed to the call of the nation, renouncing all he again embraced poverty".

Journalism

Raja Rampal Singh of Kalakankar (Pratapgadh District) was impressed by the speech and the personality of Malaviyaji, during the 2nd Congress Session in Calcutta held in 1886. He requested him to edit the Hindi daily 'Hindosthan' in July 1887. Though he was young at that time, Malaviyaji's earlier writings and speeches helped him acquire the characteristics of a journalist. His poems (sawaiyas) published (sometime in 1883-84) under the pseudonym of 'Makrand' in 'Harischandra Chandrika' magazine (brought out by the famous Bharatendu), articles on religious and contemporary subjects published in 'Hindi Pradeepa', editorial work for the English weekly 'Indian Union' (1885), work and speeches in social organizations stood him in good stead. Malaviyaji worked in the editorial of Hindi daily 'Hindosthan' (1887-1889), English daily 'Indian Opinion' (1889-), started Hindi weekly 'Abhyuday' (1907-1909 under his editorship). started English daily with the help of Motilal Nehru 'Leader' When the English Government tried to bring in the Press Act and Newspaper Act in 1908, Malaviyaji started a campaign against the Act and called an All India Conference in Allahabad. He then realized the need of an English Newspaper to make the campaign effective throughout the country. As a result, he started the English daily `Leader' in 1909 with the help of Pt. Motilal Nehru. He was associated with 'Leader' as Editor 1909-1911 and as the President 1911-1919. In 1910, Malaviyaji started the Hindi paper `Maryada'. He took active control of `Hindusthan Times' from Delhi in 1924. `Sanatana Dharma', a magazine dedicated to religious, dharmic interests, was started in 1933 from BHU.

Hindu Ideals and Religion

Malaviyaji's firm grounding in the tenets of Hindu Dharma led him to strong beliefs on right attitude, right thinking, right expression and right actions in every field of his activity. A few examples from his early years are: 1) worked as the Secretary of 'Prayaga Hindu Samaj' (in 1880), 2) active part in organizing the 'Madhya Bharat Hindu Samaj Conference' at Allahabad (in 1885), which discussed about the social good and the welfare of the nation. 3) association and lectures on Hinduism and Indian Culture in 'Bharat Dharma Mahamandal', Haridwar (from 1887 to 1902), 4) organizing a conference of 'Sanatana Dharma Mahasabha' (Prayag Kumbh in 1906), and in 1936, 5) President of the Education Committee for 10 years of 'Rishikul Brahmacharya Ashram' (started in 1906 by Pt Durgadutt Sharma) and many others of later years.

Political

Malaviyaji was catapulted into the political arena immediately after his first thrilling speech at the Second Congress Session in Calcutta, held in 1886. He served the Congress for almost 50 years and worked with 50 Congress Presidents. He was the Congress President for a record of four times- in 1909 (Lahore), in 1918(Delhi), in 1930 (Delhi) and in 1932 (Calcutta). He was actively involved with the Allahabad Municipal Board till 1916. He was a member of the Provincial Legislative Council during 1903-1918, Central Council during 1910-1920, elected member of the Indian Legislative Assembly during 1924-1930, Industrial Commission during 1916-1918 and attended the second Round Table Conference in 1931. He bid farewell to active politics in 1937. In politics, Malaviyaji was midway between the Liberals and the Nationalists, the moderates and the extremists, as the followers of Gokhale and Tilak were respectively called.

Educational

Malaviyaji visualized the importance of education and the hardships of the students early in life. He set up the 'MacDonald Hindu Boarding House' to accommodate 230 students in 1903 in Allahabad, by collecting a public donation of Rs 1.3 lakhs. This appears to be the precursor for his grand vision of the Banaras Hindu University, which he built up from a vision in 1900 to a reality in 1916. These examples show his keen analysis of a problem, ability to think of a workable solution, motivate a team to work, collect large amount of funds for a public cause and realize the dream. More of BHU separately.

Service to the Needy/Downtrodden

Malaviyaji encouraged his son Ramakant to start the Yatri Sevadal (in 1912), which became 'Deen Rakshak Samiti' (1914), and later became 'Prayag Seva Samiti' under the chairmanship of Malaviyaji (1915). By 1918, it took the form of an Akhil Bharatiya Seva Samiti with centers at many places and a broad based objective of service to the needy during Kumbh Mela, floods, earthquakes, other natural calamities. In 1918, a sub unit modelled like the 'Boy Scouts' was started under the Akhil Bharatiya Seva Samiti. The main difference was that a patriotic leader was its Chief Scout and 'Vande Mataram' was sung instead of the British National Anthem. During the dreaded plague, he struggled hard to hospitalize the sick, rehabilitate others into safer areas, arrange for mass feeding and shelter for the poor and needy. The above occasion brought out the best of the human kindness in him, a quality which could be seen in his care of the downtrodden. Malaviyaji gave mantra dik„a to the untouchables in Calcutta in 1928, much before the Harijan movement started by Gandhiji on 1st August 1933. When Gandhiji addressed the varanasi crowd on 1st August 1934, Malaviyaji lent his support. He also carried out the 'Shuddhi Movement' by initiating the Harijanas with dik–a mantra on 12th March 1936, on the banks of Godavari. He repeated the initiation ceremony of Harijans, on the banks of Ganga in Varanasi on the Shivaratri day in 1936. The initiation was preceded by a mammoth procession of elephants carrying Vedas and religious books, followed by musical parties, citizens and scholars of Varanasi. Later shuddhikaran and mantra diksha was held in Nasik, Calcutta, Prayag. He worked for the emancipation of women. He was the President of the Conference in Bombay (1932) for the removal of untouchability.

Other Social Activities

His keen interest in many social issues can be seen in examples of his involvement in : 1) The Minto Memorial Park not so well-known as it should be, was also the result of his efforts (1910), 2) opposing the construction of a dam across the Ganga in Haridwar as this would have reduced the flow of water in the canal (in 1916), and making the Govt to agree to the public proposal of maintaining an uninterrupted flow of water in the canal, 3) president of the special session of Hindu Mahasabha in Gaya in 1922, in Kashi in 1923 and his leadership till 1927, 4) starting the Cow Protection Society in 1941, 5) starting the Akhil Bharatiya Vikram Parishad in 1942.

Malaviyaji's Personality

His personality can not be condensed in a few words. Mahatma Gandhi called him pratah smaraniyaÌ, a pious person whose name when remembered in the morning would lift one out of the mire of one's sordid self. Gandhiji compared Tilak to the lofty Himalayas, Gokhale to the deep seas and Malaviyaji to the crystal clear sacred river in which he decided to have ablution! Malaviyaji's gentle, sweet, soft and graceful nature was a true reflection of his abundant love for humanity.

A British official commented that Malaviyaji 'wore the white flower of a blameless life'. Edgar Snow, a journalist, wrote that his personality radiated 'the sweetness and simplicity of a child, yet his words carried the strength and conviction of a man with a settled philosophy of life'. For all his sweetness he could still be tougher than the toughest when occasion demanded it.

Karma Yogi

Dr S. Radhakrishnan said "Pandit Malaviyaji is a Karmayogin. He is not only a representative of Hinduism but the soul of Hinduism. He had strived all through his life for the Hindu ideals and we see the combination of idealism and practical wisdom....... While preserving the imperishable treasures of our past, he is keen on moving forward with the times". Kashi's sacredness is usually described in a number of triads. To these sacred triads, we can add one more—the trinity of Ka„i, the Banaras Hindu University and Pt Madan Mohan Malaviya.

45

Shri Atal Bihari Vajpayee

Shri Vajpayee was Prime Minister of India from May 16-31, 1996, and then again from March 19, 1998 to May 13, 2004. With his swearing-in as Prime Minister after the parliamentary election of October 1999, he became the first and only person since Jawaharlal Nehru to occupy the office of the Prime Minister of India through three successive Lok Sabhas. Shri Vajpayee was the first Prime Minister since Smt. Indira Gandhi to lead his party to victory in successive elections.

Born on December 25, 1924, in Gwalior, Madhya Pradesh to Shri Krishna Bihari Vajpayee and Smt. Krishna Devi, Shri Vajpayee brings with him a long parliamentary experience spanning over four decades. He has been a Member of Parliament since 1957. He was elected to the 5th, 6th and 7th Lok Sabha and again to the 10th, 11th 12th and 13th Lok Sabha and to Rajya Sabha in 1962 and 1986. In 2004, he was to Parliament from Lucknow in Uttar Pradesh for the fifth time consecutively. He is the only parliamentarian elected from four different States at different times - UP, Gujarat, MP and Delhi. His legacy as Prime Minister is a rich one that is remembered and cherished even a decade after his term ended. It included the Pokhran nuclear tests, astute and wise economic policies that laid the foundations of the longest period of sustained growth in independent Indian history, massive infrastructure projects such as those related to development of national highways and the Golden Quadrilateral. Few Indian Prime Ministers have left such a dramatic impact on society.

Educated at Victoria College (now Laxmibai College), Gwalior and DAV College, Kanpur, Uttar Pradesh, Shri Vajpayee holds an M.A (Political Science) degree and has many literary, artistic and scientific accomplishments to his credit. He edited Rashtradharma (a Hindi monthly), Panchjanya (a Hindi weekly) and the dailies Swadesh and Veer Arjun. His published works include "Meri Sansadiya Yatra" (in four volumes), "Meri Ikkyavan Kavitayen", "Sankalp Kaal", "Shakti-se-Shanti", "Four Decades in Parliament" (speeches in three volumes), 1957-95, "Lok Sabha Mein Atalji" (a collection of speeches); Mrityu Ya Hatya", "Amar Balidan", "Kaidi Kaviraj Ki Kundalian" (a collection of poems written in jail during Emergency); "New Dimensions of India's Foreign Policy" (a collection of speeches delivered as External Affairs Minister during 1977-79); "Jan Sangh Aur Mussalman"; "Sansad Mein Teen Dashak" (Hindi) (speeches in Parliament, 1957-1992, three volumes); and "Amar Aag Hai" (a collection of poems, 1994).

Shri Vajpayee has participated in various social and cultural activities. He has been a Member of the National Integration Council since 1961. Some of his other associations include -

(i) President, All India Station Masters and Assistant Station Masters Association (1965-70);

(ii) Pandit Deendayal Upadhyay Smarak Samiti (1968-84);

(iii) Deen Dayal Dham, Farah, Mathura, U.P; and

(iv) Janmabhomi Smarak Samiti, 1969 onwards.

Founder-member of the erstwhile Jana Sangh (1951), President, Bharatiya Jana Sangh (1968-1973), leader of the

Jana Sangh parliamentary party (1955-1977) and a founder-member of the Janata Party (1977-1980), Shri Vajpayee was President, BJP (1980-1986) and the leader of BJP parliamentary party during 1980-1984, 1986 and 1993-1996. He was Leader of the Opposition throughout the term of the 11th Lok Sabha. Earlier, he was India's External Affairs Minister in the Morarji Desai Government from March 24, 1977 ,to July 28, 1979.

Widely respected within the country and abroad as a statesman of the genre of Pt. Jawaharlal Nehru, Shri Vajpayee's 1998-99 stint as Prime Minister has been characterised as 'one year of courage of conviction'. It was during this period that India entered a select group of nations following a series of successful nuclear tests at Pokhran in May 1998. The bus journey to Pakistan in February 1999 was widely acclaimed for starting a new era of negotiations to resolve the outstanding problems of the sub-continent. India's honesty made an impact on the world community. Later, when this gesture of friendship turned out to be a betrayal of faith in Kargil, Shri Vajpayee was also hailed for his successful handling of the situation in repulsing back the intruders from the Indian soil.

It was during Shri Vajpayee's 1998-99 tenure that despite a global recession, India achieved 5.8 per cent GDP growth, which was higher than the previous year. Higher agricultural production and increase in foreign exchange reserves during this period were indicative of a forward-looking economy responding to the needs of the people. "We must grow faster. We simply have no other alternative" has been Shri Vajpayee's slogan focusing particularly on economic empowerment of the rural poor. The bold decisions taken by his Government for strengthening rural economy, building a strong infrastructure and revitalising human development programmes, fully demonstrated his Government's commitment to a strong and self-reliant nation to meet the challenges of the next millennium to make India an economic power in the 21st century. Speaking from the ramparts of the Red Fort on the

52nd Independence Day, he had said, "I have a vision of India: an India free of hunger and fear, an India free of illiteracy and want."

Shri Vajpayee has served on a number of important Committees of Parliament. He was Chairman, Committee on Government Assurances (1966-67); Chairman, Public Accounts Committee (1967-70); Member, General Purposes Committee (1986); Member, House Committee and Member, Business Advisory Committee, Rajya Sabha (1988-90); Chairman, Committee on Petitions, Rajya Sabha (1990-91); Chairman, Public Accounts Committee, Lok Sabha (1991-93); Chairman, Standing Committee on External Affairs (1993-96).

Shri Vajpayee participated in the freedom struggle and went to jail in 1942. He was detained during Emergency in 1975-77.

Widely travelled, Shri Vajpayee has been taking a keen interest in international affairs, uplift of Scheduled Castes and Scheduled Tribes, women and child welfare. Some of his travels abroad include visits such as - Member, Parliamentary Goodwill Mission to East Africa, 1965; Parliamentary Delegation to Australia, 1967; European Parliament, 1983; Canada, 1987; Indian delegation to Commonwealth Parliamentary Association meetings held in Canada, 1966 and 1994, Zambia, 1980, Isle of Man 1984, Indian delegation to Inter-Parliamentary Union Conference, Japan, 1974; Sri Lanka, 1975; Switzerland, 1984; Indian Delegation to the UN General Assembly, 1988, 1990, 1991, 1992, 1993 and 1994; Leader, Indian Delegation to the Human Rights Commission Conference, Geneva, 1993.

Shri Vajpayee was conferred Padma Vibhushan in 1992 in recognition of his services to the nation. He was also conferred the Lokmanya Tilak Puruskar and the Bharat Ratna Pt. Govind Ballabh Pant Award for the Best Parliamentarian, both in 1994. Earlier, the Kanpur University honoured him with an Honorary Doctorate of Philosophy in 1993.

Well known and respected for his love for poetry and as an eloquent speaker, Shri Vajpayee is known to be a voracious reader. He is fond of Indian music and dance.

Positions Held

- **1951** - Founder-Member, Bharatiya Jana Sangh (B.J.S)
- 1957 - Elected to 2nd Lok Sabha
- **1957-77** - Leader, Bharatiya Jana Sangh Parliamentary Party
- **1962** - Member, Rajya Sabha
- **1966-67** - Chairman, Committee on Government Assurances
- **1967** - Re-elected to 4th Lok Sabha (2nd term)
- **1967-70** - Chairman, Public Accounts Committee
- **1968-73** - President, B.J.S.
- **1971** - Re-elected to 5th Lok Sabha (3rd term)
- **1977** - Re-elected to 6th Lok Sabha (4th term)
- **1977-79** - Union Cabinet Minister, External Affairs
- **1977-80** - Founder - Member, Janata Party
- **1980** - Re-elected to 7th Lok Sabha (5th term)
- **1980-86**- President, Bharatiya Janata Party (B.J.P.)
- **1980-84, 1986 and 1993-96** - Leader, B.J.P. Parliamentary Party
- **1986** - Member, Rajya Sabha; Member, General Purposes Committee
- **1988-90** - Member, House Committee; Member, Business Advisory Committee
- **1990-91**- Chairman, Committee on Petitions
- **1991**- Re-elected to 10th Lok Sabha (6th term)

- **1991-93** - Chairman, Public Accounts Committee
- **1993-96** - Chairman, Committee on External Affairs; Leader of Opposition, Lok Sabha
- **1996** - Re-elected to 11th Lok Sabha (7th term)
- **16 May 1996 - 31 May 1996** - Prime Minister of India; Minister of External Affairs and also incharge of Ministries/Departments of Chemicals and Fertilizers, Civil Supplies, Consumer Affairs and Public Distribution, Coal, Commerce, Communications, Environment and Forests, Food Processing Industries, Human Resource Development, Labour, Mines, Non-Conventional Energy Sources, Personnel, Public Grievances and Pension, Petroleum and Natural Gas, Planning and Programme Implementation, Power, Railways, Rural Areas and Employment, Science and Technology, Steel, Surface Transport, Textiles, Water Resources, Atomic Energy, Electronics, Jammu & Kashmir Affairs, Ocean Development, Space and other subjects not allocated to any other Cabinet Minister
- **1996-97** - Leader of Opposition, Lok Sabha
- **1997-98** - Chairman, Committee on External Affairs
- **1998** - Re- elected to 12th Lok Sabha (8th term)
- **1998-99** - Prime Minister of India; Minister of External Affairs; and also incharge of Ministries/ Department not specifically allocated to the charge of any Minister
- **1999-** Re-elected to 13th Lok Sabha (9th term)
- **13 Oct.1999 to 13 May 2004-** Prime Minister of India and also in charge of the Ministries/ Departments not specifically allocated to the charge of any Minister

Appendix

Specifications

The original specifications for the award in 1954 mentioned the medal to be in circular shape with the diameter of 1 D $_{8}$ inches (35 mm) and was to be made of gold. The obverse side of the medal was designed to have the Sun with the rays embossed in the centre with the words "Bharat Ratna" written in Hindi language in silver-gilt on the upper edge and a wreath on the lower edge. The reverse side was designed to have the Emblem of India in the centre with national motto of India "Satyameva Jayate" (Truth alone triumphs) written in Hindi in silver-gilt on the lower edge.

However, the original design and specification were changed to its current form a year later. The current decoration is in the form of a Peepal leaf, about 2 ^{5}D $_{16}$ inches (59 mm) long 1 ^{7}D $_{8}$ inches (48 mm) wide and ^{1}D $_{8}$ inch (3.2 mm) thick. The Sun with the rays embossed on the obverse side of the medal has a diameter of ^{5}D $_{8}$ inch (16 mm) with rays spreading out from ^{5}D $_{6}$ inch (21 mm) to ^{1}D $_{2}$ inch (13 mm) from the center of the Sun. The words "Bharat Ratna" on the obverse side and Emblem of India along with "Satyameva Jayate" on the reverse side are kept same as from the original specifications. The emblem, the Sun and the rim of the medal are made up of platinum. A 2-inch-wide (51 mm) white ribbon is attached to the medal and is designed to be worn around the neck by the recipients. In 1957, the silver-gilt decoration was changed to burnished bronze.